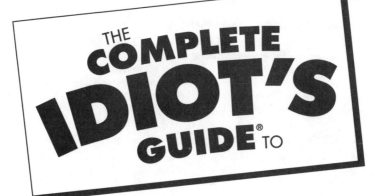

THE COMPLETE IDIOT'S GUIDE® TO

Savvy Investing

Second Edition

by Edward T. Koch and Debra DeSalvo

ALPHA

A Pearson Education Company

International Standard Book Number: 0-02-864457-3
Library of Congress Catalog Card Number: Available upon request.

04 03 02   8 7 6 5 4 3 2 1

Interpretation of the printing code: The rightmost number of the first series of numbers is the year of the book's printing; the rightmost number of the second series of numbers is the number of the book's printing. For example, a printing code of 02-1 shows that the first printing occurred in 2002.

Printed in the United States of America

Note: This publication contains the opinions and ideas of its authors. It is intended to provide helpful and informative material on the subject matter covered. It is sold with the understanding that the authors and publisher are not engaged in rendering professional services in the book. If the reader requires personal assistance or advice, a competent professional should be consulted.

The authors and publisher specifically disclaim any responsibility for any liability, loss, or risk, personal or otherwise, which is incurred as a consequence, directly or indirectly, of the use and application of any of the contents of this book.

For marketing and publicity, please call: 317-581-3722

The publisher offers discounts on this book when ordered in quantity for bulk purchases and special sales.

For sales within the United States, please contact: Corporate and Government Sales, 1-800-382-3419 or corpsales@pearsontechgroup.com

Outside the United States, please contact: International Sales, 317-581-3793 or international@pearsontechgroup.com

Publisher: *Marie Butler-Knight*
Product Manager: *Phil Kitchel*
Managing Editor: *Jennifer Chisholm*
Acquisitions Editor: *Eric Heagy*
Development Editor: *Suzanne LeVert*
Production Editor: *Billy Fields*
Copy Editor: *Amy Borrelli*
Illustrator: *Chris Eliopoulos*
Cover/Book Designer: *Trina Wurst*
Indexer: *Angie Bess*
Layout/Proofreading: *Megan Douglass, Becky Harmon*

Contents at a Glance

Appendixes

Contents

Foreword

This week my daughter wanted to lease a car. How to do it? *The Complete Idiot's Guide to Savvy Investing, Second Edition*. My wife and I are revising our estate planning and our wills. How to do it? *The Complete Idiot's Guide to Savvy Investing, Second Edition*. Taxes, household budgeting, when to buy muni bonds, stock picking, prenuptial agreements, refinancing mortgages, life insurance, and online shopping are all included—plus, of course, advice on how to invest like a pro. This book has it all. And it's not just for idiots—unless of course a Ph.D.'d economics professor who chairs a money management firm is an idiot. Come to think of it, some people think I probably am …

The book is a dream come true when you need the information. And, rest assured, you *will* need the information sometime. In fact, at one time or another you'll need most of this book's contents and you probably could use several sections of this book right now. It's all here. In my case the manuscript has already saved me a bundle within a week of reading it. How's *that* for the best investment tip of the year?

In all my years as a professor, advisor to presidents, businessman, father (of six), money manager, and just plain old inhabitant of planet Earth, I've never seen anything as down-to-earth, practical, and comprehensive as Ed Koch and Debra DeSalvo's *The Complete Idiot's Guide to Savvy Investing, Second Edition*.

Dr. Arthur B. Laffer

Dr. Arthur B. Laffer's academic specialty on tax issues and his close involvement in the tax-cutting movement around the world have earned him the distinction in many publications as "The Father of Supply-Side Economics." He was a member of President Reagan's Economic Policy Advisory Board for both of his two terms (1981–1989), as well as a member of the Executive Committee of the Reagan/Bush Finance Committee in 1984, and a founding member of the Reagan Executive Advisory Committee for the Presidential race of 1980. He also served as the first-ever Chief Economist at the Office of Management and Budget (OMB) under former Secretary of State George Shultz. He is the founder and Chairman of Laffer Associates, an economic research and consulting firm, which provides investment research services to institutional asset managers.

Introduction

Even though this book is called *The Complete Idiot's Guide to Savvy Investing, Second Edition*, we wrote it for smart people—people with the common sense to know that investing can't be all that difficult. After all, lots of people do it very successfully (even some real dimwits!). You may even have a sneaking suspicion that investing is the key to making dreams come true. Guess what? You're 100 percent correct!

You may have tried to tackle investing before and had a bad experience with a blow-hard financial advisor or a tedious, confusing book. If you threw up your hands in frustration and said "Forget it!" but can't get rid of the nagging feeling that you're missing out on something very important, well, we wrote this book for you.

This book assumes you know less than nothing about investing, but doesn't patronize you by telling you what to do. Instead, we offer you a step-by-step guide so that you can figure out exactly what investment strategies will work for your situation:

- How much you need to save to put the kids through college *and* retire happily

- How much risk you can take on and still sleep at night

- How to create a balanced portfolio of investments tailored to your financial goals

- How to manage your investments from year to year and still roll with life's changes

Questionnaires, worksheets, dreadful jokes—they're all in here. It's best to start at the beginning and work through to the end, but feel free to skip around until you get comfortable. Just remember that you'll find everything you need to know in this book to become someone who can make savvy investment decisions with calm confidence. Here's the gist ….

Part 1, "What Does 'Financial Security' Mean to You?" helps you figure out exactly that, because there's no point in investing without specific goals. You'll also take a risk tolerance questionnaire and create your own income statement and balance sheet.

Part 2, "Shore Up Your Foundation," is based on the premise that you have to know what you've got before you can get any more. Here, you'll take a close look at your job benefits and find out how to trim your taxes to the bone (so you can keep more of what you make). You'll also learn some neat tricks to keep spending down and get a grip on any debt.

Part 3, "Investing 101," is a primer in investment basics. Everything you ever wanted to know but felt too stupid to ask, from what they're really up to on Wall Street to how to pick a mutual fund from the overwhelming number available.

Part 4, "Rolling with Life's Changes," confronts the inevitable upheavals that many investment books ignore. Sure, you can steadily sock away dollars on your investment plan when life is smooth, but what about when you get married, get divorced, have kids, buy a house, change jobs? This section contains event—specific advice so that no matter what life throws at you, your investments keep growing.

Part 5, "Investing Online," gets you up and running on the Internet and shows you how to bank, trade, and track your portfolio online. You'll learn it all, from the best ways to research investments online to the best brokers on the web—this is fun stuff!

Part 6, "Advanced Investment Plays," is for readers who want to explore more complicated, alternative investments. It's also a source of answers for questions you may have when you hear words like "option" or "futures contract" bandied about.

In addition, you get a comprehensive glossary with clear, straightforward definitions of investment terms and an appendix with some recommendations for further reading and financial exploration.

One caveat: Although we have made every effort to confirm our data, accidents do happen. Equally important to keep in mind is that tax laws are under constant revision, reinterpretation, etc. So please double-check with the sources listed in the back of the book before proceeding with any financial endeavor.

Extras

If you're more a scanner than a reader, you'll appreciate our sidebars. These explain confusing jargon, help you avoid expensive mistakes, and offer super inside strategies. Look for the following boxes:

Investor's Idiom

Yes, investing has its own language, but it's not hard to learn. Peek in this box for clear, succinct explanations of any italicized terms.

Crash Alert

When dealing with money, mistakes can be costly. This box alerts you to tax issues, legal snarls, and scams, so you can steer clear.

Fiscal Facts

These little boxes contain just-for-fun facts about the financial world. Great for cocktail party chatter.

Super Strategy

These boxes outline super-smart investing strategies you can apply right away to improve your finances. Hint: Some of these strategies appear only in the box, not in the text, so don't pass 'em up!

Acknowledgments

Ed would like to thank his former associates at FleetBoston Financial. Those who came through at "crunch time" include Frances McPartland, Charlie Yue, John Bolton, Donna Todaro, Eddie Aydin, Christine Flynn, and Ben Campbell of the Columbia Management Group, and Jane Higgins of the Private Clients Group. Also, a special thanks from Ed to Skip and Elaine Howland: best friends and major support for so many years.

Finally, Ed would like to thank his family. His wife Joan, for her understanding and support when deadlines were nigh. To his daughter, Emily, and to his son, John, who fill him with pride. And last but not least, to the newest apples of "Booba's" eye: Henry, Oliver, and Ella.

Special Thanks to the Technical Reviewer

The Complete Idiot's Guide to Savvy Investing, Second Edition, was reviewed by an expert who not only checked the technical accuracy of the information in this book but also provided valuable insight to help ensure that it tells you everything you need to know to invest with ease.

Our special thanks are extended to Laura Castañeda. Laura Castañeda is a Philadelphia-based freelance writer. A graduate of the University of Southern California and Columbia University, she has worked as a staff writer for the *Associated Press*, the *Dallas Morning News*, and the *San Francisco Chronicle*. Her first book, *The Latino Guide to Personal Money Management*, will be published in May by Bloomberg Press.

Trademarks

All terms mentioned in this book that are known to be or are suspected of being trademarks or service marks have been appropriately capitalized. Alpha Books and Pearson Education, Inc., cannot attest to the accuracy of this information. Use of a term in this book should not be regarded as affecting the validity of any trademark or service mark.

Part 1

What Does "Financial Security" Mean to You?

Investing is really very simple—it's about putting your money to work for you over time. The longer your money is parked in an investment, the more time it has to grow … and grow … and grow!

But what are you growing it for? Before you choose investments, you need to choose investment objectives. Are you saving to buy a home? To put kids through school? For retirement? Or all three? How much time do you have to reach those objectives?

Next, you need to figure out how much risk you're willing to take with your hard-earned cash to try to meet those objectives. Finally, you need to take a look at what you've already got—and what you owe.

There's no point in putting yourself into some cookie-cutter investment plan. To invest really well, you've got to know yourself really well. In this section, we're going exploring in the dark cave that is your financial psyche.

Put Your Money to Work for You

In This Chapter

- ◆ How investing will put your money to work for you
- ◆ How compounding interest can build your wealth
- ◆ Using time as a money-making asset
- ◆ Forming the 10 percent habit
- ◆ The relationship between time, risk, and your sanity
- ◆ How interest rates affect your investment choices

When John D. Rockefeller was a teen—back in the mid-1800s—he lent $50 to a neighboring farmer. A year later the farmer paid him back the $50 plus $3.50 interest on the loan. The week before, Rockefeller had earned a measly $1.12 after 30 hours of backbreaking work hoeing potatoes for another neighbor. "From that time on," Rockefeller wrote in his autobiography, *Random Reminiscences*, "I was determined to make money work for me."

Putting your money to work for you is the essence of investing—and anyone can learn to do it well. Think for a moment about what you envision a successful investor to look like. Maybe you picture someone in a power suit, up at the crack of dawn checking stock quotes in *The Wall Street Journal* before he or she has even had coffee. A real mover and shaker. Well, toss that picture right out of your head and take a walk over to the closest mirror. See that good-lookin' person looking back at you? *That's* what a successful investor looks like. It's anybody. It certainly could be you. You just need a few tools to get you up to a savvy speed.

"But where am I going to get the money I need to start investing?" you may be thinking. That's simple: Any dollar you aren't using to pay bills is money you can invest. Luckily, you have a lot more investment options than young Rockefeller did. On the other hand, separating the wheat from the chaff is going to be a little more complicated for you than it was for our boy on the farm. Before you start threshing your investment opportunities, you'll need to lay a little groundwork.

Become an Educated Investor, Not Just a Consumer

At this point in the history of the stock market, there are a lot of educated consumers, but not many educated investors. The stock market's unusually strong performance during the 1990s was splashed across the covers of all the new financial magazines, convincing individual investors to "come on in, the water's fine!" All the raving about how fabulously the stock market performed created a new class of investment consumers who jumped into the stock market feet first.

> **Fiscal Facts**
>
> The word **millionaire** is believed to have first come into use in Paris around 1720. A number of French noblemen invested in shares of The Mississippi Company and became fabulously (temporarily) wealthy. They were called "millionaires." The Mississippi Company was a contemporary of the equally initially profitable South Sea Company in England ... and both bubbles burst!

These are the same investors who panicked and dumped their stock holdings—collectively losing millions—when the market went sour in 2002 due to revelations that some important and heretofore respectable corporations were cooking the books. Fact is, the stream of accounting scandals was a direct result of the unbridled exuberance of the market during the 1990s, when the stock of many Internet-based companies (the shiny new "dot-coms") took off like rockets—even when the companies were wildly unprofitable.

So What Went Wrong When the Market Went Bust?

The Internet culture encouraged a new tolerance in the formerly staid business culture of some funky bookkeeping tactics. As C. Michael Armstrong, the CEO of AT&T said in *The New York Times* ("New Economy" by Tim Race, July 1, 2002), "The Internet created a culture and the culture got excited in and of itself." This culture, according to Armstrong, invented its own ways of measuring business success. Instead of profit and loss, companies touted their page hits, for example. And the money kept pouring in.

Understandably, executives from all types of business saw investors flocking to even the most unprofitable Internet-based companies and wanted to divert some of that cash flow to their companies. Excited by what was going on in the dot-com universe, they created new businesses based on the new technology—and also began playing fast and loose with their numbers. The result: Falsely inflated earnings covered up financial weaknesses, particularly among telecommunications giants like WorldCom and Global Crossing who rolled questionable new businesses onto the information superhighway without the capital structure in place to fund them. Meanwhile, the once-solid energy giant Enron got itself into trouble as it ventured into attempting to trade bandwidth as a commodity.

When certain companies were found to have been defrauding their stockholders, investors righteously dumped these stocks, but many of the newly minted investors who had been delightedly tallying up their big wins during the 1990s panicked and dumped *all* their stocks. Even the stock of perfectly decent companies. The idea is to buy low and sell high, folks, not to buy high and sell low!

> **Crash Alert**
>
> The single most important thing you can do for yourself as an investor is to develop a long-term perspective. This will inoculate you against persuasive pitches to buy the latest hot investment and prevent you from selling based on bits of news and rumors.

Ah well … live and learn. Given a lengthy time frame, the stock market *is* a great investment, but you have to educate yourself about the risks involved—especially over shorter time frames, when something like accountants getting arrested or war breaking out can cause terrifying dips in the value of your holdings.

This book will help you protect yourself emotionally and financially from periods of reversal. In the next few chapters, you will transform yourself from an educated consumer to an educated investor. We're going to demystify the world of investing by helping you develop an understanding of the relationships that drive the financial markets. Let's begin with a concept that will soon be near and dear to your wallet: compounding interest.

The Miracle of Compounding

If the first miracle is life, the second would have to be compounding interest. Simply put, compounding *interest* is the interest you earn on your interest. Instead of spending the interest you are earning on money you lend to corporations, banks, or neighborhood farmers, reinvest it. This is a simple but very effective way to build wealth.

Investor's Idiom

Interest is payment you receive for lending someone your money. Interest is also the fee you pay when you borrow money.

To see how compounding works its magic, compare these three examples:

1. Fred earns 5 percent per year on his investment of $100,000. He spends that 5 percent on meals at gourmet restaurants. What does Fred have after 10 years? Love handles, some nice memories, and $100,000.

2. Mary earns 5 percent per year on her investment of $100,000 and puts her interest income in a shoe box. What does Mary have after 10 years? Well, first, here's a quick lesson on percentages for those of us who spaced out during math class!

Percent means *out of a hundred*. Five percent, therefore, means five out of a hundred. A dollar comprises 100 pennies, so 5 percent of a dollar is five pennies. Five out of a hundred is written as 5 percent.

When you divide five by 100, you get .05. This is another way to express any percentage—simply move the decimal point two places to the left.

- 5% is also .05

- 10% is also .10

- 39.6% is also .396

Expressing 5 percent as a decimal makes it super easy to figure out what Mary earned on her $100,000 in one year. Just whip out your handy calculator and multiply $100,000 by .05.

$$\$100,000 \times .05 = \$5,000$$

Mary earned $5,000 per year on her investment for 10 years, so she earned $50,000 total in interest. Add that to her initial $100,000 investment, and Mary ended up with $150,000 in 10 years.

Super Strategy

You can save yourself a math step when calculating compound interest. Simply multiply the investment amount by one plus the interest percentage. If the interest on an investment is 10 percent, for example, first convert the percentage to a decimal. Ten percent becomes .10. Then add one to .10, which gives you 1.10. Now, multiply your investment by 1.10. If your investment is $50,000, for example:

$$\$50,000 \times 1.10 = \$55,000$$

You'll have a total investment of $55,000 after the first year of compounding.

---

3. Helen also earned 5 percent per year on an initial investment of $100,000, but she had the good sense to reinvest the interest that she earned each year. The first year, Helen's investment earned $5,000, so she started the second year with $105,000. The second year she earned $5,250 ($105,000 × .05 = $5,250). She started the third year with $105,000 + $5,250, or $110,250. After 10 years of earning interest on her interest (i.e., compound interest), Helen has a whopping $162,890!

An Easy Way to Figure Compound Interest

I'll bet you're already thinking, "Well, that Helen was smart, but I really don't want to do ten tedious calculations to figure out how much my money will earn in ten years of compounding." This, my friend, is why the Almighty invented charts.

The Future Value Chart below shows you how much one dollar will be worth over a certain time period if it is compounded at a given interest rate. In Helen's case, she let $100,000 compound at 5 percent over 10 years. Run your finger down the left side of the chart under "Years" until you find "10." Okay, now move your finger across that row until you're under "5 percent." There's your answer. Every dollar Helen invests will become $1.6289 dollars in 10 years compounded at 5 percent. If she invests $100,000 dollars, she'll earn $162,890. Use this chart to stoke your financial fantasies.

Investor's Idiom

Compound interest is the money you earn on interest you earned in a previous period. Compound interest enables your money to grow exponentially (okay, a lot!).

The Future Value of Money (Amount of $1 at Compound Interest)

Rate Years	1%	2%	3%	4%	5%	6%	7%	8%	9%	10%	11%	12%
1	1.0100	1.0200	1.0300	1.0400	1.0500	1.0600	1.0700	1.0800	1.0900	1.1000	1.1100	1.1200
2	1.0201	1.0404	1.0609	1.0816	1.1025	1.1236	1.1449	1.1664	1.1881	1.2100	1.2321	1.2544
3	1.0303	1.0612	1.0927	1.1249	1.1576	1.1910	1.2250	1.2597	1.2950	1.3310	1.3676	1.4049
4	1.0406	1.0824	1.1255	1.1699	1.2155	1.2625	1.3108	1.3605	1.4116	1.4641	1.5181	1.5735
5	1.0510	1.1041	1.1593	1.2167	1.2763(1)	1.3382	1.4026	1.4693	1.5386	1.6105	1.6851	1.7623
6	1.0615	1.1262	1.1941	1.2653	1.3401	1.4185	1.5007	1.5869	1.6771	1.7716	1.8704	1.9738
7	1.0721	1.1487	1.2299(2)	1.3159	1.4071	1.5036	1.6058	1.7138	1.8280	1.9487	2.0762	2.2107
8	1.0829	1.1717	1.2668	1.3686	1.4775	1.5938	1.7182	1.8509	1.9926	2.1436	2.3045	2.4760
9	1.0937	1.1951	1.3048	1.4233	1.5513	1.6895	1.8385	1.9990	2.1719	2.3579	2.5580	2.7731
10	1.1046	1.2190	1.3439	1.4802	1.6289	1.7908	1.9671	2.1589	2.3674	2.5937	2.8394	3.1058
11	1.1157	1.2434	1.3842	1.5395	1.7103	1.8983	2.1048	2.3316	2.5804	2.8531	3.1518	3.4785
12	1.1268	1.2682	1.4258	1.6010	1.7959	2.0122	2.2522	2.5182	2.8127	3.1384	3.4984	3.8960
13	1.1381	1.2936	1.4685	1.6651	1.8856	2.1329	2.4098	2.7196	3.0658	3.4523	3.8833	4.3635
14	1.1495	1.3195	1.5126	1.7317	1.9799	2.2609	2.5785	2.9372	3.3417	3.7975	4.3104	4.8871
15	1.1610	1.3459	1.5580	1.8009	2.0789	2.3965	2.7590	3.1722	3.6425	4.1772	4.7846	5.4736
16	1.1726	1.3728	1.6047	1.8730	2.1829	2.5403	2.9522	3.4259	3.9703	4.5950	5.3109	6.1304
17	1.1843	1.4002	1.6528	1.9479	2.2920	2.6928	3.1588	3.7000	4.3276	5.0545	5.8951	6.8660
18	1.1961	1.4282	1.7024	2.0258	2.4066	2.8543	3.3799	3.9960	4.7171	5.5599	6.5435	7.6900
19	1.2081	1.4568	1.7535	2.1068	2.5269	3.0256	3.6165	4.3157	5.1416	6.1159	7.2633	8.6127
20	1.2202	1.4859	1.8061	2.1911	2.6533	3.2071	3.8697	4.6609	5.6044	6.7275	8.0623	9.6463
21	1.2324	1.5157	1.8603	2.2788	2.7860	3.3995	4.1405	5.0338	6.1088	7.4002	8.9491	10.8038
22	1.2447	1.5460	1.9161	2.3699	2.9252	3.6035	4.4304	5.4365	6.6586	8.1403	9.9335	12.1002
23	1.2572	1.5769	1.9736	2.4647	3.0715	3.8197	4.7405	5.8714	7.2579	8.9543	11.0262	13.5523
24	1.2697	1.6084	2.0328	2.5633	3.2251	4.0489	5.0723	6.3412	7.9111	9.8497	12.2391	15.1785
25	1.2824	1.6406	2.0938	2.6658	3.3863	4.2918	5.4274	6.8484	8.6231	10.8346	13.5854	16.9999
26	1.2952	1.6734	2.1566	2.7725	3.5557	4.5494	5.8073	7.3963	9.3991	11.9181	15.0798	19.0399
27	1.3082	1.7069	2.2213	2.8834	3.7334	4.8223	6.2138	7.9880	10.2450	13.1099	16.7385	21.3247
28	1.3213	1.7410	2.2879	2.9987	3.9201	5.1117	6.6488	8.6271	11.1670	14.4209	18.5798	23.8837
29	1.3345	1.7758	2.3565	3.1186	4.1161	5.4184	7.1142	9.3172	12.1721	15.8630	20.6235	26.7497
30	1.3478	1.8113	2.4272	3.2434	4.3219	5.7435	7.6122	10.0626	13.2676	17.4493	22.8921	29.9597
31	1.3613	1.8476	2.5001	3.3731	4.5380	6.0881	8.1451	10.8676	14.4616	19.1942	25.4103	33.5549

Rate Years	1%	2%	3%	4%	5%	6%	7%	8%	9%	10%	11%	12%
32	1.3749	1.8845	2.5751	3.5080	4.7649	6.4533	8.7152	11.7370	15.7632	21.1136	28.2054	37.5815
33	1.3887	1.9222	2.6523	3.6484	5.0032	6.8405	9.3253	12.6759	17.1819	23.2250	31.3080	42.0912
34	1.4026	1.9607	2.7319	3.7943	5.2533	7.2510	9.9781	13.6900	18.7283	25.5475	34.7519	47.1422
35	1.4166	1.9999	2.8138	3.9461	5.5160	7.6860	10.6765	14.7852	20.4138	28.1022	38.5746	52.7993
36	1.4308	2.0399	2.8983	4.1039	5.7918	8.1472	11.4238	15.9680	22.2510	30.9125	42.8178	59.1352
37	1.4451	2.0807	2.9852	4.2681	6.0814	8.6360	12.2235	17.2454	24.2536	34.0037	47.5277	66.2314
38	1.4595	2.1223	3.0748	4.4388	6.3854	9.1542	13.0791	18.6251	26.4365	37.4041	52.7558	74.1792
39	1.4741	2.1647	3.1670	4.6163	6.7047	9.7034	13.9947	20.1151	28.8157	41.1445	58.5589	83.0807
40	1.4888	2.2080	3.2620	4.8010	7.0399	10.2856	14.9743	21.7243	31.4092	45.2589	65.0004	93.0503

(1) To find the future value, take a given rate, go down column to correct year; multiply this by your actual number; e.g., $28,000 growing at 5% for 5 years: $28,000 x 1.2763 = $35,736.40.

(2) Can also be used for inflation impact; e.g., what does $5,000 have to grow to in 7 years to offset 3% inflation? $5,000 × 1.2299 = $6,149.37.

The "Blow-Your-Mind-by-Adding-Time" Chart

I'll bet you've already guessed that the longer your money compounds, the more deliciously rich you'll get. Letting time work for you is the key to growing your green. The earlier you start investing, the better off you'll be. In fact, the difference between someone who starts investing at age 22 and someone who waits until age 28 is really dramatic, as illustrated here:

♦ Person A invests $2,000 a year for 6 years at 12 percent, starting at age 22. Person A's total investment is $12,000.

♦ Person B spends her first six years out of college blowing her salary on facials and designer suits. But then she settles down and invests $2,000 a year for the next 35 years at 12 percent. Her total investment is $70,000.

Now, here's the "blow-your-mind-by-adding-time" moment. If you read standing up, you might want to sit down. Get this—at age 62, Person A, who only invested $12,000, has earned $959,793. Person B, who invested $70,000, has earned $966,926. Person A earned nearly as much as Person B even though she invested $58,000 less! Ah, but Person A started early ....

What's the moral of the story? All together now, kids: Start early. Let time work for you!

The 10 Percent Habit

In the likelihood that you're over the age of 22, don't despair. (Between you and me, how many 22-year-olds do you know who are investing in anything but having fun?) If you are in your early 20s, though, I hope you're feeling fired up enough to start investing—if only so you can spend your 30s feeling smug. There's a great psychological advantage to starting early. It's easier to get into the investing habit when you're unencumbered by kids. You may be sharing an apartment and making a fairly low income, but you don't have to send anyone to college and you're certainly not staring down the barrel of retirement.

> **Fiscal Facts**
>
> An easy way to figure out how long it will take an investment to double is to use the "Rule of 72." Take any fixed annual interest rate, and divide it into 72 (the average life span nowadays). The result will be the number of years it will take your investment to double. If you expect to earn 6 percent, for example, divide 6 into 72. Your investment will double in 12 years!
>
> Bear in mind that this formula is based on the assumption that the interest rate never changes.

No matter what your age, the sooner you get in the habit of investing 10 percent of every paycheck, the more time your investment plan will have to work. Why 10 percent? It's not a big chunk, but it's not insignificant either. Most people can find ways to cut their spending by 10 percent pretty easily (we'll get into cutting expenses in Chapter 6).

Now, back to time. When talking about investing, time is simply how long you can let your investment program work. Time affects your investment decisions in two ways:

1. The more time you have, the longer your investment has to compound.

2. The more time you have, the more risk you can handle.

Time, Risk, and Your Sanity

One definition of risk is the chance that you'll lose money. Here's a real, extreme example from the stock market of the interrelationship between time, risk, and your sanity.

A *stock* is simply a share of ownership in a corporation. A stockholder literally owns a piece of a company. When you buy AT&T stock, for example, you become one of many owners of AT&T. This, in turn, entitles you to a share of AT&T's profits (or losses!). That share is paid to stockholders as a dividend. Just like an interest payment, you can reinvest a dividend or spend it.

Corporations issue stock to raise money to finance everything from the building of factories to the creation of new divisions or products. This is called *equity* financing, because equity means ownership, and a corporation that sells stock to raise money is selling ownership. Money raised for business purposes is called *capital*.

Assume it is the end of October 1987 and you are heavily invested in stocks. You've witnessed the following sickening drops in the stock market:

- In one day, October 19, 1987, the *Dow Jones*, an average of a group of stock prices used to monitor the stock market, dropped 20 percent.

- Within 10 days, the market had dropped 34 percent.

- By the end of October, the market was down 21.5 percent.

If one month was your time frame, you were one unhappy camper. Putting your family's Christmas money into the stock market in September would have been a lousy idea, because you didn't have time to recover from the crash.

But what if you were in the stock market for the long haul? Let's expand the time frame. Including the crash of Black October, let's see how well you would have done over the last 10 years. Take a look at the following chart to see how investing 10 years in the stock market stacks up against investing 10 years in treasury bonds and treasury bills. FYI: The *S&P 500* is a group of 500 stocks that a Wall Street rating company called Standard & Poor's tracks to get a picture of the stock market. Treasury bonds (T-bonds) and Treasury bills (T-bills) are very safe (i.e., low-risk) investments that are backed by the U.S. Government (we'll talk more about these later in Chapter 3).

Investor's Idiom

When you own **stock,** you own a piece of the company that issued it. Like any owner, you are entitled to a share of the company's profits. The share is paid to stockholders as a **dividend.** You are also vulnerable to the company's losses. Corporations issue stock to raise **capital,** which is a fancy word for money used for business purposes. Raising capital this way is called **equity** financing. Equity means ownership.

Investor's Idiom

Stocks are bought and sold on the **stock market.** The stock market doesn't exist as a physical place—stocks are traded at various stock exchanges, such as the New York Stock Exchange or the American Stock Exchange. The **Dow Jones Average (DJIA)** is an average of 30 well-known companies, such as AT&T or McDonald's, chosen by the editors of *The Wall Street Journal* to represent trends in the stock market.

Total Returns[1]: Periods Ending 10/31/87

	S&P Stocks	Treasury Bonds	Treasury Bills
1 year	+6.6%	−2.3%	+5.6%
10 years compound annual return	+15.9%	+9.2%	+9.2%
Total Percent Change	+337%	+140%	+141%

Wow! Even including the crash, stocks were a superior investment for investors who had the time to ride out the ups and downs.

Want more recent numbers?

Total Returns[1]: Periods Ending 12/31/01

	S&P Stocks	Treasury Bonds	Treasury Bills
1 year	−11.9%	+3.7%	+3.8%
10 years compound annual return	+12.9%	+8.7%	+4.6%
Total Percent Change	+237%	+131%	+56%

(1) Market price increase (decrease) + income (dividends or interest). Source: Calculated using data presented in Stocks, Bonds, Bills and Inflation® 2002 Yearbook, ©Ibbotson Associates, Inc. Based on copyrighted works by Ibbotson and Sinquefield. All rights reserved. Used with permission.

Double Wow! Even with the negative return of 12 percent in 2001, stocks still did substantially better than bonds and bills over the 10 year period. And that's the secret to successful investing: Holding stocks and/or stock mutual funds for at least 10 years.

The Fed's Balancing Act: Dampening Inflation Without Dumping on Us

Probably the most fundamental relationship you'll need to learn about is the one between interest rates and the markets. Maybe at times you've wondered how interest rates are determined.

You've probably heard of the Federal Reserve. That's our country's central bank, and it monitors the activity of all banks in the nation. The Fed is charged with only one task, but it's a doozy. The Full Employment Act of 1946 and the Humphrey-Hawkins Act demand that the Fed keep the economy stoked so people can find jobs, yet also control inflation. This is an almost impossible task—like squeezing a balloon at one end without the other end blowing up with air.

Inflation, as you probably know, is an overall increase in prices. Inflation tends to occur when, as economists love to say, "too much money is chasing too few goods." If everyone in the country has a job and is earning plenty of money to spend, a situation may arise where companies are not able to make enough products to satisfy the demand for them.

If you own a factory that makes stereos and your stereos are flying off the shelves, you will want to make more to satisfy the demand. Only problem is, with full employ-ment, you can't find any workers to hire. So you can't make more stereos. "Well," you think, "all those flush consumers really want to buy my stereos, so I could definitely make some money here. I can't find anyone to help me make more stereos, but I'll bet if I raise the price, people will pay it." This is how full employment can fan the fires of inflation.

Investor's Idiom

The **S&P 500** is a group of 500 stocks that the Wall Street rating company Standard & Poor's tracks to get a picture of the stock market.

The Problem with Inflation

The problem with inflation is that once it takes off, it can outpace wages and lower living standards. If you can buy a bag of groceries in August for $60 and by December the same groceries cost you $75 but your salary hasn't budged, well, you're going to have to start eating less or going to fewer movies or playing fewer rounds of minia-ture golf on the weekend. Now that's no fun!

When the Fed sees evidence of inflation building up, it takes the one action it can, which is to raise interest rates. If you're one of those folks rushing out to throw a new stereo on your credit card and your credit card com-pany informs you that your rate has gone up from 12.5 percent to 14.5 percent, you may give that purchase a second thought. When the Fed raises interest rates, spending calms down a bit and inflation is dampened.

How does the Fed raise rates? Well, every bank in the country is required to keep at least 20 percent of its customers' deposits in its vault overnight. But sometimes a bank runs short at the end of the day and has to borrow money

Investor's Idiom

The Fed manipulates the interest rates we pay for auto loans, mortgages, and like in two main ways. It raises or low-ers the **discount rate**, which banks must pay when they bor-row from the Fed. If the banks have to pay more, they'll turn around and charge you more. The Fed can also indirectly affect the **funds rate** that banks charge each other by adding or drain-ing cash from the banking sys-tem.

from another bank. The rate that banks charge each other for these short-term loans is called the *federal funds rate*.

Okay, stay with me now. The Fed doesn't set the funds rate directly but can affect it by adding or draining the cash reserves to or from the bank system.

In the same way that too much money chasing too few goods causes inflation, if the Fed drains reserves from the system, banks have fewer dollars on hand to lend each other overnight. Since they have less to lend, there will be pressure on the funds rate to rise.

The Fed can also directly control interest rates by raising and lowering the *discount rate*. This is the rate at which banks borrow from the Fed.

Now, the one thing you can count on is that when it costs a bank more money to borrow money, it'll turn around and charge you more money to borrow. So when the funds rate or the discount rate rises, every other interest rate in the country starts to climb. Suddenly, it costs you more money to buy that stereo or a new house. You slow down your spending. Factories slow down their hiring. The economy begins to contract.

Investor's Idiom

A **bond** is an I.O.U. that a corporation or government issues when it wants to borrow money for more than 10 years. The issuer agrees to pay back the bond holder at a specified **maturity** date, with interest.

Conversely, when interest rates fall, it encourages borrowing, expansion, spending, and hiring. When the Fed thinks inflation is under control but jobs are scarce, it encourages the economy to grow by adding reserves to the banking system. This increases the cash available for banks to lend each other, and the funds rate comes down. Interest rates start to decline—people start buying again and companies start expanding and hiring. The economy begins to expand.

What Do Interest Rates Have to Do with Stocks and Bonds? Glad You Asked!

What does all this have to do with stocks and bonds? Plenty! You've already learned that stocks are a form of equity financing—corporations sell ownership in the form of stock to raise capital. Well, bonds are simply a different instrument corporations use to raise capital. A *bond* is a form of debt financing.

When you buy a bond, you are *lending* money to a corporation for a specified length of time, not buying ownership. In return, the company promises to pay back the value of the bond at *maturity* with interest. We'll get into this in more detail later, but for now all you need to know is that if you buy a $100 bond today, when the bond matures in, for example, five years, you will get that $100 back, plus interest. Nothing more, nothing less.

But what if inflation has risen so much during those five years that your $100 only buys $80 worth of groceries? Bonds don't protect investors from inflation at all. That's why when investors hear economic news that makes them worry about inflation, they tend to become more interested in stocks. Inflation can really degrade the value of a bond. Stock prices, on the other hand—just like all other prices in the economy—tend to rise over time, so if you are worried about inflation, you'll find stocks more attractive than bonds because they offer some protection from the corrosive effect of inflation.

Both the stock and bond markets react to changes in interest rates, which in turn affects expectations about inflation—which in turn affects investors' decisions. If you understand that, you're on your way to becoming an educated investor.

Your Personal Time Frame

You could hold one stock forever and either:

- Make a lot of money

- Lose a lot of money

- Break even

Add another stock and, statistically, you will make less or lose less. Keep adding stocks until you own the S&P 500 and you will earn close to the market return. Over periods of 20 years or more, investors have always made money from a market-like portfolio. The average return over that time is around 10 to 12 percent. During a shorter time period, however, the likelihood increases that you will make a lot less or a lot more than 10 to 12 percent. On one day, October 19, 1987, the stock market declined 20 percent. But for the year, it was up 5 percent, and for that decade it was up nearly 16 percent. Go figure!

What does this all mean? Simply, that the risk you assume decreases the longer your time frame is. Risk is reduced as time is added. Here is the relationship between time, risk, and return.

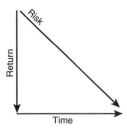

In other words, the later you start investing, the less risk you can afford to take. If you're 60 and hope to retire at 65, and you do some calculations on the back of an envelope and realize you'll be $50,000 short of income when you retire, you shouldn't turn to the stock market because you aren't giving yourself enough time to ride out its risk. If you start to invest for retirement at a young age, on the other hand, you can put a high percentage of your savings in the stock market because you have time to ride out the highs and lows. A good rule of thumb is to give your investments at least 10 years to ride out stock market volatility.

Given a decent time frame, though, stocks have historically performed quite well. Here's the data going back to 1926, when the forerunner to the Standard & Poor's 500, the Standard & Poor's 90, was first tabulated:

Compound Annual Return 1926–2001

Standard & Poor's 500 Stock Index	+10.7%
Long-Term Government Bonds Index	+5.3%
U.S. Treasury Bills Index	+3.8%
Inflation (Consumer Price Index)	+3.1%

(Source: Ibbotson Associates, Inc. Stocks, Bonds, Bills and Inflation® 2002 Yearbook. All rights reserved. Used with permission.)

As you can see, the total return for stocks was 2 times that for risk-free government bonds and 3.5 times the inflation rate for the last 76 years. Looks like stocks are worth the risk, if you can hold them for at least 10 years.

Every investment goal will have a different time frame, though. It depends on what your personal short- and long-term goals are. You might want to buy your first house in five years, for example. Your savings for that goal would have to be in investments that won't fluctuate too much during that short time period. Perhaps you just got married, and, although there might not be a child on the scene for a couple years, you want to begin a 20-year savings plan for his or her college education. In this case, you have a lot more freedom in how to invest.

In general, what you invest in depends on your investment time frame. The less time you have to achieve your goal, the less you should invest in riskier investments like stocks. If you have a longer time frame, your chances of success on the market will increase. We'll go into your personal time frames in much greater depth in Chapter 2. But first, let's figure out how you *really* feel about risk.

The Least You Need to Know

- Instead of spending any money you earn on an investment, reinvest it and let compounding interest build your wealth.

- Start to invest as early in life as you can by making a habit of saving and investing 10 percent of your salary.

- Riskier investments, like the stock market, can make you a lot of money, but only if you have time to ride out the ups and downs.

- Expectations about inflation affect the financial markets and investors' decisions.

- The later you start investing, the less risk you can afford to take.

How Do You Really Feel About Risk?

In This Chapter

- ◆ How much risk is too much for you?
- ◆ How to figure out your return on any investment
- ◆ Understanding the relationship between risk and return
- ◆ Getting a grip on your own risk tolerance
- ◆ Evaluating your unique time frame

Jumped out of any airplanes lately? Or are you the type who white-knuckled it and sucked down three drinks during your last commercial flight?

Whether we perceive a given situation as exciting or terrifying has to do with our tolerance for risk. Many of us like to kid ourselves about how much risk we're willing to accept. We dream of jumping out of a plane or skiing top-speed down a sheer slope—but when we find ourselves at the door of that plane or the top of that slope, we wish we had our feet firmly planted on terra firma.

You can chicken out of skydiving or skiing with only your pride to salvage, but if you make investments that require more risk tolerance than you have, you'll be a miserable, sleep-deprived wreck. So the first step before you invest in anything is to analyze and get comfortable with your risk tolerance. The investment world is no place for false bravado.

What Is Return?

In investing, risk doesn't mean credit risk or the risk of bankruptcy, but rather the risk that an investment's return will disappoint or surprise you. When you invest in something, you decide to do so because you expect to get more money out than you put in. The difference between the amount you put in and the total amount you receive at the end of the investment period is your *return*.

Return on investment (ROI) is also called rate of return. It's typically expressed as a percentage of the original investment. Let's say your little brother asks to borrow $500 to buy an old car that he intends to fix up and resell. When he sells the car for $1,000, he gives you back your $500 and splits the $500 profit with you. You get $500 plus $250, or $750. Since $250 is half of $500, for every dollar you invested, you earned 50¢. Your ROI is 50 percent.

What You Made, What You Paid

Here's a formula you can use to calculate the return on any investment:

1. The total you receive at the end of the investment period is your end-of-period wealth (A).

2. Your original investment is called your beginning-of-period wealth (B).

3. If you subtract your beginning-of-period wealth (B) from your end-of-period wealth, you'll get your return: A – B.

Investor's Idiom

Risk is the chance that your investment's return will either disappoint or pleasantly surprise you.

Return is the amount you earn from an investment over a given period of time. Generally, higher returns require the investor to assume greater risk.

Return on investment (ROI) is also called rate of return, and is expressed as a percentage of your original investment.

Now that you've figured out your return, you can easily calculate your ROI. Use the following formula to figure out your return as a percentage of your original investment (B).

$$\frac{[A - B]}{B} \times 100 = ROI$$

Applying the formula to the preceding example, you get:

$$\frac{[\$750 - \$500]}{\$500} \times \$100 = \frac{\$250}{\$500} \times 100 = .50 \times 100 = 50\%$$

Hopefully, this doesn't look too hard to you. But if it does, an easy way to remember this formula is the following:

What you made (e.g., $250) over what you paid (e.g., $500), divided by what you paid, times 100.

Fear of Heights: The Higher the Return, the Greater the Risk

When you lent your brother the money to buy that car, you took on the risk that a number of things could have gone wrong:

- He might not have been able to sell the car.

- The car might have been stolen or vandalized before he sold it.

- He could have sold it for a disappointing return.

Before lending him the money, you calculated your ROI in your head—even if you didn't know that's what you were doing!—and found it acceptable payback for the risk you were accepting. If your brother lives in a neighborhood where cars are stolen every night, maybe you would have decided not to risk your $500. Then again, if he swore to you that he could resell the

Fiscal Facts

When the word *on* shows up in a business term, it means "divided by." So return *on* investment really means return *divided by* investment. Looking at the formula for ROI, this becomes clear. Return is A–B, which is then divided by B, giving you the investment amount. We just multiply by 100 to express the result as a percentage.

car for $1,500, making your return $500 instead of $250, maybe you'd have gone for it anyway. After all, a 100 percent return on investment is nothing to sneeze at.

In this case: $\dfrac{[\$1,000 - \$500]}{500} = \dfrac{\$500}{500} = 1 \times 100 = 100\%$

You've just uncovered an unimpeachable rule of investment: the higher the return, the greater the risk. If you ever had a coach whose mantra was "No pain, no gain," you've already digested this concept. No matter what someone tries to tell you, the higher the return you are offered on an investment, the greater the risk.

CAUTION Crash Alert

Now that you understand the relationship between risk and return, you'll never be fooled by investments that promise a high return with little or no risk of losing your money. Remember, if someone is offering you a high return on your investment, it's because the investment is high risk. There's no such thing as a low-risk investment that generates high returns.

The rate of return from investing in a small business, for example, can be very high. But roughly one out of every seven small businesses fails, so the risk of losing your investment is very high as well. In contrast, the return banks offer on savings accounts is typically very low—3 or 4 percent. But the risk that you will lose your money if you put it in a savings account is also very low.

In addition, you learned in Chapter 1 that risk is reduced as time is added because over time ups and downs in your investment have a chance to even out. In other words, risk falls as time passes—and this increases your chances of superior returns. The relationship between risk, return, and time looks like this:

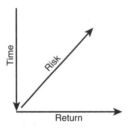

The Tools of the Trade

To control risk, investment professionals use several tactics, which you can apply yourself to your own portfolio of investments.

Before we discuss these tactics, let's look at a basic tenet of investment theory: *standard deviation*. Don't panic. No need to fear scary flashbacks of the math section of the SAT. It's just a mathematical term that helps to frame the likelihood (or, in math terms, probability) of a given number recurring.

Standard Deviation and a Podunk Potato

Freddie has played third base for the Podunk Potatoes for the past 12 years. His batting average each year has been:

1) .290	5) .390	9) .330
2) .380	6) .320	10) .340
3) .300	7) .270	11) .350
4) .310	8) .370	12) .370

What will he bat in his thirteenth year? Let's look at his average. To calculate the average of any group of figures, simply add them together and divide by the number of figures—12, in this case.

Freddie's average is .335. But maybe in years two and five, Freddie got lucky and his batting average was boosted by a stew of easy pitches.

And, let's say he was bothered by injuries in years one and seven, when he did particularly badly. These aren't normal situations, so why don't we just throw out those four years? This is similar to what figure skating and gymnastics judges do when scoring a routine—they throw out the highest and lowest scores. This is also what financial analysts do when they are trying to find a pattern in a bunch of numbers. They disregard the very highest and the very lowest numbers. Analysts usually dump about a third of the numbers they are given, which is what we're doing in this case by getting rid of four out of 12 of Freddie's batting averages.

If we get rid of years one, two, five, and seven, Freddie's lowest score turns out to be the .300 he batted in year three. His highest score becomes the .370 he batted in year 12. The difference between those two years, or the spread, is:

$$.370 - .300 = .70$$

Investor's Idiom

Your **portfolio** is the mix of assets in which you have invested. A portfolio contains investment instruments that you've selected to achieve your financial goals, such as common stocks, bonds, Treasury bills, etc.

An **asset** is any item of value—from baseball cards to stocks—that you own.

A **liability** is a debt you owe, while an asset is something you own.

So we could think of Freddie as someone who tends to bat between .300 and .370. If we divide that .70 difference in half, we could say that Freddie bats his average of .335 plus or minus .35. That "plus or minus .35" is called the *first level standard deviation*. It gives you a pretty clear picture of Freddie's potential future performance: His batting average in a given year can *deviate* up or down from the overall average by .35.

Deviant Behavior

We can follow the same procedure with the stock market by looking at the annual returns for the market as far back as we want to go. Let's assume that for a single year, the stock market returned 12 percent with a standard deviation of plus or minus 15. This would mean that stocks returned between +27 percent (12 + 15) and –3 percent (12 – 15) that year.

That same year, bonds returned 5 percent and money market instruments returned 3 percent. Well, if the stock you were holding was at the low end of the stock market return, you would've actually lost –3 percent and probably would've been happier with your money parked in bonds or even in a savings account.

What's interesting, though, is that when we look at stock market returns over a 20-year period, the standard deviation really comes down from +/–15 to closer to +/–3. This means stock investors who stay in the market for 20 years could expect returns of 12 percent +/–3. The low would be 12 percent –3, or 9 percent. The high would be 12 percent +3, or 15 percent. This means that, for investors with a 20-year time horizon, stocks have historically performed very well. Also, for each and every 20-year period, stocks have returned more than bonds. Over time the returns from stocks smooth out and the deviation drops.

Basically, the longer you hold a high-risk investment like stock, the smaller the standard deviation will become. Over time all the fluctuations matter less and less. What matters is how the investment performs over the long run, not the short term. Historically, stocks have been very volatile over short periods, but have performed very well over 10–20 year horizons. The more time you have, therefore, the more risk you can handle.

Fiscal Facts

A huge amount of wealth is invested in the stock market. The estimated value of American stocks is $11.3 trillion, according to Herbert Barchoff, who's been around long enough to see the confidence Americans have in the stock market go from zero to today's somewhat unrealistic level. Barchoff was a member of the President's Council of Economic Advisor's during the Truman Administration. (Source: *The New York Times*, June 19, 1998.)

Therefore, we can say that the standard deviation (risk) of the highest risk/highest return investment declines as the time frame increases. This is a key concept in investment theory and, for your purposes, asset allocation.

How does this all apply to you? Well, once you understand how time, risk, and return interact, you can begin to think about how to allocate your investment assets. Simply put, if your time frame is short, you shouldn't own much common stock. If you have a long time frame, you should have a substantial portion of your assets allocated to stock, because over time the ups and downs in the stock market—as represented by the standard deviation—tend to cancel each other out.

The Three Broad Investment Classes

There are basically three broad classes of investments from which you can choose when you build your portfolio:

1. Common Stocks

2. Bonds

3. Money Market Instruments

As you learned in Chapter 1, common stocks represent shares of ownership in a company. Corporations sell ownership in the form of stock to raise capital. This is called equity financing.

As an owner, you are entitled to the fruits of the company's success: higher cash dividends and, ultimately (and hopefully), a higher stock price. On the other hand, you are vulnerable to the costs of failure: a reduction in (or even elimination of) the cash dividend and a lower (perhaps substantially lower) stock price.

Bonds, you'll recall from Chapter 1, are a form of debt financing. When you buy a bond you are lending money for a specified length of time.

Money market instruments pay rates that vary from day to day, week to week, or month to month. They are very liquid. This means they can be converted to cash easily and quickly. A savings account or a money market fund can be

Investor's Idiom

When a corporation issues stock, it is essentially selling pieces of ownership (called "equity") in the company. When you buy a share of GM common stock, you become an owner of General Motors. You are now entitled to a share of the company's profits, which are paid to stockholders **as dividends.** Most stock is simply **common stock,** but some is preferred. The owners of **preferred stock** get their dividends first.

Investor's Idiom

An investment is considered **liquid** if it can be converted into cash quickly and easily. Money market instruments offer liquidity, because they can be converted to cash right away or within 24 hours.

cashed in any day for the same price you paid. Treasury bills can be sold within 24 hours. To liquidate a bond (or stock), on the other hand, might take some time because you have to find someone to buy it. The purpose of money market instruments is to provide instant (or close-to-instant) liquidity in your portfolio.

Stocks are riskier investments than money market instruments or bonds, but because they are riskier, they generate higher returns.

Variety Is the Spice of Life

What's life without a little diversity? Well, in the world of investing, diversity can mean the difference between taking off or crashing and burning. *Diversification* is another method investment pros use to increase your portfolio's ability to handle greater risk—and thereby earn greater returns.

In Chapter 1, we discussed how if you keep adding stocks to your portfolio until you own the 500 stocks in the S&P 500, you will earn close to the average market return. The reason for increasing your number of stock holdings is to help minimize *event risk*. This is the risk that one event could really damage the value of a stock you own.

Investor's Idiom

Diversification is a method of decreasing risk by increasing the variety of assets in a portfolio. If you own lots of different stocks, for example, your whole portfolio won't tank if one company goes bankrupt.

In 1997, while the S&P 500 Stock Index was up 33 percent, McDonald's stock rose only 6 percent. Why? Well, the Arch Deluxe didn't exactly fly off the grill, if you recall. There was also some media flap about the quality of your average McDonald's meal. So, if you had all your money in McDonald's stock, you were probably too queasy to eat a dozen Arch Deluxes for the sake of saving your investment.

On the other hand, in the first six months of 1998, the S&P was up close to 18 percent, but McDonald's stock price skyrocketed 50 percent. Why? McDonald's went on a campaign to solve its problems—dumping the loser burger and running some popular specials, like its Beanie Baby™ giveaway. Now here's what's really interesting—over that year and half, the returns for the S&P 500 and for McDonald's stock are very close. The S&P 500 didn't perform as spectacularly as McDonald's did in the first six months of 1998, but neither did it drop as dizzyingly in 1997. This is the value of diversification—over time it may dampen the highs, but it cushions the lows.

Quiz Thyself to Know Thyself: Risk Tolerance Quiz

The key to successful investing is to determine how much risk you can handle, taking into consideration:

♦ Your future obligations, such as children, a mortgage, or a business.

♦ Your liquidity constraints, for example, if you don't have health insurance and you break your leg, you'll need cash to cover the medical bills.

♦ Your growth requirements, such as the standard of living you want to maintain when you retire. Social Security probably won't do it for you, so you'll need some investments that really grow, like stocks.

♦ Your investment objectives—such as keeping your investments safe—growth, and income.

♦ Your investment philosophy, i.e., how willing are you to take risk? How much time do you have?

Investor's Idiom

Risk tolerance is how much risk an investor is willing to assume in order to increase the level of potential reward.

But how do you know whether you can ride out the bumps and take the lumps that long-term investors in high-risk, high-return investments like stocks have to tolerate? How do you know what your risk tolerance level is? To complete the quiz, simply make a check mark next to the statement that best describes your feelings. To score the quiz, simply add up the numbers next to your check marks. Then look up your score on our handy Risk Chart.

A. ____ 1) I'd be willing to do without some of the potential to earn more money on my investments in order to receive some minimal assured rate of return.

____ 2) I'm much more concerned with getting solid, consistent results on my investments than superior investment returns.

____ 3) Hey, you've got to be in it to win it! I can accept fluctuating year-by-year returns in order to achieve higher total returns in the long run.

B. ____ 1) Although I may not get as much income right now on my investment, I'm interested in preserving what capital I have and don't want to see the market value of my securities decrease. When it comes to my future, I like to play it safe.

____ 2) When it comes to my investments, show me the money: Current income more important than capital preservation.

_____ 3) Sure, I'm interested in preserving my capital, but I can take some decrease of market value to increase the income I'm earning on my investments right now.

C. _____ 1) Even looking at dice gives me the willies! I am definitely not much of a gambler. I'm more concerned in preserving the value of my current assets than in investing in riskier securities that have the potential to increase in value later on.

_____ 2) Growth of my assets in the future is as important to me as preserving the value of my current assets.

_____ 3) I am more concerned with providing greater future growth than playing it safe now and preserving my current assets.

D. _____ 1) Keeping risk very low is more important for me than taking a chance in order to achieve superior investment returns.

_____ 2) Hey, there's chance in everything. Some market risk is inevitable in order to get the growth I deem necessary from my investments.

_____ 3) The final result is more important than how I got there. If I have to risk a bad year to meet my goal, that's okay.

E. _____ 1) I feel I can make a fairly accurate prediction of what my future liabilities will be.

_____ 2) Well, I may not have a crystal ball, but I think I can accurately predict some of my future liabilities. Other possible liabilities are subject to rough estimates.

_____ 3) Do I look like a fortune teller? I am relatively uncertain about what my future liabilities will be.

F. _____ 1) I don't like to put my eggs in one (or two) baskets. I believe in keeping my investment portfolio well diversified.

_____ 2) I don't like complications. I think it's best to keep the investment process simple. I use one or two types of investments with which I am comfortable. That's all I need.

_____ 3) You don't get to be a billionaire by playing it safe. The final result is more important than how it was derived. Diversification is not a major issue for me.

G. _____ 1) The Blue Chip (high quality) stocks of solid, mature companies give me the perfect combination of income and stability. I don't need to have superlative growth on my investments to be satisfied.

_____ 2) Blue chip companies are great, but I don't necessarily need to be that conservative with my investments. The stocks of solid companies in growing businesses will give very good results with a level of risk I can tolerate.

_____ 3) Entrepreneurship is where it's at. Small companies' stocks may be more   volatile, but I prefer them because they reward me with the highest long-term rates of return.

> **Fiscal Facts** _____
>
> Interestingly enough, the term **blue chip** was coined in nineteenth century poker games. The blue chip is the one with the highest value.

H. Given the choice of the following three investments identical in every other respect, I would choose:

_____ 1) Investment 1: 100 percent chance of a 5 percent rate of return per year over the next 5 years.

_____ 2) Investment 2: 75 percent chance of a 10 percent rate of return per year, 25 percent chance of a 4 percent rate of return per year over the next 5 years.

_____ 3) Investment 3: 50 percent chance of a 20 percent rate of return per year, 50 percent chance of a 0 percent rate of return per year over the next 5 years.

I. Use the following graph to answer the following question.

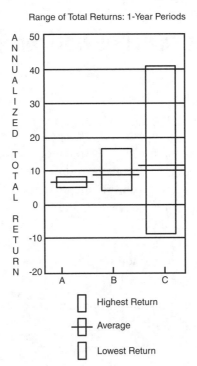

Range of Total Returns: 1-Year Periods

ANNUALIZED TOTAL RETURN

Highest Return

Average

Lowest Return

Assuming the expected rate of inflation over the next year is 4 percent, which investment option would you choose for a one-year time horizon?

_____ 1) Investment A would be the most appropriate of the three alternatives for my needs.

_____ 2) Investment B would be the most appropriate of the three alternatives for my needs.

_____ 3) Investment C would be the most appropriate of the three alternatives for my needs.

Calculate Your Score:

Your Risk Tolerance Rating

Point Total	Risk Level		
	Low	Medium	High
9–14	X		
15–21		X	
22–27			X

Got the Time? Take the Time Horizon Quiz

Are we done? Can you go to sleep now? Not quite. We haven't addressed time frame.

Each of us has our own attitude toward time, and before you invest a dime, you need to determine yours. Believe it or not, though, almost everybody is a short-term, medium-term, and long-term investor simultaneously. How so? You might be saving for retirement, investing to send your kids to college, *and* saving for a vacation all at once. Each of these savings plans has its own time horizon; that is, each has a limit as to how much time is needed to reach the intended goal. How do you figure out what this time horizon is? Well, sometimes you may find that your investment priorities conflict. The manner in which you most consistently opt to resolve those conflicts indicates your true investment time horizon. Take the following quiz and check your results on the scale. Again, simply add up the numbers next to each question and find where you fall on the Time Frame Chart:

A. Considering time to be the most important factor distinguishing the three investments shown on the following page:

_____ 1) Investment A would be most appropriate for my needs.

_____ 2) Investment B would be most appropriate for my needs.

_____ 3) Investment C would be most appropriate for my needs.

B. _____ 1) It is most important to grow assets in an investment fund in the next 1 to 2 years.

_____ 2) It is most important to grow assets in an investment fund in the next 5 years.

_____ 3) It is most important to grow assets in an investment fund in the next 10 years or longer.

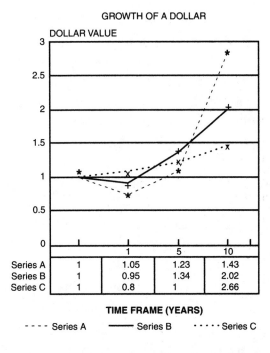

GROWTH OF A DOLLAR

	1	5	10
Series A	1	1.05	1.23	1.43
Series B	1	0.95	1.34	2.02
Series C	1	0.8	1	2.66

TIME FRAME (YEARS)

- - - - Series A   ——— Series B   · · · · Series C

C. _____ 1) I'm not one to jump to conclusions. I don't feel it's necessary to make decisions based on individual quarterly rates of return. However, four consecutive disappointing quarters may cause me to rethink my investment strategy.

_____ 2) I do not make decisions based on one year of investment returns. However, two consecutive disappointing years or a disappointing 5-year period may weaken my confidence in my current investment strategy.

_____ 3) I know that good things are worth waiting for. Ten years is my preferred barometer for measuring investment results.

Investor's Idiom _____

In the investment world, the year is divided into three-month **quarters.** Companies are required to report their financial performance to stockholders every quarter. the **quarterly rate of return** is the return on investment for one quarter, as opposed to **annual return,** which is an investment's return over one year. Companies and mutual funds report results both quarterly and annually.

D. ____ 1) My concerns lie in the here and now. I am most interested in maintaining my current financial position.

____ 2) I've done fairly well over the past 5 years. Why not continue in that progress over the next 5 years?

____ 3) Time is on my side. My financial position has barely started to reach its potential. I look forward to rapid growth.

E. ____ 1) Safety first, I always say. If I can get high yields from bonds, I will forgo the future potential for gains in stocks.

____ 2) I don't need to totally play it safe, but I would be willing to accept lower levels of growth over a period of 5 years in order to hold on to consistent year-to-year returns.

____ 3) You've got to take the bad with the good. I'm willing to accept one year with a negative rate of return (for example, between –5 percent and –10 percent) in order to provide greater total returns over a period between 5 and 10 years.

F. Given a choice between receiving $100,000 this year or $300,000 10 years from today:

____ 1) I would accept $100,000 this year.

____ 2) I consider both offers to be equally attractive.

____ 3) I would accept $300,000 10 years from today.

Check Your Score:

Your Time Horizon Score

Point Total	Time Frame		
	Short (0–2 yrs.)	Intermediate (2–10 yrs.)	Long (over 10 yrs.)
6–9	X		
10–13		X	
14–18			X

If you had any difficulty getting through these quizzes, don't panic. You're just going with your gut reaction right now. In fact, for those who are intimidated, we recommend that you return to them after you've read a few more chapters and feel a little more confident. Once you've completed these quizzes and found yourself on the tables, you should have a much clearer picture of your time frame and how you really feel about risk. Now your personal investment philosophy is shaping up.

The Least You Need to Know

- ◆ Return is the amount you expect to earn from an investment.

- ◆ The higher the promised return on an investment, the greater the risk that you will be disappointed in the investment's performance.

- ◆ To reduce risk, you can increase both the time you give your investments to perform and the diversification of your portfolio.

- ◆ There are three broad investment classes: stocks, bonds, and money market instruments.

- ◆ Money market instruments, unlike stocks and bonds, offer liquidity; that is, they can be easily and quickly changed into cash.

Are You a Grasshopper or an Ant? Selecting Your Investment Objectives

In This Chapter

◆ Getting your investment objectives straight right now

◆ How to build your emergency fund

◆ Where to keep your rainy day cash

◆ How best to juggle your present and future investment objectives—without dropping any balls

◆ What does comfortable retirement mean?

◆ Pros and cons of retiring early

Remember Aesop's fable of the ant and the grasshopper? In a nutshell, the grasshopper mocks the hard-working ant for wasting a beautiful summer afternoon toiling away storing food for the winter. Of course, the warm summer rays give way to colder northern winds. As the grasshopper gets stuck out in the cold with nothing, nada, zip to eat, the ant is happily feeding his face in his warm anthill.

The moral of the story is, of course, if you don't prepare now, you're going to be one sorry grasshopper later. But does this mean you can't have any more fun? Of course not. It just means that if you want to have *any* fun in the future, you'd better get your investment objectives straight now. For instance, most people don't think about retirement planning for the simple reason that they've got plenty of other really important things to think about and plan for right now. And then there are the other near-future goals looming ahead, like getting married, buying a house, or sending the kids (whether you have them now or are planning to soon) to college. How do you juggle your multiple financial goals and pressures and still save for a comfortable retirement? Read on!

Just-in-Case Cash

Most investors either never get around to establishing a plan for retirement, or if they do they deviate from it. Think of your financial plan as a stroll down a beautiful trail in the woods. If you stay on the path, you'll eventually reach your destination, but if you chase every butterfly or every storm sends you running for shelter, you'll get lost and may never find your way back to your path.

Hospitalizations, funerals, weddings, auto or home repairs, gifts, taxes, etc., don't show up programmed on a calendar. They occur with little or no advance warning, and you either have funds set aside to cover them or you go into debt. And going into debt, both financially and psychologically, can take the fun out of a happy event or make a sad one even sadder.

Your umbrella for those times when life drenches you with unexpected expenses is your emergency fund. This should be roughly 10 percent of your annual income or $10,000, whichever is greater. Some experts recommend keeping half your annual salary in an emergency fund, but that's a bit extreme. If you're making $50,000 a year or less, it's awfully hard to save $25,000. These days—what with low down payments available on homes and easy car financing—few emergencies require $25,000, as long as you have health insurance. Ten percent or $10,000 should cover you for most of life's financial emergencies. This is the single most important thing you can do to secure your financial future; an emergency fund ensures that you never have to touch your investments.

> **Super Strategy**
>
> Don't forget the 10 percent rule: Put aside 10 percent of every paycheck and you'll be able to painlessly create your emergency fund.

Mattresses Are for Sleeping, Not Stashing

It's important to save money for emergencies—but it's equally vital that you have immediate access to that money when a serious situation does arise. (And, no, keeping your cash under the mattress is *not* the best place, even if it is immediately accessible!) So what investments are available that combine liquidity and safety for amounts under $100,000? (We assume you are not John D. Rockefeller.) You basically have four options:

- ◆ Treasury Bills
- ◆ Certificates of Deposit
- ◆ Savings Accounts
- ◆ Money Market Funds

All these investments are called cash equivalents, because they can be quickly and easily turned into cash.

> **Investor's Idiom**
>
> **Liquid investments** are those which can be turned into cash within 24 hours. Treasury bills, CDs, savings accounts, and money market funds are all **cash equivalents** that are highly liquid.

Treasury Bills

You can park your emergency fund in Treasury bills (or T-bills) and earn a nice return on your money while you enjoy the security of knowing that your funds are now a direct obligation of the U.S. Government. This means that, if necessary, the Treasury will turn on the printing press to make sure you receive your principal. Treasury bills are sold at a discount that reflects their yield, or interest. A $10,000 six-month T-bill, for example, might be sold for $9,750. You buy the bill for $9,750 and six months later you get $10,000.

To figure out the yield, simply apply our old pal, the ROI (return on investment) formula:

$$\$10,000 - \$9,750 \div \$9,750 \times 100 = 2.564\%$$

That's the return for six months; the annual return would be 2.564 percent times two, or 5.1282 percent.

> **Investor's Idiom**
>
> **Treasury bills,** or **T-bills,** are essentially I.O.U.s from the U.S. Government. They are available in three-month, six-month, and one-year maturities and are used by the U.S. Treasury Department to finance the national debt and day-to-day government cash flow crunches. They are fully guaranteed by the government and can be sold within 24 hours.

Bills are sold by the Treasury at sales called "auctions." They are usually available in 4-week, 13-week, 26-week, or 1-year maturities. The minimum purchase is $1,000. Auction purchases for 13- and 26-week T-bills are typically held every Monday and settled on Thursday. The settlement date is the day you must actually pay for your bill purchase. Sales proceeds are available on a next-day basis.

You may purchase bills directly from the U.S. Government via the Treasury Direct Program or via banks or brokers, usually for a service fee. If you buy directly from the Treasury, you can do so in person, by mail, by phone (1-800-722-2678) or via the Internet at www.publicdebt.treas.gov/sec/secinvsr.htm. To utilize the latter two alternatives, you will need to provide a signature to open your account.

Certificates of Deposit

"CDs" are issued by banks or thrifts (another term for savings and loans), with the first $100,000 insured by the federal government. Terms typically are for a fixed maturity ranging from 3 months to 10 years. If you need your funds before maturity, you will pay a penalty that may run as high as three months of interest for CDs maturing within one year, and six months of interest for CDs maturing after a year. The minimum purchase required is $1,000, but any dollar sum above $1,000 is acceptable ($1,100.21, for example).

When using CDs you have to stay on top of your maturity dates or the bank will automatically roll it over for another period. Prior to maturity, the financial institution will usually inform you in writing of the upcoming maturity date and give you three options:

- ◆ Collect the proceeds
- ◆ Roll over the sum due
- ◆ Change the amount or the maturity

Crash Alert

Although you can always cash Treasury Bills within 24 hours, if you sell before the maturity, you may receive less than the maturity value, and perhaps even less than the amount you invested!

Investor's Idiom

The **yield** on a Treasury bill is its return on investment; it's a way of expressing as a percentage the difference between the discount price and the value at maturity of the bill. You place an order to buy Treasury securities at auctions and actually pay for them on the settlement date.

Crash Alert

If you cash in a CD early, you will be penalized. For example, the typical six-month $1,000 CD might incur a penalty of around $12 if you cashed it at three months. If the CD was paying 4 percent interest, you would have expected a return of $40 for a year or $20 for six months, so that $12 penalty sucks up more than half of what you'd hoped to have earned.

Usually the CD is rolled over into a new CD of like maturity if you do nothing. If you invest in CDs, just be aware that banks love to automatically roll them over when they mature. If you don't tell your bank prior to maturity that you want to collect the proceeds of your six-month CD, for example, the bank will automatically lock you into another six months and you won't be able to withdraw your money before then without paying a penalty. And the penalties for early withdrawal can be pretty stiff.

Savings Accounts

Savings accounts offer one advantage over T-bills and CDs—same day deposit and withdrawal. With T-bills and CDs it takes 24 hours to get at your emergency fund. Like CDs, saving accounts are insured by the federal government up to $100,000. Rates typically run 1–2 percent below other money market fund rates. Interest checking accounts pay even less (e.g., 1–2 percent) but are very convenient.

Money Market Funds

Money market funds (MMFs) are mutual funds that invest only in safe, short-term money market instruments, such as Treasury securities, CDs, or short-term debt (called commercial paper) issued by creditworthy corporations.

Shares in a money market fund are bought and sold on a daily basis and are priced at $1 each. Although these funds are not insured or guaranteed, no money market fund wants to "break the buck" or admit to being unable to pay your $1 per share price if you want to cash in your shares. In those few instances where an asset was in question, the fund stepped in to insure the $1 price.

If you want greater assurance, limit your choice to money market funds that only buy Treasury or other government securities, without *repos*. Repos are securities the fund lends to broker-dealers who pledge assets to cover the loan equal to typically 102 percent of the sum borrowed. Much as a bank earns interest by lending out your deposits as loans, the MMF earns interest on these repos.

Fiscal Facts

The Federal Deposit Insurance Corporation (FDIC) was created in 1933 to furnish insurance protection for depositors in the event that their bank fails. Savings and checking accounts, and certificates of deposit are all protected up to $100,000 by the FDIC.

Investor's Idiom

Money market funds are mutual funds that invest in safe, short-term investments like Treasury securities or CDs. Some also invest in commercial paper, which is short-term debt issued by corporations to raise cash. Some MMFs lend the securities in their funds to broker-dealers in order to earn more interest. These securities are called repos.

The other catch with repos is that you can't deduct all the interest on your state tax return. The interest earned by the repos is taxable.

The Wall Street Journal lists approximately 880 taxable money market funds and approximately 350 tax-free funds. The *Journal* also lists the average maturity of the assets in each fund. Look in *The Wall Street Journal* on Thursdays under Money Market Mutual Funds in the Money & Investing Section. Your local newspaper also probably lists MMFs.

CAUTION

Crash Alert _____

If you have mutual funds, don't use them for emergencies. Many folks get so excited about investing that they run out and purchase mutual funds before setting up emergency funds. But if your adventurous significant other wrenches his or her back while skydiving in Zimbabwe and you suddenly need a $2,000 airplane ticket and don't have an emergency fund, you'll have to sell your mutual fund. That's a taxable act, bud, so not only will you trash your investment program, you'll pay the Feds for the privilege.

For a minimum balance, your money market fund may provide you with a free checking account. Checks usually have to be for at least $250. If you have a brokerage account, your broker may offer you a limited choice of MMFs. You may also open an account directly with some money market funds, such as The Vanguard Group (flagship. vanguard.com/VGApp/hnw/PersonalHome), for example. Some people really like the convenience of opening a brokerage account with their local bank and transferring funds between the brokerage account and their checking account. Before you take this route, investigate the fees, if any, your bank will charge for transfers and other services.

Eenie, Meenie, Minie, Mo

Let's take a moment to evaluate these four options, as they pertain to your emergency fund:

	Pros	Cons
Savings Account	Insured, liquid	Low rates
CD	Insured, competitive	Fixed rates and maturity, penalty if redeemed before maturity
Money Market Account	Liquid, competitive rates	Not insured
Treasury Bills	Liquid, competitive rates	Can lose some principal if sold before maturity, min. purchase required

Before deciding where to keep your emergency fund, think, above all, about what's most convenient for you:

◆ How easy or inconvenient is it for you to get to your bank?

◆ Does it offer all the services you desire, such as Treasury securities, savings bonds, CDs, automatic teller machines (ATMs), brokerage services, etc.?

◆ How do the interest-earning rates on liquid accounts at your bank compare to others? Can you earn more somewhere else? Is it convenient?

◆ Would you prefer to let a bank reinvest (roll over) your CDs rather than have to call or see your broker when T-bills mature?

How Can I Bring Home the Bacon, Fry It Up in a Pan, and Have Some Left Over?

You want cash for a rainy day. You want to chill out on a warm beach when you hit 65 because, hell, you deserve it. But what about all the in-between stuff? You want a nice house. You want smart, well-educated kids. Maybe you even have dreams of becoming your own boss one of these days. These aren't such lofty goals—but achieving them will require some careful planning. We're going to go into greater detail about these topics later on, but for now, let's take a quick look at these near-future investment objectives.

And Baby Makes How Much?

New parents dote on their kids, live and breathe for their kids, usually; at least until the little darlings hit surly adolescence and start applying Goth makeup. That's perfectly fine and how it should be, but be careful that your children don't become butterflies that delight you but lure you off your financial path into dark and spooky woods.

When you have children, it's natural to want to plan to send them to the finest schools in the land and to save for their education first and foremost. At the risk of heresy, though, let's agree that your retirement needs must take precedence over your children's education. Remember, first, that their admission to the college of their (or your) choice is driven as much by their secondary school achievements as by the size of your checkbook.

> **Super Strategy**
>
> A good habit to establish early in your family's beginnings is to dump all cash gifts for the children from relatives and friends into their educational funds.

In addition, there are many more options available to fund a college education—such as loans, grants, gifts from relatives, scholarships, work/study programs, and summer jobs—than there are for retirement. And if you *really* want to secure a happy future for your children, don't saddle them with destitute elderly parents. Risking your financial security to ensure your child's college education does not make sense. (The same advice applies to grandparents who are involved in financing their grandchildren's educations.)

Also remember that you will have devoted much love and support to bringing them to the point where they are eligible for college. Let them help you share the next step by contributing money from summer or part-time jobs to their college funds. Their own contributions might make their college experience more meaningful to them, grumble as they may. As Dear Abby (Abigail Van Buren) once counseled: "If you want your children to turn out well, spend twice as much time with them and half as much money."

Having said all that, of course you should save for your children's education. But first establish your emergency fund. By the time you've done this, you should have established a pretty steady habit of saving 10 percent of your salary for investment purposes. From this sum, target 20 percent for educational purposes from the time of the birth of your first child until the graduation from college of your last child. So, for every $10 of your salary you save, invest $2 in education and put $8 toward retirement.

Crash Alert

The biggest financial planning error new parents make is to put saving for their children's education ahead of saving for their own retirement. It's much wiser to put your own financial security first. A great rule of thumb is to divide the 10 percent of your salary you should be saving for the future so that 2 percent of it goes to college funds and 8 percent goes toward your retirement.

This time frame means that if you're going to work for 40 years, for about half of those years you can save 10 percent exclusively for retirement. The remaining 20 years you will probably be splitting the 10 percent 20/80 between education and retirement. We'll take a close look at the best places to put your education dollars in Chapter 16.

Oh, Give Me a Roof

Another big expenditure you may face, besides retirement and college, might be the down payment on a home. But if you think of this expense properly, it needn't throw you off your path to retirement savings.

First off, think of a home as shelter, not as investment—no matter how many ex-baseball pitchers you've heard extolling second mortgages on TV. A home down payment, ideally, would come from the $10,000-plus in emergency savings you've already set aside. We'll get into home ownership in greater detail in Chapter 15.

Who's the Boss? You!

Are entrepreneurial dreams occupying your unconscious nocturnal activity? You may think you need to use every ounce of capital you have to start your own small business. Before you go cracking open the piggy bank, though, remember this: it is akin to buying shares in a business, and you might be tempted to rationalize the use of equity dollars from your retirement plan for this purpose. Bear in mind our discussion in Chapter 2 about diversification, though. Do you really want to sink your retirement dollars into one business—even if it is your own? Would you feel comfortable buying only Sears & Roebuck stock for your portfolio? Undiversified equities are high risk and you would be mortgaging your retirement by resorting to this approach—not to mention the unpleasant fact that many business start-ups fail. In fact, most successful entrepreneurs have had several failed businesses under their belts before hitting one out of the park. As Henry Ford said, "Failure is a chance to begin again more intelligently."

How Gold Do You Want Your Golden Years to Be?

If planning for retirement is the farthest thing from your mind, you're not alone. According to the *1998 Retirement Confidence Survey* conducted by The Employee Benefit Research Institute, only 45 percent of all workers have figured out how much they'll need to retire—up from 32 percent the prior year. What's more:

 ◆ Half of all baby boomers born between 1946 and 1953 haven't given it a thought, reports The Institute's Paul Yakoboski (Source: *Pensions & Investments Magazine*, Arleen Jacobius, June 29, 1998).

 ◆ Among boomers born between 1954 and 1964, 47 percent are investigating their retirement savings needs this year, up from 32 percent last year.

 ◆ Only 33 percent of Generation X-ers have looked into retirement, up a mere 3 percent since 1997.

And for some weird reason, the percentage of smug individuals who say they are "very confident about retirement" has remained flat at 20 to 25 percent for the last six years. (Who are those people, anyway?) This means that three quarters of us have either blocked the entire disconcerting business out of our minds or toss and turn enough at night to wrinkle our wrinkle-free sheets.

Unless you want to spend your twilight years pushing a shopping cart around town looking for recyclables, you must add retirement into your overall investment-objective picture. Your logical next step in planning your financial future is to figure out how much money you need to put aside so you can not only retire, but retire comfortably.

What does this mean, exactly? Just this: A comfortable retirement is the manner in which you will maintain your present standard of living without heading off to the salt mines 40 plus hours a week. Presently, you probably don't often have to do without or scrimp; you have the means to eat well and entertain when you wish. When you retire, you'll have roughly the same expenses, with four possible exceptions.

The good news is there are four categories of expenses in which you will probably save money once you retire:

◆ **Car expense.** If you have two cars now and one is primarily used for commuting, you might be able to get by with one after retirement. This'll mean significant savings on car payments, insurance, gas, and maintenance.

◆ **Home expense.** If you have a four-bedroom colonial, you might consider moving to a smaller house or condo when the kids leave the nest. This would free up capital and reduce monthly payments and taxes.

◆ **Clothing expense.** Not going to work means not having to wear a different snazzy suit or dress everyday; Bermuda shorts and Converse hi-tops are a lot cheaper.

◆ **Taxes.** Income tax will come down as your income declines; property taxes can be reduced if you sell a large home.

Because these expenses are likely to be reduced once you retire, and because the dollars you're saving now for retirement will become dollars you can consume, a good rule of thumb is to expect that you'll require an annual retirement income of 50 to 70 percent of your present salary. The range accounts for a mortgaged home versus one owned free and clear. So, for example, if you live comfortably now on $60,000 a year and you expect to pay off your home by the time you retire, you need to save a pool of money that will generate 50 percent of $60,000, or $30,000, per year for your retirement.

Now the question is do you spend down that pool of money you have accumulated by age 65, or do you leave it to your heirs? It's probably wiser to assume that you'll spend it to zero by, say, age 85. If you include your savings as part of your retirement support (and face the gruesome fact of your own actuarial mortality!), you'll have to save far less to reach your goal. It's very important when planning your financial security to set realistic, reachable goals. If you establish a goal that requires too much scrimping and saving, you'll eventually shrug your shoulders and say, "Well, whatever happens, happens." Better to set a goal you recognize as doable. Start now, save consistently, get reasonable rates of return, and you'll have that pool of money when you retire.

In Chapter 4, we'll figure out exactly how much you will need to save in order to retire comfortably.

The Least You Need to Know

- ◆ Before you invest in anything, set up an emergency fund, so you never have to dip into your investments to cover unexpected expenses.

- ◆ Keep your emergency fund in a liquid account or investment you can cash within 24 hours.

- ◆ The amount of income you'll need to retire is about 50 to 70 percent of what you need now to live comfortably.

- ◆ For every 10 percent of your salary you save to invest, put 2 percent toward your children's education and 8 percent toward retirement.

Chapter 4

What Have You Got Right Now—and What Are You Going to Need?

In This Chapter

- ◆ Determining your Social Security benefits
- ◆ Figuring out your employment retirement benefits
- ◆ Saving the right amount for retirement
- ◆ Creating a personal balance sheet
- ◆ Creating a personal income statement
- ◆ Real-life examples of personal financial statements

Believe it or not, over 80 percent of the 77 million baby boomers (those born between 1946 and 1964) think they're going to keep working at least part-time after age 65, according to a survey published in the July/August 1998 *AARP Bulletin*. Of these boomers who intend to stay in the harness,

52 percent claim they're going to do it for fun, while 13 percent cop to fearing that they'll need to work into their dotage just to keep up payments on the Beamer.

When you consider that only 12 percent of people over 65 hold jobs today, you have to wonder whether the boomers who say they intend to work as seniors are deluding themselves out of fear that they won't be able to fund decent retirements. In fact, as long as you start reasonably early, it's not that difficult to fund retirement. In the same issue of the *AARP Bulletin*, William M. Mercer Inc. calculated that, assuming an 8 percent return, the following savings are required to accumulate $100,000 by age 65.

- ◆ At age 25: $7.14/week
- ◆ At age 35: $16.32/week
- ◆ At age 45: $40.40/week
- ◆ At age 55: $127.61/week

As you can see, the person who waits until age 55 to start saving for retirement will have to save almost eight times as much per week as the person who starts at 35. So if your head has been in the sand, pull it out and let's take a look at what you have—right now—and what it'll take to make your dreams of a great retirement come true.

So What Will Social Security Do for Me, Anyway?

Half of the baby boomers surveyed by AARP said they had no faith that Social Security would be there for them when they retire. But the fact is, Social Security is one of our most revered social programs, and no young congressional firebrand is going to be able to dismantle it anytime soon. At least not with fearsome senior groups like the Gray Panthers ready to storm the Capitol with Uzis in hand. No politician wants to have anything to do with abolishing Social Security.

On the other hand, there's a Bush in the White House again and he's got a bee in his bonnet about privatizing Social Security. During his presidential campaign George W. Bush proposed that workers be allowed to use part of their payroll taxes to set up voluntary investment accounts—a move that would turn the government-run Social Security system into a partially privatized program. On taking office, he gleefully (well, we think he was gleeful!), sicced a 16-member commission on the issue and they drew up a blueprint for privatization. It landed with a thud in Congress, however, for a few reasons:

- ◆ Some members of Congress (okay, Democrats) are never gonna go for privatization.

- ◆ Bush's panel had to admit that setting up private investment accounts for every working American was a pricey proposition that could only be funded by large government subsidies and cuts in benefits for future SS recipients (uh, that could be you).

- ◆ Federal surpluses that Bush could have used to subsidize the shift to privatization have dried up.

- ◆ In the late 1990s the stock market seemed like a money machine, but by 2000, people realized that they could actually lose money on stocks (what a shocker!).

So is privatization a dead issue? Nope, There's a lot less political risk than there used to be in considering changing Social Security. There are discussions in Congress now that range from allowing you to invest a portion of your Social Security benefits yourself to allowing the government to invest some of the Social Security pool in stocks, which it can't at the moment. For now, include Social Security payments as a portion of your retirement income. Just don't plan to live on Social Security alone, unless you have a fondness for cat-food casserole.

Investor's Idiom _____

Social Security is a system managed by the federal government that provides money to people who are retired or are not able to work due to disability.
FICA stands for the Federal Insurance Contributions Act.
Medicare is included under Social Security. This is a national health program that pays certain medical and hospital expenses for elderly and disabled people. The Social Security system is funded by employees, employers, and the government.

Figuring Out Your FICA

Look at your paycheck. See the section marked FICA? That's how much you pay each week into the Social Security system, which pays out Social Security and Medicare benefits. If you are employed, your employer pays an amount equal to 7.65 percent of your income to Social Security. The other 7.65 percent comes out of your paycheck, for a total of 15.3 percent of your income each year, up to a salary of $84,900. After that, only Medicare is deducted, which is 1.45 percent of your salary.

The Social Security Administration can tell you what your Social Security benefits will be based on when you retire. Call them at 1-800-772-1213 or visit their website at www.ssa.gov to obtain Form SSA-7004, the Request for Social Security Statement (formerly known as the Request for Earnings and Benefits Estimate Statement). You will receive, by mail, your Statement. The left page shows how much you have contributed to Social Security and to Medicare for every single year you've been employed. On the right page are your estimated Social Security benefits. This shows how much you can expect to receive each year from Social Security:

Fiscal Facts

To estimate what Social Security will pay you during your leisurely retirement years, call 1-800-772-1213 or visit the Social Security website at www.ssa.gov. You'll need to fill out Form SSA-7004. Social Security will send you your very own Social Security Statement. Check it carefully for bureaucratic boo-boos.

- ◆ If you retire at age 62 (reduced benefit)
- ◆ If you retire at full-retirement age, e.g. 65
- ◆ If you work until age 70

Check to see if there are any mistakes. If, for example, you know you earned about $30,000 in 1989 and your Social Security Statement shows $0 for that year, call the Social Security Administration and go through your statement carefully with someone. It's a good idea to get this statement updated every five years.

Getting a Handle on Your Retirement Benefits by Pestering Human Resources

Now let's figure out what, if anything, you've built up in retirement benefits at your job. Stop by your employer's personnel or human resources department and ask them to calculate your retirement benefits for you. (They probably won't be thrilled, but hey, this is your future we're talking about here.)

Do this only if your employer offers a defined benefit or pension plan, or *DB*. A DB is simply an employer-financed retirement plan that promises to pay you a certain sum annually at retirement, with the sum dependent upon when you retire, how long you worked, and how much you received in salary. (If your employer doesn't have a DB, you can skip the rest of this section.)

Ask your HR representative two questions:

1. "What would my annual benefits be (if any) at age 65 if I left the firm tomorrow?" If you haven't put in the minimum time (e.g., five years), tell them to assume that you have. Having put in the minimum time is called *vesting*, or *being vested*.

2. "What would my annual benefits be at 65 if I continued to work here until 65?" Have human resources either use your present salary or assume a 3 percent annual raise.

Investor's Idiom

A **pension** is simply a regular payment made to you (or your family, if you've passed away) by your employer that reflects how much you earned and how many years you worked at your job.

A **defined benefit plan,** or **DB,** is an employer-financed retirement plan that will pay you an annual sum upon retirement. Pensions typically require you to have worked for the employer at least five years before you are considered **vested,** or eligible, for the pension.

A **defined contribution plan** is a retirement plan that allows *you* to define how much is contributed to it. You tell the company how much to take from your check and put into your retirement plan.

Generally, the second number is going to be bigger than the first number. For our purposes in this chapter, use the smaller number. If you've had several jobs where you've earned retirement benefits, go back to each of the human resources departments and repeat the above procedure. You may get snarled at, but that's a small price to pay to get a grip on your finances.

Help, I'm Self-Employed!

If you are self-employed, you make (or should be making!) quarterly estimated tax payments. Included in these tax payments is a federal self-employment tax that covers Social Security and Medicare.

When you work for an employer, it is required to contribute a sum equal to 7.65 percent of your income into the Social Security system. The other half is deducted from your paycheck. Self-employed people pay the whole amount, which is presently 15.3 percent of income, themselves. On the plus side, self-employed

Fiscal Facts

According to the American Association for Retired People (AARP), the average annual benefit for retired workers is $9,180. The maximum benefit available from Social Security for someone retiring at age 65 is $18,888 ($18,240 after deducting for Medicare). So if you want to have fun when you're retired, better start your own plan!

people get to deduct half of this self-employment tax from their income tax. If you're running your own business, you must pay self-employment tax if you earn more than $400 per year after expenses, even if you have another job. (Oddly, you also must pay self-employment tax if you performed services for a church as an employee and received income of $108.28. Who comes up with this stuff?!)

If you are fully or partially self-employed, check in with Social Security to find out how your retirement benefits are shaping up.

Creating Your Own Fabulous Pension Plan

Whether you work for yourself part-time or full-time, you are entitled to create a pension for yourself, since an employer isn't creating one for you. You can choose from special Individual Retirement Accounts (IRAs) for self-employed people, or a Keogh Plan. An IRA is basically a shell that protects any investment you put underneath it from taxation. It's the government's way of encouraging us to save for retirement.

If you own a small business, you can create pensions for yourself and your employees. This is also a great way to reduce your income tax, as contributions to self-employment retirement plans are deductible up to a point. We'll get into this in more detail in Chapter 5, but you have four options:

- ◆ **SEP-IRA.** This is a Simplified Employee Pension, which is very easy to set up with most banks, mutual funds, brokers, or insurance companies. All you have to do is complete Form 5305-SEP, which your bank can supply, or you can download it from www.irs.gov.

- ◆ **Keogh Plan.** These are primarily for small-business owners who need to set up retirement plans for themselves and employees. Keoghs require a lot of paperwork, so you'll probably need professional help. There are two types of Keogh plans: the profit sharing and the money purchase plan. You must make the same percentage contribution to a money purchase plan each year, whether you have profits or not. The contribution to a profit sharing plan can change each year. Money-purchase plans contributions are limited to the lesser of $40,000 or 25 percent of your self-employment income. Profit-sharing Keogh contributions can vary in a given year from 0–20 percent of new business income, maxing out at $40,000.

- ◆ **SIMPLE-IRA.** SIMPLE stands for Savings Incentive Match Plan for Employees. This seems to be taking the place of the SEP-IRAs. An employer can match up to 3 percent of your total compensation. Your contribution is presently limited to $7,000 annually but will increase $1,000 each tax year thereafter until it reaches $10,000 in 2005.

◆ **Owner-only 401(k).** The Uni-K Plan (from Pioneer in Boston) is a hot new product that lets you max out contributions at $40,000 ($41,000 if you're over 50). More about this in Chapter 5.

A Super-Easy Way to Figure Out How Much You Need to Save

Now that you know how much will be coming in from Social Security and any retirement plans, you're ready to figure out how much you need to save and invest each year to retire, using the worksheet below. This worksheet gives you two options. One assumes that you'll own your house by retirement, so you'll only need 50 percent of your current annual income. The other assumes that you may still be paying a mortgage and will need 70 percent of your current annual income.

1. Present Annual Salary $_____ $_____

2. Times Percent at Age 65 _____ .50 _____ .70

3. Gross Amount Required _____

4. Less: Social Security[1] _____

5. Less: Pension (if any)[2] _____

6. Less: Existing Savings & Investment Income[3] _____

7. Equals: Add'tl Income Required _____

   (1) *Get this number from the Personal and Benefit Estimate Statement sent to you by Social Security.*

   (2) *Get this number from your employer's personnel office. If you have worked there fewer than five years, request that they use five years in the calculation. Do the same with all previous employers. Enter the total on Line 5.*

   (3) *Do not use your savings account balances here; what you want is the current annual income that savings and all other investments are generating annually. An easy way out is to simply multiply your total balances by .04 and use that sum for Line 6.*

Your total in Line 7 is how much additional income you will need each year of retirement to supplement what you will be receiving from Social Security and any existing pension. Your goal now is to save and invest a pool of money that will generate that additional income.

Let's say, for example, that you are a 35-year-old making $30,000, and your worksheet looks like this:

1. Present Annual Salary	$30,000	$30,000
2. Times Percent at Age 65	.50	.70
3. Gross Amount Required	$15,000	$21,000
4. Less: Social Security[1]	$7,000	$7,000
5. Less: Pension (if any)[2]	$5,000	$5,000
6. Less: Existing Savings & Investment Income[3]	$0	$0
7. Equals: Add'tl Income Required	$3,000	$9,000

You need at least $15,000 per year of retirement income, and your Social Security ($7,000) and pension benefits ($5,000) add up to $12,000. That means when you retire, you'll be $3,000 short per year. Uh-oh.

Let's say you had $37,500 in investments that generated 8 percent income. You would get an extra $3,000 per year from those investments. That's exactly what you need. But you don't have $37,500 in investments, do you? So you have to grow it by saving over the next 30 years.

Let's say you invest these savings at 8 percent, and assume inflation is going to eat 4 percent per year. How much should you invest each year? Well, we can multiply $37,500 by 1.04 (4% = .04; $100 that earns 4% = $104, or $100 × 1.04) each year for 30 years or just sneak a peak at our old friend the Future Value of Money Chart back in Chapter 1. Either way, we'll find out that $37,500 today will have to grow to $121,627 by age 65 for you to avoid having your savings eroded by inflation. Remember, a dollar tomorrow won't buy as much as a dollar does today, but you want to be able to maintain your standard of living. You need to include inflation, therefore, when you calculate how much money you'll need to retire happily. If $37,500 a year would be enough for you today, you'll need $121,627 in 30 years to buy the same stuff.

So how much will you have to invest each year, assuming it will grow at 8 percent per year, in order to reach $121,627 by age 65? Well, we can do a whole bunch of calculations or we can look on the following "Annual Savings Required" table. (Note: This table assumes you are earning 8 percent per year on your investments.) Look down the "Residual Needs" column until you get to $3,000, which is the annual amount you're looking to cover during retirement. Now, if you're 35, you have 30 years until retirement, so look under the "30" column across from $3,000 and there's your answer: You'll need to save $1,074 a year to create a pool that will generate $3,000 a year once you retire.

Annual Savings Required

Residual Needs[6]	Years to Retirement							
	40	35	30	25	20	15	10	5
$ 2,000	463	573	716	912	1,197	1,658	2,555	5,185
3,000	659	859	1,074	1,367	1,796	2,487	3,832	7,777
4,000	927	1,145	1,431	1,823	2,394	3,316	5,109	10,369
5,000	1,158	1,431	1,789	2,279	2,993	4,145	6,386	12,962
6,000	1,391	1,717	2,148	2,732	3,593	4,974	7,663	15,553
7,000	1,623	2,003	2,506	3,187	4,192	5,803	8,940	18,145
8,000	1,855	2,289	2,864	3,642	4,791	6,632	10,217	20,737
9,000	2,087	2,575	3,222	4,097	5,390	7,461	11,494	23,329
10,000	2,319	2,861	3,580	4,552	5,989	8,290	12,771	25,921
11,000	2,551	3,147	3,938	5,007	6,588	9,119	14,048	28,513
12,000	2,783	3,433	4,296	5,462	7,187	9,948	15,325	31,105
13,000	3,015	3,719	4,654	5,917	7,786	10,777	16,602	33,697
14,000	3,247	4,005	5,012	6,372	8,385	11,606	17,879	36,289
15,000	3,479	4,291	5,370	6,827	8,984	12,435	19,156	38,881
16,000	3,711	4,577	5,728	7,282	9,583	13,264	20,433	41,473
17,000	3,943	4,863	6,086	7,737	10,182	14,093	21,710	44,065
18,000	4,175	5,149	6,444	8,192	10,871	14,922	22,987	46,657
19,000	4,407	5,435	6,802	8,647	11,380	15,751	24,264	49,249
20,000	4,639	5,721	7,160	9,102	11,979	16,580	25,541	51,841
21,000	4,871	6,007	7,518	9,557	12,578	17,409	26,818	54,433
22,000	5,103	6,293	7,876	10,012	13,177	18,238	28,095	57,025
23,000	5,335	6,579	8,234	10,467	13,776	19,067	29,372	59,617
24,000	5,567	6,865	8,592	10,922	14,375	19,896	30,649	62,209
25,000	5,799	7,151	8,950	11,377	14,974	20,725	31,926	64,801
26,000	6,031	7,437	9,308	11,832	15,573	21,554	33,203	67,393
27,000	6,263	7,723	9,666	12,287	16,172	22,383	34,480	69,985
28,000	6,495	8,009	10,024	12,742	16,771	23,212	35,757	72,577

continues

Annual Savings Required (continued)

Residual Needs[6]	Years to Retirement							
	40	**35**	**30**	**25**	**20**	**15**	**10**	**5**
29,000	6,727	8,295	10,382	13,197	17,370	24,041	37,034	75,169
30,000	6,959	8,581	10,740	13,652	17,969	24,870	38,311	77,761
31,000	7,191	8,867	11,098	14,107	18,568	25,699	39,588	80,353
32,000	7,423	9,153	11,456	14,562	19,167	26,528	40,865	82,945
33,000	7,655	9,439	11,814	15,017	19,766	27,357	42,142	85,537
34,000	7,887	9,725	12,172	15,472	20,365	28,186	43,419	88,129
35,000	8,119	10,011	12,530	15,927	20,964	29,015	44,696	90,721
36,000	8,351	10,297	12,888	16,382	21,563	29,844	45,973	93,313
37,000	8,583	10,583	13,246	16,837	22,162	30,673	47,250	95,905
38,000	8,815	10,869	13,604	17,292	22,761	31,502	48,527	98,497
39,000	9,047	11,155	13,962	17,747	23,360	32,331	49,804	101,089
40,000	9,279	11,441	14,320	18,202	23,959	33,160	51,081	103,681
42,000	9,743	12,013	15,036	19,112	25,157	34,818	53,635	108,865
44,000	10,207	12,585	15,752	20,022	26,355	36,476	56,189	114,049
46,000	10,671	13,157	16,468	20,932	27,553	38,134	58,743	119,233
48,000	11,135	13,729	17,481	21,842	28,751	39,792	61,297	124,417
50,000	11,599	14,301	17,900	22,752	29,949	41,450	63,851	129,601
52,000	12,063	14,873	18,616	23,662	31,147	43,108	66,405	134,785
54,000	12,527	15,445	19,332	24,572	32,345	44,766	68,959	139,969
56,000	12,991	16,017	20,048	25,482	33,543	46,424	71,513	145,153
58,000	13,445	16,589	20,764	26,392	34,741	48,082	74,067	150,337
60,000	13,919	17,161	21,480	27,302	35,939	49,740	76,621	155,521
62,000	14,383	17,733	22,196	28,212	37,137	51,398	79,175	160,705
64,000	14,847	18,305	22,912	29,122	38,335	53,056	81,729	165,889

(6) From Line 7 on Annual Savings Required Form

This works out to about $83 per month. That's not a whole lot, when you think about it. Of course, this is what you'll need to meet your *minimum* requirements for retirement. If you want to really be secure and comfortable, you may want to save enough to generate the $9,000 in additional income you'll need if you follow the far right side of your worksheet. If you look on the table under $9,000 and 30 years, it says you'll have to save $3,222 per year.

Use the 401(k) Plan, Stan

So how do you save this much? Well, if your employer offers a groovy matching 401(k) or 403(b) pension plan, it's a great start. Many companies offer plans where for every $1 you contribute, the company will put in 50¢ (or 25¢ or 75¢, depending on the company—companies aren't *required* to contribute anything). That's free moolah for you. If you are lucky enough to be in this situation, contribute the maximum of pre-tax earnings—usually around 6 percent of your annual gross income.

The Economic Growth and Tax Relief Reconciliation Act of 2001 upped the amounts we are allowed to contribute to retirement accounts. As of 2002, all employees regardless of age who have a 401(k) may contribute up to $11,000. This maximum increases each tax year until it reaches $15,000 in 2006. If you are 50 or older, you benefit from a new provision in 2002 that allows you to contribute an additional $1,000 per year, for a $12,000 total.

Now, if your employer contributes half of that, or 3 percent, that's 9 percent (which is really close to the 10 percent we recommend you invest, anyway). Just increase your deductions to 7 percent by continuing to have that 6 percent taken out of your pre-tax earnings and ask the personnel department if it can arrange for you to invest another 1 percent of your after-tax earnings in your company's plan. Voilà! You're painlessly on your way to establishing the 10-percent habit—and you don't even have to contribute all of it yourself. Just remember that the 10-percent rule applies as your salary increases, giving you a growing pool of assets that benefit from the magic of compounding interest each and every year.

Investor's Idiom

Many corporations offer **401(k)** plans to their employees. Under this type of retirement savings plan, employees who are eligible are allowed to choose how much of their pay is to be deducted for investment purposes. They also decide how the dollars are to be invested. The **403(b)** is a version of the 401(k) used by public employers, such as schools, hospitals, and other nonprofit organizations.

Use your employer's plan first, if offered. There are tax advantages in that you may be able to shelter up to 15 percent of pre-tax earnings in an employer's plan depending on your salary and other restrictions. That's pretty cool—it means some of your hard-earned money escapes the clutches of the IRS by going straight into your tax-sheltered retirement plan. In addition, there are usually partial company matching dollar contributions.

Get an IRA!

Of course, you can also shelter money for your retirement in an IRA. As of 2002, all individuals, regardless of age, can put up to $3,000 annually into a traditional IRA. If you are over 50, you are allowed to contribute an extra $500, for a $3,500 total. The cap will rise in 2005 to $4,500 for people over 50, going up to $6,000 in 2008. Again, this is the government's way of encouraging you to get on the stick.

You can contribute up to $3,000 per year as of 2002 to a regular IRA or a Roth IRA. The Roth IRA is named after Senator William V. Roth Jr., then-chairman of the Senate Finance Committee, and a result of the Taxpayer Relief Act of 1997. The Roth IRA provides no deduction for contributions, but if you meet certain require-ments, *all earnings are tax free* when you or your beneficiary withdraw them. The rules governing these tax-free distributions are pretty complicated but basically they come down to this: Once you've kept your money in your Roth IRA for five years, if you are buying a home for the first time, you can take money out of your Roth IRA without paying taxes on it.

Trust Us, You Really Don't Want to Wait

Now let's look at an annual savings worksheet for someone age 50 earning $50,000. She'll need 50–70 percent of her annual salary for retirement, or $25,000–$35,000. Social Security and retirement benefits will be greater than those for our 35-year-old, but not dollar-for-dollar, because there is a cap on annual Social Security benefits.

Let's assume that her combined benefits are $18,000. She needs to self-fund at least $7,000 per year. Assuming a return on investment of 8 percent, she'll need a pool of $87,500 to generate $7,000 per year in retirement income. Assuming 4 percent infla-tion, she'll actually need $157,583 ($87,500 × 1.04 for 15 years).

So how much does she need to invest at an 8 percent return per year to reach $157,583 in 15 years? More than $5,000 per year, or $417 per month. Argh! That's a hefty chunk—five times the annual investment needs of our 35-year-old. Plus, age 50 is a time when you are usually deep into college expenses for the kiddies and can least afford to put aside retirement dollars. Yet put them aside she must.

But My Circumstances Will Change ... Won't They?

Of course, we all pray for raises, promotions, lottery winnings, and the like to lift us out of our present standard of living. How do you account for higher income over time when figuring out your retirement savings needs? By using a *fixed percent*, not a fixed dollar sum, of salary for retirement planning.

Back to our example of using you as a 35-year-old putting aside 3 percent of $30,000. If you get a 3.5 percent raise every year, by age 50, your salary will be about $50,000. You wouldn't need to change a thing about your investment strategy. In fact, if you get a 3.5 percent raise every year and continue to invest a steady 3 percent per year of your salary (and earn 8 percent on it per year), you'll have accumulated $34,792 by age 50 and $154,354 by age 65. Trust us, we did the math! That's pretty close to what we calculated as the pool you'll need to generate as additional required retirement income.

You still need to redo your annual savings worksheet periodically, though, to see if a higher or lower percent is warranted. The best time to do this is every year on your birthday. This is also the time to have Social Security and pension benefits recalculated. You may need to start saving more, but never set aside less than the percent of salary with which you started.

> ### Crash Alert
>
> Whatever you do, don't wait to start investing for retirement. Every 10 years the amount you'll have to put aside goes up drastically. A 50-year-old will have to invest roughly **seven times** the amount a 35-year-old will invest to get the same results. Plus, remember that the older you get, the less risk you can afford to take by holding stocks. This means you have to turn to investments that don't earn as much as stocks usually do—slowing down the growth of your retirement pool further.

Stagger Your Debt

In *Hamlet*, Shakespeare wrote: "Neither a borrower nor a lender be." These are wise words to heed these days, as we are strongly encouraged by advertising and tempting credit card offers to live debt-heavy lives. But if you're earning 8 percent on your investments and paying 18 percent in credit card and other debt, you're never going to get ahead.

The two biggest debts you are likely to take on are the following:

> ### Fiscal Facts
>
> Many early American homes have a knob on the top of the banister that leads to the second floor, which signifies that the home was owned free and clear. Some early Americans even hollowed out the banister and inserted the paid-off mortgage!

- ◆ College loans for you or your children

- ◆ Your home mortgage

Try to avoid incurring both at the same time. A great rule of thumb is this: Pay off your student loans before assuming a mortgage, and pay off your mortgage before incurring children's educational loans. The good thing about both education and home mortgage loans is they are used to finance assets that will probably increase in value over time. An education will ideally increase earning capacity and a home should appreciate over the years. Try timing your indebtedness something like this:

Age 21 Take out student loans

Age 30 Pay off student loans

Age 30 Buy a home

Age 45 Pay off mortgage

Age 45 Take out loans for first child's college education

Crash Alert _____
Avoid taking on loans to finance assets that lose value over time, such as home furnishings, clothing, and cars.

Of course, this is idealistic for most people, but it's a good idea to at least start thinking this way!

We'll get more into how to dig yourself out of debt in Chapter 7.

Your Personal Balance Sheet: A Snapshot of Your Finances

Some people spend less than they earn, but most do not. How do you enter into the category of the frugal former? Make it your goal to spend 10 percent less than you earn.

Investor's Idiom _____

A **balance sheet** is like a photograph of your finances at a given moment in time. It shows what you own (your **assets**) and what you owe (your **liabilities**).

Your **net worth** is the difference between assets and liabilities. Net worth can be positive (if assets are greater than liabilities) or negative (if liabilities are greater than assets). Each side of the balance sheet should "balance," or have the same total.

An **income statement,** in contrast, shows the flow of money through your life. It allows you to compare your income with your expenses.

Your first reaction is probably: "Are you kidding? I can hardly make ends meet now." Well, you can find that 10 percent, but only if you know where your money is coming from and going to right now. The best way to do that is to use simple versions of the same financial statements corporations use: a balance sheet and an income statement.

Let's do the balance sheet first. A balance sheet shows your assets, liabilities, and net worth. Your *net worth* is the difference between your *assets* (what you own) and your *liabilities* (what you owe). It's sort of a snapshot of your finances.

To create a personal balance sheet for you or your family, fill out the worksheet on the following page. Make a habit of doing this every year on your birthday.

John Q. (and Suzie Q.) Personal Balance Sheet as of 00/00/02 (Your Birthday)

Assets	Liabilities
Cash _____	Credit Card Debt _____
Checking Account Balance _____	Student Loans _____
Savings Account Balance _____	Other Personal Loans _____
Individual Investments _____	Home Mortgage _____
Profit Sharing (401[k], 403[b], etc.) _____	Car Loan _____
Home (best-guess value) _____	
Car (best-guess value) _____	
Collectibles (antiques, stamps, etc.) _____	
Furnishings (best-guess value) _____	
Total _____	**Total** _____

Your first goal is to get your assets to exceed your liabilities. Your ongoing goal is to continually widen that spread so that you maximize your net worth.

On the asset side, we have left out two potential retirement benefits that some financial advisors would include: Social Security and earned pension benefits. You may add them in if you are close (e.g., five years or less) to retirement, but otherwise exclude them because:

1. They cannot be converted to cash if necessary.

2. They don't technically belong to you right now. In some cases, a former employer may offer to meet your earned pension sum by offering a lump-sum

payment. In that case, you would transfer the sum to an IRA rollover and include it under the profit-sharing line.

Get a Grip with a Personal Income Statement

So much of financial planning is just getting a clear view of your situation. Before you can get a handle on your spending, you'll need to tally up your expenses and compare them to your income. If your expenses are 90 percent of your income, great! If they are equal to or are greater than your income, well, now you know what you're dealing with.

Creating a personal income statement which clearly sets out your income and expenses will help you bring your expenses in line. While a balance sheet is a snapshot of your finances that is typically prepared once a year, income statements track your finances over time. If you prepare an income statement once a month, you can really get a grip on how much money is coming in and how it's being spent. Before you fill out the worksheet below, you might want to make 20 or so copies of it. Fill out one using yearly figures and use the others to create an income statement each month.

John Q. (and Suzie Q.) Personal Income Statement Twelve Months Ending 00/00/02 (Your Birthday)

Income	Expenses
Salary _____	FICA, etc. _____
Gifts to you/yours _____	Federal Taxes _____
Income from Savings[1] _____	State Taxes _____
Alimony Received _____	Life Ins. Premiums _____
	Rental/Mortgage Payments _____
	Real Estate Tax[2] _____
	Food _____
	Clothing _____
	Alimony Paid _____
	Medical/Dental _____
	Entertainment _____
	Gifts Given _____
	Auto Payments _____

Income	Expenses
	Student Loan Payments _____
	Credit Card Payments[3] _____
	Other Loan Payments _____
	Auto Related (gas, service, etc.) _____
	Home Repairs _____
	Furnishings _____
	Vacation _____
	Utilities (gas, electric, phone) _____
	Education Related _____
	Other _____
Total _____	**Total** _____

(1) *Limited to savings for car, etc.*

(2) *If not included in mortgage payment*

(3) *Deduct sums covered elsewhere (e.g., clothing, etc.)*

Now that you have your expenses broken down and on paper, you'll be prepared to tackle reducing them when you reach Chapter 6.

On the income side, there are a few things you can do right away:

♦ Divert any raises you get at work toward your 10 percent goal.

♦ Make sure your savings are with the bank that offers the highest savings interest rate in your area.

♦ If you have a five-year target for a home down payment, find the safest investment that will earn you the most interest. For instance, if Treasury notes yield 1-2 percent more than Treasury bills or money market funds, go for it. Or maybe your bank has a "teaser" rate on CDs that is significantly higher than money market funds or Treasury bills. However you do it, be sure to keep your emergency savings fund in the most liquid and marketable investments available, which means money market funds or Treasury bills. It's not likely that you'll be able to postpone surgery to match up with a Treasury note to mature so you can get your principal back!

♦ Be sure to put any cash gifts into your savings/investing accounts. This is "found" money for you. And you might hint to family members that you would prefer cash to gifts going forward. It all counts toward that 10 percent goal.

A Happy Couple on the Right Track

If you've had a little trouble filling out your balance sheet, here's an example from real life. Let's call this couple "Bill and Mary." They are both 33 years old, with one 3-year-old child. They own their condo. Bill is a private school teacher and Mary works part-time at a retail firm. Credit cards are paid off in full each month.

Balance Sheet–Bill and Mary   July 15, 2002

Assets			Liabilities	
Savings		$20,000	Student Loans	0
Investments			Other Personal Loans	0
Bill (403b)	$12,000			
Pension	$5,600			
Mary (401k)	$600			
Child	$5,000			
Roth IRA	$2,000	$25,200		
Home		$240,000	Mortgage	$99,000
Auto		$5,400	Auto Loans	0
Total		$290,000	Total	$99,000
Net Worth: $191,600				

Income Statement–Bill and Mary   July 15, 2002

Income				Expenses	
Salary:	Bill	$37,000		Mortgage	$8,184
	Mary	$11,000	$48,000	Real Estate Tax	$1,416
Investment Income			$800	FICA	$702
Gifts (cash)			$1,000	Medicare	$684
				Federal Tax	$6,004
				State Tax	$2,950
				Medical Plan	$1,344
				Pension	$2,064
				Gifts	$1,000

Income		Expenses	
		Auto Repair	$1,000
		Credit Cards	$200
		Home Insurance	$783
		Auto Insurance	$510
		Phone	$672
		Electric & Gas	$1,192
		Food	$5,200
		Clothing	$6,500
		Home Repairs	$2,000
		Entertainment	$2,600
		Vacation	$1,000
		Balance Savings/Investments	$3,795
Total	**$49,800**	**Total**	**$49,800**

Incidentally, Bill and Mary are still young enough to be able to keep all their investments in stock, and therefore can take advantage of the high returns available. Their investments are structured as follows:

Bill's 401(k): All equity (TIAA-CREF Growth Fund—Teachers Insurance and Annuity Association College Retirement Fund)

Mary's 401(k): All equity (70 percent Growth, 20 percent SmallCap, 10 percent International)

Roth IRA: All equity (50 percent S&P 500 Index, 50 percent Int'l Index)

Child's Savings: All equity (US Equity Market Index)

Looking good!

Your Typical Young Guy Living Hand to Mouth

Here is another real-life example. Fred is also a teacher, but he's 30 and single. You can see how the unpaid balance on student loans hinders his opportunities for savings and investment.

Fred's Balance Sheet as of 7/02

Assets		Liabilities	
Checking	0	Car Loan	$1,000
Retirement Plan	$7,088	Student Loans	$36,400
Car	$2,000	Student Loans	$1,000
		Credit Cards	$325
	$9,088		$38,725
Net Worth: ($29,634)			

Income Statement as of 7/02 (Monthly)

Income		Expenses	
Salary	$2,517	Federal Tax	$275
Other	$147	State Tax	$170
Gifts from	$90	FICA	$165
		Medicare	$39
		Workers Comp	$2
		Union Dues	$51
		Retirement Plan	$160
		Student Loans	$164
		(e.g. 8%)	$243
		Credit Cards	$15
		Rent	$615
		Gifts to	$35
		Auto Insurance	$70
		Auto Club	$5
		Gas	$50
		Telephone	$40
		Electricity	$50
		Cable	$45
		Water & Sewer	$12
		Food	$170
		Entertainment	$200

Income		Expenses	
		Other	$20
		Auto Loan	$58
		To Savings	$100
	$2,754		$2,754

Fred has a negative net worth, and pretty much lives hand to mouth on a month-to-month basis. The student loans are his big handicap, but the first one will be paid off in November (saving Fred $164 per month). Unfortunately, payments on the other loan increase to $318 per month, so his net savings will be $89 per month.

Fred's very first goal must be to build up an emergency savings balance. Any of life's blips would put him deeper in debt (auto repairs, etc.).

His second goal must be to work off the remaining student loan. Although the interest rate (8 percent) is reasonable, the size of the debt is going to prevent him from getting ahead. But the good thing about looking unflinchingly at your finances like this is it forces you to face your problems—and every problem has a solution. In Fred's case, for example, he might consider taking a part-time job for one or two years to knock off that loan. He could take a roommate to lower his rent.

Fred's situation is typical of recent college graduates. They need to catch a break, get a promotion and/or raise, inherit some cash, or all of the above in order to cross over into financial security. Let's hope all three happen to Fred so he can shore up his foundation, which is the focus of our book's next section.

The Least You Need to Know

- You can request a statement from Social Security that will show exactly how much per month you can expect to receive from Social Security upon retirement.

- Ask your personnel department to figure out how much you stand to receive from your company retirement plan.

- You can start financing your own retirement plan to make up the difference between what Social Security and your employer's plan will give you and what you will need.

- The sooner you start saving for retirement, the less you'll need to save.

◆ Figure out what percentage of your salary you need to save to meet your goals and stick to it.

◆ Try to stagger college loans and your home mortgage so they don't all hit you at once.

◆ Create a personal balance sheet and income statement at least once a year—on your birthday.

Part

Shore Up Your Foundation

Um, we have a personal question: What's the interest rate on your maxed-out credit card? Eighteen percent? Youch! So what if your investments are earning a whopping 20 percent if you're paying 18 percent to those sharks at First Credit of North Dakota? Kinda defeats the purpose, wouldn't you say?

Well, you're in luck, because this section is about wiping out debt, trimming your taxes, cutting your spending, and maximizing your job benefits; swabbing your deck and hoisting your sails ... sorry, got carried away there for a moment.

The point is, this section will help you get your financial ship in strong and seaworthy shape.

Chapter 5

A Closer Look at Employment Benefits

In This Chapter

- ◆ Determining your retirement benefits
- ◆ IRAs
- ◆ Pensions vs. 401(k) plans
- ◆ What if you change employers?
- ◆ Self-employment retirement benefits
- ◆ Evaluating stock options

How many of you reading this book have invested in an employer-sponsored retirement plan? Can we see a show of hands? Okay, not bad. Now for the real question: How many of you, upon leaving a job and receiving a lump-sum payment out of your retirement account, invested it in your new employer's plan? And, um, how many of you spent it?

That's what we thought. Well, if you did, you're not alone. At least a third of the people who receive lump-sum payments of their retirement savings when they change jobs fail to roll the money over into other tax-deferred accounts, according to the *AARP Bulletin*. And approximately one third of employees who qualify for 401(k) plans don't bother to contribute to them at all.

If you haven't yet contributed, it's probably because you don't really know what employer-sponsored retirement plans are and what they can do for you. And you've been too busy to really pay attention to the whole deal anyway. Well, since you've taken the time to crack open this book, let us make it easy for you. Let's take a look from the ground up at the kinds of retirement plans that employers offer and the role these plans should play in your investment strategy.

Retirement Plans 101

Millions of people in this country contribute to retirement accounts sponsored by their employers. There are several types of plans, but they all work on the same basic principle: You don't have to pay taxes on the money you put in your retirement plan until you start taking it out to support yourself during retirement. And no tax is due while it grows. That's why they are called tax-deferred plans.

A corporation is under no legal obligation to set up a 401(k) plan for its employees—it's a perk, part of your total package of employee benefits. In the past, most retirement plans offered by employers were defined benefit plans. The employer promised you a specific pension upon retirement (in other words, the "benefit" was defined) and invested money with insurance companies or bank trust departments in order to be able to provide that benefit.

Defined Contribution Plans at a Glance

Today, most employers offer plans that allow you, the employee, to decide how and where you want to invest your tax-deferred retirement savings. You choose from a menu of investment options offered by the employer. These types of plans are called *defined contribution plans* because the employee decides ("defines") how much he or she is going to contribute. The *benefit* (your retirement income) is not defined because it depends on how much you contribute and how well your investments perform.

The most popular of these plans are 401(k) and 403(b) plans. If you recall from Chapter 4:

- ◆ *401(k)* plans are for employees of private companies.
- ◆ *403(b)* plans are tax-deferred annuities for employees of nonprofits, such as public schools, philanthropic foundations, and hospitals.

♦ Eligible state or local government employees have so-called Section 457 plans ("457s"). Named for Section 457 in the IRS Code, they are set up similar to 401(k)s.

Tens of millions of employees in this country contribute to 401(k) and 403(b) plans, mainly because many employers add 25¢ or 50¢ or even more to every dollar an employee puts into his or her plan. If your employer contributes to your 401(k) plan like this, there's one simple rule for you to follow: Fund it to the max! This is *free money* you're getting here—and how rare is that?

Defined Benefit Plans at a Glance

The other main family of retirement plans is *defined benefit plans*. In a defined benefit plan the employer guarantees the sum and is liable if the actual assets are less than the required sum. It differs from a defined contribution plan as follows:

♦ In a defined benefit plan, the amount of the employee's pension is established but the employer's contribution is not. It is dependent upon the degree to which the plan is funded. If it's overfunded, no contribution by the employer is necessary.

♦ In a defined contribution plan, the employer's contributions are fixed, but the amount of the employee's pension is not.

Now let's get into the various types of plans available in more depth.

> **Investor's Idiom**
>
> In a **defined contribution plan,** the employee decides ("defines") how much he or she is going to contribute. The most popular defined contribution plans are 401(k) and 403(b) plans.
>
> In a **defined benefit plan,** an employer guarantees the sum, or pension, and is liable if the actual assets are less than the required sum.

Defined Benefit Plans

As we mentioned in Chapter 4, defined benefit plans are employer-financed plans that promise to pay you a certain sum annually upon retirement. This is the traditional corporate pension plan that many of our parents probably retired on. Employees with pension plans don't contribute to them or help decide how to invest the money in them. Defined benefit plans are more expensive for companies to run than defined contribution, which is why companies have moved away from them. In addition, defined contribution plans, such as 401(k)s, offer employees the opportunity to choose the investments for their retirement plans.

Most defined benefit plans have four characteristics:

♦ A vesting schedule requiring that you work a minimum number of hours per year—a thousand, for example. This eliminates part-timers.

♦ A minimum number of years must be vested before qualifying for the pension— five years is common. This is to discourage job hoppers. The total of vested years you've accumulated is called "credited service."

♦ The value of the pension increases as you put more years in at the company.

♦ The value of the pension is weighted so that if you work at the company until you retire, the last five years or so before you retire earn you a big chunk of your pension. This is to encourage you to stay at this company until you retire. You maximize your pension by staying put.

How the Amount of Your Monthly Pension Is Determined

In the end, the amount of your pension is based on a formula that takes all these factors into consideration. For example, Ralph's Dog Biscuit Company figures out its employees' monthly retirement benefit based on the following convoluted formula:

♦ Take 2 percent of final average monthly pay.

♦ Multiply it by number of vested years (credited service) up to a maximum of 35 years.

♦ Subtract $1^{2}/_{3}$ percent of Social Security benefit and then multiply the resulting number by credited service up to a maximum of 30 years.

♦ Finally, subtract the latter from the former.

♦ This equals the monthly benefit at age 65.

Fiscal Facts

Just in case some of you have forgotten how to convert a mixed fraction to a decimal, here's the trick: Multiply the denominator (the bottom number of the fraction) by the whole number. Add the resulting number to the numerator (the top number of the fraction). Now, divide the denominator by the new numerator. For example, for the mixed fraction $1^{2}/_{3}$:

3 (the denominator) × 1 (the whole number) = 3;

3 + 2 (the numerator) = 5, giving you a new fraction of $^{5}/_{3}$;

5 ÷ 3 = 1.66

Whew!

Let's look at an example. Assume loyal Ralph's Dog Biscuit Company employee Scooter Snodgrass will be 65 on January 1, 2003, and will have 20 years of fully vested, credited service at that time. Let's say his Social Security benefit in 2003 is $1,007 a month. Let's also assume that his final average pay is $2,500 a month ($30,000 a year). Now we can apply the formula from hell.

Figure out 2 percent of $2,500 (final average monthly pay), and multiply it by 20 (total vested years of slaving away).

2% = .02

2,500 × .02 = 50.00

50.00 × 20 = $1,000

Then, subtract 1²/₃ percent of $1,007 (the S.S. benefit), and multiply that by 20 (those hard-earned years again): 1²/₃ percent expressed as a decimal is 1.66.

1,007 × 1.66 = $16.72

16.72 × 20 = $334.40

1,000 − 334.40 = $665.60

Monthly Benefit = $665.60

Mr. Snodgrass will receive a monthly pension of $665.60, as well as $1,007 per month from Social Security. His total monthly retirement income, unless he has other investments, will be $1,672.60.

A Whole Lotta Lumps or Just One: the Lump-Sum Option

Pensions are a promise or guarantee from your employer to you to pay a certain sum at a certain age until death. A regular payment over time like this is called an *annuity*. In some cases, you may be given a choice between either the monthly pension payment or receiving the entire pension upon retirement as a *lump sum*.

How can you tell if the lump sum is better than the monthly payment? Well, first it depends on how involved you want to be. Some people are simply intimidated by large sums of money and are grateful to get a monthly check from their former employer. But you could shop the lump sum to several reputable insurers for their annuity rates and then compare. Many insurers "write" annuities and may offer you a better deal (i.e., higher monthly payment) for your lump sum than your employer's plan does. You can also use your broker or friendly banker to help in the process.

However, you will not be given all the time in the world to decide which plan is best for you, so be aware that you need to give this some thought before the day of your retirement party.

If You Choose the Lump-Sum Option

If you choose the lump-sum option, you will want to invest it in something that will generate regular interest payments so that you have income to live on. To do so, you can buy an annuity from an insurance company. You can call up any insurance company and ask about its annuity plans. Ask friends and neighbors to recommend a good insurance agent.

Insurance company annuities can be expensive, though. Check out the no-load annuities available from companies like Vanguard (www.vanguard.com), Schwab (www.schwab.com), or T. Rowe Price (www.troweprice.com).

You also used to be able take your lump sum and invest it in a long U.S. government Treasury bond. By "long," we mean a bond that takes 20 to 30 years to mature. However, the Treasury Department hasn't offered a bond since its decision in October 2001 to suspend issuance of the 30-year bond. But just in case that changes, we'll tell you how using a long bond for retirement income would work.

> **Investor's Idiom**
>
> An **annuity** is an investment that yields fixed payments during the investment holder's lifetime or for a stated number of years. Payments are typically made monthly. A **lump sum,** in contrast, is the entire value of the investment taken in cash at once.

Long bonds make interest payments twice a year. So if you want monthly interest payments, you could buy six bonds with different semiannual interest-payment dates. Bond #1 would pay interest in January and again six months later in July; Bond #2 would pay in February and August; Bond #3 would pay in March and September, and so on. Kinda neat, huh?

How can you tell when a bond pays interest? Check the maturity date. That tells you one of the two interest dates. The second interest date is six months later. For example, if you buy a bond with a maturity date of January 31, 2005, the two interest-payment dates are January 31 and July 31. This way, you have income coming in every month.

If Your Employer Drops the Ball

Note that a defined benefit plan like a pension is a promise to pay on the part of the employer. The employer, or plan sponsor, is totally responsible for providing pension payments to retired employees. Traditional profit-sharing plans only tie the employer's contribution to the plan to the level of profitability of the corporation: no profit, no contribution.

The employer is supposed to be making annual contributions to the company's retirement fund and investing this money wisely. If the CEO embezzles the fund and splits for Rio or the company goes bankrupt—or anything else happens to the employer's ability to pay—the obligation to provide pensions for retirees of the company is turned over to a federal agency called the Pension Benefit Guaranty Corp. (PBGC). Probably not who you expected to be handling your future, but at least it's a back-up plan.

Investor's Idiom

There are three basic types of securities issued by the U.S. Treasury: **bills, notes,** and **bonds.** Bills are short-term investments; that is, they mature in under a year. Notes have longer maturities—from 1 year to 10 years. Bonds mature over 10 years. Historically, the Treasury has issued 20- or 30-year bonds, however the Treasury hasn't offered a bond since its decision in October 2001 to suspend issuance of the 30-year bond.

Defined Contribution Plans

Defined contribution plans, unlike defined benefit plans, limit the employer's role and responsibility. With a 401(k) plan, for example, the employee, if eligible, determines how much of his or her pay is to be deducted for investment purposes, and decides how the dollars are to be invested.

Your employer may offer matching contributions equal to a percentage of how much you contribute to your 401(k) or 403(b). Some employers put in 25¢ or 50¢ for every dollar you contribute. Others might match, for example, up to 100 percent of the first 6 percent of salary contributed by the employee.

Defined contribution 401(k) and 403(b) plans limit the maximum amount that an employee can contribute on a *pretax-dollar* basis to $11,000 (as of 2002). If you are investing in a 403(b), you will be offered basically a menu of tax-sheltered annuities provided by insurance companies. New annual deferral (employee contributions) limits for the 401(k) and 403(b) plans are as follows:

Fiscal Facts

Safeguards to prevent pension plans from defaulting on paying retirement benefits to employees were an important reason for the passage of the Employee Retirement Income Security Act of 1974 (ERISA). ERISA also codified 401(k) and 403(b) plans and prohibited employers from conducting certain transactions with retirement plan dollars.

Annual Deferral Limits for 401(k) and 403(b)

Year	Under age 50	Over age 50
2002	$11,000	$12,000
2003	$12,000	$14,000
2004	$13,000	$16,000
2005	$14,000	$18,000
2006+	$15,000	$20,000

This is to prevent the very highest-salaried employees from being able to shelter a much higher share of their income than lower-salaried employees can. It also encourages companies to offer a higher level of matching funds. If the fat cats at the top of your company could shelter huge chunks of their salaries in retirement accounts and the company had to pay them, say, 50¢ on every dollar they saved in their 401(k) plans, pretty soon the company might decide it can only afford to pay 25¢ on the dollar, thus lowering the retirement benefit for everyone.

Investor's Idiom

The money that is deducted from your pay before taxes are applied is called **pre-tax dollars**. These enable you to avoid paying taxes on whatever you contribute to your 401(k) or 403(b).

Investor's Idiom

An **IRA** is an Individual Retirement Account. Basically, it's a shell that protects money you put in it from taxation until you start to take money out. A **rollover IRA** is used to shelter money that was in a 401(k) or cash pension plan at your old job when you change employers and find you have nowhere else to put it.

Cash Pension Plans

These plans are increasingly popular (and somewhat controversial). The idea behind them is that they ensure younger employees annual, tangible benefits and portability should they leave their employer. In most cases, it also saves employers money and does away with unfunded liabilities. However, there is a downside for older employees (e.g., those five years from retirement) and upon conversion from the traditional pension to the cash pension plan. The traditional pension tends to be back-end loaded, with the last five years or so of employment having a significant impact on the amount of money you get during retirement.

Here is how a typical cash pension works:

Employee age and service	>39	40–49	50–59	60–69	70–79	80+
Up to $80,400 base salary	3.0%	3.5%	4.5%	5.5%	6.5%	7.5%
Over $80,400 base salary	6.0%	7.0%	9.0%	11.0%	13.0%	15%

So an employee whose age and service equals 55, and whose salary was $50,000 would have $2,250 credited to his/her account ($50,000 × .045% = $2,250). The existing account balance earns interest using a short-term measure, such as 90-day Treasury bills.

If Your Employer Matches, Invest the Max

Why wouldn't everybody invest the max? This is "found" money! If your employer offers a 401(k) with any matching percent contribution, contribute to get the full benefit. Don't hesitate, don't quibble, just do it.

To be perfectly clear, talk to your personnel or HR representative and confirm the maximum employer contribution and the maximum amount you can contribute and still have the sum deducted before taxes from your salary.

If your employer does not offer a matching contribution but does offer a 401(k), it's still a good idea to make it part of your retirement plan. Your best bet will probably be some combination of a traditional IRA, Roth IRA, and the 401(k). (Don't worry, we're going to get into this more later.) For now, all you need to know is that IRA stands for Individual Retirement Account. It's an account you set up for yourself, as opposed to something arranged by an employer. IRAs also offer some really nice tax deductions.

So, you may want to put most of your yearly contributions into an IRA and contribute to your 401(k) any additional sum you can afford. Why not just bypass the 401(k)? Because even if your employer's not offering matching funds, that menu of investment options it offers has been carefully chosen and is probably quite solid. Managers of mutual funds and other investments compete quite intensely to convince corporations to offer their funds as 401(k) plan options.

Can I Borrow from My 401(k)?

Can you take or borrow any of this money? Yes, but only under certain conditions enforced by the employer (and dictated by the federal government). If you borrow it,

you will have to pay competitive interest rates established by the employer. It is strongly recommended that this option be utilized only for a dire emergency, and that any sum borrowed be repaid ASAP!

You can borrow from your 401(k) for any reason. You can borrow up to half of your total vested amount (typically in increments of $100). There's usually a minimum amount (e.g., $1,000) and a maximum (usually the lesser of 50 percent of what's vested or $50,000). The interest rate you are charged when you borrow from your 401(k) is competitive and you can choose a repayment period of anywhere from 3 to 54 months. But if you don't pay back the loan according to its terms, the amount of the loan will be considered a taxable distribution to you and you will owe taxes!

What If I Change Employers?

What if you leave your employer? What happens to your 401(k)?

♦ You could leave your 401(k) with your old employer. Some employers allow you to maintain your account in their 401(k).

♦ If your old employer won't allow you to do that, or you don't want to, you could transfer your 401(k) assets into your new employer's 401(k) plan. No tax will be generated by this transfer.

♦ You could establish a separate IRA account and transfer your assets to this account. You have 60 days to do this before the assets will be taxed and subject to a 10 percent penalty. Because you are _rolling over_ his assets into another account, this is called a rollover IRA.

♦ Finally, you could cash out your IRA (after your employer deducts taxes and penalties) and buy a new car. But would we recommend that? Noooooooo!

Once you create a rollover IRA, you can't move those funds in the future to a traditional IRA or a 401(k) plan.

Should You Put All Your Eggs in the Company Basket? Ask the Folks at Enron ...

Often, a company will offer its employees an opportunity to buy its stock as part of the menu for its 401(k) plan. At first glance, this might seem like a pretty good idea. Why not have your company act as a stockbroker for you? You give them all your blood, sweat, and tears, why not let them work for you? Well, because on closer examination this may not be such a great idea. Even if the stock is being offered to you at a discount, you'll be putting all of your eggs in the company basket. Your future is already heavily invested in the success of your company—you work there! To invest your savings with it, too, goes against the principle of diversification we introduced in Chapter 2.

When Enron, the energy conglomerate, came under investigation by the SEC in 2002, about 62 percent of the funds held in the 401(k) plans of 11,000 employees were invested in Enron stock. That money was wiped out when Enron's stock tanked, and so were the retirement dreams of many Enron employees. Surprisingly, it's not unusual for company employees to hold so much company stock. According to a survey by DC Plan Investing, General Electric employees are 77 percent invested in G.E. paper, and Procter & Gamble's fund is almost 95 percent company stock. Common, yes. Smart, no.

Crash Alert

We've seen several instances where employees had all of their 401(k) or profit-sharing money in company stock and the company went bankrupt, leaving them with nothing. We're not trying to scare you, and you may work for one of the biggest and sturdiest companies in the world, but dire consequences can affect any company.

If you do want to own some company stock in your 401(k), you should limit it to what you would invest in if you were creating your own equity portfolio. A good rule of thumb is to invest no more than 4 percent of your portfolio in the stock of any individual company, so apply that rule to your company's stock. And don't worry, your employer can't punish you for taking minimal or no participation in the company stock option. There are laws against that. Don't let 'em pressure you (it was widely rumored that Enron execs were pushing their employees to buy more Enron stock while dumping it out of their own retirement accounts). One advantage of share ownership, though, is that it entitles you to receive annual reports and other information that goes to stockholders, so you can keep current on your company and its fiscal healthiness (or lack thereof), if you so desire.

What About Stock Options? Go for It.

If your company offers you *stock options*, as opposed to stock, go for it. These can be very profitable. You'd be amazed how many top executives in corporate America own little or no stock in their companies, but have large stock option grants.

Because there is no risk—you don't exercise your option unless the exercise price is less than the current price and you can make a profit—stock options are really a form of compensation.

If you are eligible for stock options, there are two things you can do with them:

♦ **Buy and sell on the same day.** You immediately exercise your option because the strike price is less than the current price and you can make a profit. You purchase the shares and sell the shares on the same day. This saves you the trouble of having to raise the money to buy the stock. You simply go to your human resources person and say you want to exercise your stock option. Your profit is taxed at ordinary income tax rates (which can be as high as 39.1 percent, depending on your tax bracket). You pay tax on the *capital gain* resulting from the difference between the exercise price (sometimes called the "strike" price) and the sales price.

♦ **Hold on to the stock now, sell later.** You can buy the stock and hold it, hoping that its price will go up and you can sell at a profit. First, you'll need the money to buy the stock. It can come either from your own savings or by borrowing from your friendly banker. Then you exercise your option, or buy the stock. If you hold the stock for at least one year, you are taxed at capital gains rates (maximum of 20 percent), which is probably lower than your income tax rate. You just have to keep your fingers crossed that the stock's price will go up and stay up.

Investor's Idiom

A **stock option** is the right, but not the obligation, to buy a stock at a fixed price after a specified period of time (usually 12 months) for a fixed period of time (10 years). Prices and time periods are all specified in the option contract.

Investor's Idiom

A **capital gain** is any money you take in from an investment. If you've held the investment longer than one year, the capital gain is not subject to income tax; instead, it's subject to capital gains tax, which is typically lower.

What would we do? Well, we prefer the bird in the hand rather than trying to search through those darn bushes, so we'd probably choose the same-day transaction and deal with the ugly income tax. But, hey, this is your decision: You know your inclination, you know the company's prospects, and you know your personal financial situation. Take all of these factors into consideration before you make your decision.

Managing Your 401(k)

Investing in a 401(k) is a great way to save for retirement; just don't put your 401(k) on cruise control. Every time you get your 401(k) statement, go through it and ask yourself the following questions:

1. Are there any mistakes?

   Were all your paycheck deductions actually put into the 401(k)? Were they invested as you had requested? If you took a loan from the 401(k), is the remaining outstanding balance correct? An antifraud campaign by the U.S. Department of Labor found that some employers misuse employee contributions by holding onto the money too long. Make sure your deductions are being invested right away.

2. How much am I being charged in mutual fund fees?

   The manager of your mutual funds should not be charging you more than 1 percent of your fund's value per year in fees or expenses. If you have any questions, call the customer service representatives for the fund manager and have the fees explained to you.

3. When do I plan to retire? Should I manage my 401(k) more aggressively?

   If you are over 50, you need to be rebalancing your 401(k) annually, moving away from aggressive stock funds and toward more secure investments because you're going to be cashing out fairly soon. Remember, in Chapter 1 we explained that over time the stock market's volatility evens out, but the key phrase is "over time." In the short run, stock market swings can wipe you out. If you don't have 15 years, start moving out of stocks. Don't worry, we'll teach you more about that topic later in the book.

4. Am I overinvested in any one company or sector?

   Make sure you don't make the Enron mistake (investing too much in one company, even if it's your own), and don't put all your eggs in one sector, such as technology or health care, either. Diversify! Still don't know what that really means? Don't worry, in Part 3 we'll give you a plan to follow that'll have you diversifying like a savvy investor.

No Company Plan? Create a Pension with an IRA

What's an IRA? Nope, it's not the Irish Republican Army, although it can pack the same punch. As we mentioned in Chapter 4, IRA stands for Individual Retirement Account. This is a retirement account that you set up for yourself, as opposed to a 401(k) or 403(b), which would be set up by your employer.

The IRA itself is not an investment, it's a tax-sheltered account into which you put money that you can then invest as you choose. You don't have to pay taxes on the money that accumulates until you start taking it out after retirement. Whether you choose a traditional IRA or a Roth IRA, a working spouse can contribute $3,000 per year for him- or herself, and an additional $3,000 per year for a nonworking spouse to an IRA set up in the nonworking spouse's name. If you are over 50, you can contribute $3,500 as part of the government's "catch-up" plan.

There are several different kinds of IRAs, each with its own quirks and purpose:

◆ *Traditional IRA*—developed in 1975 to help people who were not covered by an employer-sponsored retirement plan to save for retirement. As of 2002, all individuals, regardless of age, can put up to $3,000 annually into a traditional IRA. If you are over 50, you are allowed to contribute an extra $500, for a $3,500 total.

◆ *Rollover IRA*—used to shelter retirement savings that have been taken out of a 401(k) or cash pension due to a job change.

◆ *Roth IRA*—these were created in 1998 to give people a little more flexibility when saving for retirement, buying a house, or financing children's education. For example, if you've invested in a Roth IRA for at least five years, you can take up to $10,000 out to make a down payment on a first home.

◆ *SEP-IRA*—stands for Simplified Employee Pension. It allows an employer to make deductible contributionis for the benefit of participating employees (including the employer him/herself). The contributions are made to individual retirement accounts (IRAs) set up for participants in the plan (again, including the employer). The maximum contribution for 2002 is the lesser of 15% of the employer's compensation or $30,000. It is more complicated for the employer or a self-employed person, because you have to adjust (reduce) the compensastion figure for the self-employement tax deduction. The IRS has a special worksheet you can use to do the calculation. Incidentally, your employer's SEP-IRA contributions are excluded from your *gross income* for tax purposes. They will not show up on your W-2!

◆ *SIMPLE-IRA*—the Savings Incentive Match Plan for Employees is another option for small employers, including self-employed people, that has been growing in popularity because it is very easy to use. An employer can match up to 3 percent of your total compensation or your contribution, whichever is less. (Remember, if you're self employed, *you* are the employer and the employee!) Your contribution is presently limited to $7,000 annually, but will increase $1,000 each tax year thereafter until it reaches $10,000 in 2005. Add $500 if you are age 50 or older for 2002, $1,000 for 2003, and up to $2,500 in 2006.

Whatever IRA best suits your purpose, you can set it up with a bank, broker, or a mutual fund company.

When Is a Roth IRA the Right Choice?

In general, the younger you are and the less money you make, the more attractive the Roth IRA option is. Your *adjusted gross income* (AGI) must be less than $110,000 (or less than $160,000 combined for married working couples) for you to be eligible for a Roth IRA. So if you earn more than that, guess what? You can skip this section!

Traditional IRAs have no income limit, so if your income fluctuates, you may want to set up both a Roth and a traditional IRA. That way you can contribute to the Roth IRA in the years your income is low enough for you to qualify and contribute to the traditional IRA when your income is higher. You can invest up to $3,000 in a Roth IRA starting in 2002, $3,500 if you are 50 or older.

The *Roth IRA* offers three huge advantages:

◆ Flexibility

◆ No taxes on earnings/asset growth

◆ An opportunity to pass money on to your children tax free

Let's look at each advantage in more depth.

Investor's Idiom

Your **gross income** is the income reported on your W-2 form, plus interest income, rents, royalties, alimony, and so on. To calculate your **adjusted gross income** (AGI), the IRS makes a few minor adjustments, such as medical account deductions. Gross income and AGI are usually pretty similar.

Investor's Idiom

The **Roth IRA** is a new type of IRA that is more flexible than the traditional IRA, but is only available to individuals earning under $110,000 (or families under $160,000) a year. You can't take money out of a traditional IRA before age $59^1/_2$ without being penalized, but as long as your Roth IRA has been open for at least five years, you can withdraw up to $10,000 to buy a first home.

Wiggle Room

Traditional IRAs allow you to start taking money out as early as age 59$\frac{1}{2}$ and require you to begin distributions by age 70$\frac{1}{2}$. In addition, if you take money out of a traditional IRA before age 59$\frac{1}{2}$, you'll be hit with taxes and a substantial penalty.

In contrast, there is no age at which you are required to start spending down your Roth IRA, and as long as your Roth IRA account has been open at least five years, you can take out up to $10,000, penalty free, to buy a first home.

No Taxes on Asset Growth—Whoopee!

When you start withdrawing money from a traditional IRA, you pay taxes on the earnings (not the contributions) as if it's ordinary income. With the Roth IRA, any gains that your invested dollars have earned are tax free upon withdrawal, provided that the account has been open for at least five years and you are older than 59$\frac{1}{2}$.

Passing Along the Wealth

If you don't need the money you put into your Roth IRA to keep you in golf balls during retirement, the Roth offers an amazing tax break for your heirs. First, you don't have to start taking distributions at 70$\frac{1}{2}$, like you do with the traditional IRA. So you can leave your kids quite the tax-sheltered pile.

If you name a child (or children) as beneficiary, the monthly distributions from a traditional or a Roth IRA will go to that child upon your death. With the traditional IRA, the distributions are taxable. With the Roth, they aren't. And, of course, the money passed onto them continues to grow tax free.

Converting a Traditional IRA to a Roth IRA

If you decide to convert your traditional IRA to a Roth IRA, be aware that you will have to pay taxes on the earnings in the traditional IRA. Remember, the government will tax that money as soon as it comes out from under the IRA tax-protection shell. In addition, you must pay these taxes from a source other than the IRA.

Be aware, though, that the amount of money coming out of the traditional IRA during conversion is added to your adjusted gross income. If it's added all at once, this can really screw things up by putting you over the $110,000 income limit required for you to be eligible to open a Roth IRA.

Converting an existing IRA to a Roth requires that taxpayers have less than $110,000 in adjusted gross income (whether single or married).

	Roth IRA	Traditional IRA
Maximum Annual Contribution per Person	$3,000 ($3,500 if over 50)	$3,000
Who Is Eligible	Earned income below $110,000 (single) and $160,000 (joint); $3,000 applies to any combination of Roth and traditional.	Unlimited income; anyone under age 70½.
Tax Advantages	Investment grows free from federal income tax.	Growth is tax-deferred; taxes paid on earnings when money is withdrawn.
Tax Deductibility	Not tax deductible.	Based on adjusted gross income of $33,000–43,000 (single) and $53,000–63,000 (joint).
Withdrawal of Assets	Free from federal income tax if account open 5 years *and* age 59½ *or* purchase of first home ($10,000 lifetime cap) *or* permanent disability or death.	Penalty-free withdrawals before age 59½ *only* for first-time home or higher education. Taxes apply on earnings withdrawn. Other withdrawals before age 59½ subject to 10% penalty tax.
Age Limit for Contributions/ Distributions	None.	No contributions after age 70½. Distributions must begin at age 70½.
Rollovers and Transfers	Can roll over traditional IRA to Roth if adjusted gross income no more than $110,000. Sum subject to taxation.	Can transfer to and from other traditional IRAs. Can roll over from employer plans (e.g., 401[k]).

The Two Best Investments for Your IRA: Stocks and STRIPs

Okay, so you've set up your retirement accounts and now the question is this: What the heck should you put in them? No need to rack your brain, because we've got the answer: stock mutual funds and Treasury STRIPs. We'll explain STRIPs in the next section, but first, let's look at stocks.

Stocking Up

If you look at consecutive 10-year periods of time going back 40 to 50 years, stocks made investors more money than Treasury bonds and T-bills 80 percent of the time.

You can use this little nugget of financial history to your advantage when investing for your IRA. First, you'll want to spread out your retirement savings among a broadly diversified list of stocks. Why? So you minimize the risk of any one company going under and taking your savings with it. To be truly diversified, you should own at least 25 stocks, ideally 50. If we assume that you're going to own 100 shares of each stock and that the average stock prices are $25 to $50 a share, the minimum diversified portfolio would require between $62,500 and $125,000. Do you have this amount of savings to invest in common stocks?

Most of us don't. So the best place to get stock for your IRA is from *mutual funds.* Stock mutual funds companies collect money from many investors, pool it, and use the pool to buy stocks. Yes, you could pick your own stocks, but do you have the time, and do you think you will beat an established mutual fund? Probably not. Mutual funds provide the small investor with far greater diversification than he or she could achieve alone. With a mutual fund, you own a share of the fund, and the fund may own hundreds of stocks. Don't forget, you're probably only eligible to contribute $3,000 a year.

We'll get into mutual funds in Chapter 12, but for now just think about looking for funds with:

♦ At least $100 million in assets.

♦ Low expenses—some "active" funds charge for expenses as high as 1.5 percent, and these expenses come right out of your return.

Investor's Idiom

A **mutual fund** is a company that collects money from investors and invests on their behalf, usually in diversified securities. A fund is headed by a board of directors, or trustees, who hire an investment advisor. In some cases the advisor sets up the fund, e.g. Putnam and Putnam Growth Fund. In others the fund hires an outside advisor (Vanguard often does this).

Your investment could be earning 10 percent, but if the fund takes 1.5 percent, your return is only 8.5.

◆ At least a five-year or, more ideally, a 10-year history, a consistent investment approach, and a manager who has been associated with the fund for at least five years.

STRIP Tease

Your IRA should also include some bonds (also referred to as fixed-income securities) to balance out your stock or stock mutual fund holdings. For the fixed-income (bond) portion of your IRA, we recommend *Treasury STRIPs*.

If you recall our discussion earlier in this chapter about Treasury bonds, you'll remember that they pay interest income twice a year. Upon maturity, you'll also get your principal back.

Investor's Idiom

A **fixed-income investment** provides income that doesn't fluctuate (like stock prices do, for example). Bonds are fixed-income investments because when you buy a bond you are promised regular, steady interest payments called "coupons." You get these payments two times per year, six months apart. At maturity, you also receive the principal, which is the dollar amount of the original investment. **STRIPs,** which stands for **Separate Trading of Registered Interest and Principal,** are simply pieces of Treasury securities, such as coupons or principal payments.

A STRIP is one piece that has been "stripped" from a Treasury note or bond. For example, let's take a 20-year Treasury bond. It consists of 40 coupons (those two interest payments a year we mentioned earlier) and the principal payment. So that's 41 blocks of money. A STRIP is one of those 41 blocks of money. It could be the 13th coupon, it could be the 20th coupon, it could be the principal payment—it doesn't matter. What you're buying is that Treasury STRIP.

If the coupon can be redeemed at maturity 20 years from now, at, say, $100,000, it'll sell for around $20,000 to $25,000 now. That's its "discount price." You buy it today for that price knowing that you'll get $100,000 for it 20 years from now. You would buy it at a discount and redeem it at maturity for its full price.

The advantage that Treasury STRIPs have over other fixed-income options is you don't have to do anything but hold the STRIP until it matures. So whatever percentage of bonds you decide to hold in your IRA, think about Treasury STRIPs, because they're no-brainers for tax-sheltered accounts.

What to Do When You're Small and Solo

Small businesses are defined as businesses ...

- ◆ With fewer than 100 employees.

- ◆ With annual revenues below $1 million.

Whether you are self-employed or an employer with a limited number of employees, you are entitled (but not required) to set up a retirement plan for yourself (and your employees, if you choose). If you are a sole proprietor without employees, your best retirement-plan choice is a *SEP-IRA* or *SIMPLE-IRA*. If you have employees, however, a *Keogh* plan could be a better bet.

> **Super Strategy**
>
> The new inflation-indexed bonds are also tempting because they represent insurance in the event that inflation flares up once again. If inflation rises dramatically, the profit from your $100,000 STRIP may not be able to purchase as much time on the golf course as you'd hoped in 20 years. How about a combination for your IRA: ¾ STRIPs, ¼ inflation-indexed Treasuries? Works for me!

A Keogh is a pension plan that allows business owners to shelter more income than SEPs or SIMPLEs do and to create vesting schedules and pensions for employees.

A SEP-IRA, or Simplified Employee Pension, as discussed earlier in this chapter, is essentially an IRA for someone who is self-employed. A SEP is like a 401(k), but as of 2002 contributions are limited to 15 percent or $30,000, whichever is less—a good retirement-plan choice for a sole proprietor who doesn't have employees.

A SIMPLE-IRA, or Savings Incentive Match Plan for Employees, is a new option for self-employed people that's growing in popularity because it is very easy to use.

A Keogh has two advantages over a SEP-IRA for anyone who has a few employees, but not enough to go through the hassle and expense of setting up a 401(k):

- ◆ An entrepreneur with employees can set up vesting schedules, which require employees to remain with the company a number of years to qualify for full retirement benefits. Part-timers are typically not qualified, for example.

♦ Because these are qualified plans, you (or your employee) can "roll over" the assets into another company's qualified plan.

Keoghs are a lot cheaper to set up than 401(k) plans, which can be too costly for a small business to handle. But there's a lot of paperwork because a Keogh is a qualified plan, meaning it is specifically approved by the Internal Revenue Service. Because the Keogh is a qualified plan, the employer (or self-employed individual) must fill out and file specific forms each year for the IRS. Either you hire a specialist to draw up your plan, or you can use a prototype that is offered by a number of banks. The prototype will save you money.

As of 2002, you can choose the lesser of either 100 percent of your employee's compensation (up to a $200,000 limit) or $40,000. You can contribute up to 15 percent of your earned income (if you're self-employed) or 15 percent of your employees' salaries, subject to a $40,000 maximum.

Adding a Money Purchase Pension to the Mix

Typically, you would set up a Keogh by establishing a traditional profit-sharing plan. In addition, if you wish, you can also establish a *money purchase pension trust*. You are still limited, however, to a total of $40,000 combined for the two plans.

The profit-sharing plan defines under what circumstances a contribution will be made for qualified employees. You could decide that qualified employees are those with at least 1,000 hours of work for two consecutive years. The employer contributes and the employee benefits, but the benefit is not defined, and the employee has no voice (unless self-employed) in how the contribution is invested.

Quick quiz: This means a profit-sharing plan is …

a. A defined contribution plan.

b. A defined benefit plan.

If you answered "a," congratulations! A profit-sharing plan is indeed a defined contribution, rather than a defined benefit, plan.

Investor's Idiom

A **sole proprietor** is someone who owns a business and has no partners. A SEP-IRA or SIMPLE-IRA is usually a good retirement plan choice for a sole proprietor who doesn't have employees. An entrepreneur with partners or with employees should look into Keogh plans, which allow business owners to shelter more income than do SEPs or SIMPLEs and to create vesting schedules for employees.

A money purchase pension plan is also a defined contribution plan, in that no benefit is defined. However, it differs from a straight profit-sharing plan because a contribution must be made each year to each qualified employee. With a profit-sharing plan, the amount the business owner decides to contribute is not set in stone; with the money-purchase pension plan, it is set—unless you go through the hassle of amending the plan. Once you decide to contribute a certain percentage to a money purchase pension plan, you must do it. These plans are most popular, as a result, with clinic doctors, lawyers in small firms, or other professionals who have pretty high, relatively stable, incomes.

Whew! Aren't you glad you learned all that? Dazzle 'em at your next cocktail party.

Meet the New Kid on the Block

There's a tasty new option that's especially smart for owner-only businesses (those with no employees save the owner) called the Uni-K plan. In our first edition, we introduced you to Section 529 College Education Plans. We think the Uni-K could be the star new product of this edition.

Prior to the Tax Relief Act of 2001, there was a cap on the amount that an employee and employer could jointly contribute to an employee's 401(k). This cap was 15 percent of up to a maximum pay of $170,000, which is $25,500. Of this sum, the employee deferral (that's fed language for contribution) maxed out at $10,500 in 2001. Under the new law, however …

♦ Annual deferral limits rise.

Year	Under Age 50	Over Age 50
2002	$11,000	$12,000
2003	$12,000	$14,000
2004	$13,000	$16,000
2005	$14,000	$18,000
2006+	$15,000	$20,000

♦ The 15 percent of pay cap goes up to 25 percent in 2002, and the max pay rises to $200,000.

♦ The employee deferral will not be included in the 25 percent pay cap. That means the employer's portion increases significantly.

This is a great opportunity for owner-only businesses. Our research indicates that the developer of the Uni-K, Pioneer Funds of Boston, Massachusettes, has a jump on the competition with their product. We strongly urge you or your accountant to contact Pioneer at 1-800-225-6292, or visit www.pioneerfunds.com (click on Uni-K), and check out this option if you own and are the sole employee of your business.

Here are two tables developed by Pioneer Funds that compare contribution retirement plan options. As you can see, Uni-K offers higher limits than other plans, and contributions are flexible and can vary at your discretion from year to year. Pretty nifty.

2002 Maximum Deductible Contributions for Unincorporated Businesses

Self-Employment Income	$10,000	$50,000	$100,000	$150,000
SEP-IRA	$2,000	$10,000	$20,000	$30,000
Profit Sharing	$2,000	$10,000	$20,000	$30,000
Money Purchase	$2,000	$10,000	$20,000	$30,000
SIMPLE IRA				
Under age 50	$7,300	$8,500	$10,000	$11,500
Age 50+	$7,800	$9,000	$10,500	$12,000
Pioneer Uni-K				
Under age 50	$10,000	$21,000	$31,000	$40,000
Age 50+	$10,000	$22,000	$32,000	$41,000

Source: Pioneer Investment Management, Inc.

The Least You Need to Know

- If your employer contributes to your 401(k) plan, fund it to the max.
- Ask human resources to help you figure out your monthly pension, if you have a defined benefit plan.
- If you take a lump-sum retirement payment, invest it in something that will generate income for you to live on.
- Don't overinvest in your company's stock.
- Stock options can be very profitable employment benefits.
- In general, the younger you are and the less money you make, the more attractive the Roth IRA option is.
- The best investments for your IRA are stock mutual funds and Treasury STRIPs.
- Keogh plans are good for small-business owners with employees and/or significant income to shelter.

Chapter 6

Cutting Expenses *Is* Investing!

In This Chapter

- ◆ Getting a grip on your spending
- ◆ Figuring your marginal tax rate
- ◆ Fresh ideas on how to cut expenses
- ◆ Little things that add up

Believe it or not, it's a lot easier to spend $1 less than to earn $1 more. How so? Well, to earn more, you either have to work longer hours or take greater risks with your investments (remember the relationship between risk and return from Chapter 1). What's more, you pay taxes on each additional dollar you earn on your job—but saving is free!

Someone once said that the best exercise for losing weight is to push yourself away from the table. The same is true of savings: Just push yourself away from that sales counter! Spending can be addictive for many people, but learning to "just say no" is one of the best things you can do for your financial security.

Become a Hunter/Gatherer

In Chapter 4, we provided two real-life illustrations of personal balance sheets and income statements. One set was for Fred, a young man who, if you recall, was not in great financial shape. The other was for Bill and Mary, a happy couple on the right track. One set of financial statements took about 20 minutes to compile, while it took over a day to sort out the expense side for the other set. Can you guess which set took longer to compile? (Hint: Who was in the bigger mess?)

You can't save if you don't know what you have, and the only way to figure it out is to gather information on your spending habits. So, be a gatherer! Get a notebook and create a page for each spending category (clothing, groceries, and so on), and total them up each month. Use the personal income statement we provided in Chapter 4 to make a monthly income statement for yourself. After 12 months, you'll see some patterns emerging. Was the August clothing bill higher because you took advantage of summer markdowns, or because of heavy back-to-school purchases? Did you notice your entertainment costs rising with the barometer in the summer because it was too hot to put on the stove and you ate out a lot? How about the holidays? Did your credit card bills double because you made all of your purchases in November and December?

> **Super Strategy**
>
> Learn to buy off-season. For instance, purchase your holiday cards in January or a winter coat in April. Because no one else is thinking about purchasing these items during the off-season, the demand is low and the price is right!

Pay close attention to these patterns. Once you start getting a grip on your spending, you will become addicted to saving because it gives you both dollars and personal satisfaction. It all begins with the monthly drill of accumulating and tabulating your expenses. It's your money, and you work hard for it. Why not work just a little harder to hold onto it?

Your Tax Bracket Is Higher Than You Think

Saving becomes even more attractive when you realize that because income tax is graduated, you pay more tax on the last few dollars you earn than you do on the bulk of your income. For example, if you earn $35,000 a year and pay $3,500 in federal income tax, that doesn't mean you are in the 10 percent tax bracket. It means you pay an average of 10 percent in taxes on your income. But in reality, you pay no income tax on the first few thousand and probably closer to 35 percent on the last few. Now, if you were given a raise of $2,000, you'd pay nearly $500 of it for federal income tax and $153 to Social Security. That's $653 in federal tax on $2,000. That's a tax bracket of around 33 percent! So, for every additional dollar you earn, you have to pay at least *a third* in taxes. Ouch! This tax rate is called your *marginal tax rate*.

Figuring Your Marginal Tax Rate

We love to move from the theoretical to the painfully real in this book, so dig out your tax return from 2001 and let's figure out your marginal tax rate. If you look at your tax return (we know, it brings back painful memories, but bear with us), you will see a line at the bottom of the first page that is repeated at the top of the second page. This is called *adjusted gross income*, or AGI. Next, you will see a line for your deductions, either *standard* or *itemized*. The *net difference* is the amount of your income that

was subject to taxes. Now you are ready to compute your tax owed. Let's assume your income subject to taxes is $100,000 and you are "married filing jointly." What is your tax, your tax rate, and your marginal tax rate?

Your tax is $21,850. How did we get this? The tax on the first $45,200 is $6,780. (Please refer to the 2001 Tax Rate Schedule on page 71 of the instructional booklet for IRS Form 1040. You can also find this form online at www.irs.gov.) Reading across, though, it's clear that you are taxed at 27.5 percent for sums over $45,200. This is your marginal tax rate.

Investor's Idiom

Our income tax is progressive (as opposed to flat), meaning the more money you make, the more tax you pay per dollar. You pay no tax, in fact, on the first few dollars you earn and progressively more tax as you earn more. The rate you pay on the last few dollars you earn is your **marginal tax rate**.

Now, $100,000–$45,200 = $54,800. This is the amount of your earning that is taxed at the marginal rate of 27.5 percent. So the amount of tax you pay on that $54,800 is $54,800 × .275 = $15,070. The total amount of tax you pay, therefore, is the $6,780 due on the first $45,200 plus the $15,070 due on the remaining $54,800—or $21,850. Your average tax rate is $21,850 ÷ $100,000, or 21.85 percent. Every additional dollar of income over $45,200 (up to the next bracket at $109,250), however, is taxed at 27.5 percent, which is your marginal tax rate. There are state and local taxes affecting you as well, which can drive the taxes on those additional dollars as high as 50 percent!

If your income subject to taxes is less than $100,000, you can just look up the tax due from the tax tables found on page 59-70 in IRS Form 1040. We still want you to calculate your taxes, however, so that you will be familiar with both your tax rate and your marginal tax rate.

Why is it important to know your marginal tax rate? Because it will encourage you to spend less money! Given your tax situation, a penny saved is more than just a penny earned. It could be up to two pennies earned! Maybe you don't need to earn more; after all, every new dollar you earn is subject to that hefty marginal tax rate. Maybe you can pile up a nest egg to invest by saving.

> ### Crash Alert
>
> Federal (and state) tax withholding represents another area of potential savings. Many people overwithhold so they get a nice refund check after the tax year is over. But this lets the government, rather than you, earn interest on that money. Consider a $1,200 tax refund. If you had saved the $100 per month at 5 percent interest, instead of letting the government hold onto it, you'd be $30 ahead, because you'd get to use the money for about six months.

Risk-Free Saving Where You Least Expect It

Saving is actually one of the best investments around! The coolest thing about saving is that it's the one investment activity that breaks the rule about high returns requiring you to take on greater risk. Let's say you have a newborn and you run through five packs of diapers a week. Buying them individually, each pack costs $5, so you spend $25 a week on diapers. Zowie, that's $100 a month on diapers. Turns out, the store sells a case of diapers, which is one month's worth, at a 20 percent discount. On $100 worth of diapers, that discount is $20. The case of diapers costs $80. Hmmm … let's figure out your return on this investment.

Before, you paid $25 a week for diapers. Now, you're putting out $80 for a month's worth. Your discount on every pack of diapers is $1 ($5 – $4 = $1). Over a year, that will add up to a savings of $260 (i.e., $1 × 5 packs = $5 × 52 weeks = $260). So, for investing a measly $80 in discount diapers each month, you earn a return of $260. If we apply the ROI formula from Chapter 2, that's a return on investment of more than 20 percent!

> $1,040 (actual annual expense) – $1,300 (annual full price) ÷ $1,300 × 100 = 20 percent

And the only risk is that your baby will become miraculously toilet trained before you get a chance to use up that case of diapers (you wish!). Even better, the government doesn't get its hands on that $260. It's tax free and it's yours, all yours. If you really want to feel like a hotshot, figure that if your marginal tax rate is around 30 percent, you would have had to earn $260 plus $78 to cover the taxes to come up with $260. Saving money wherever you can is definitely the road to riches. The rest of this chapter should give you some fresh ideas on how to cut expenses on things like the following:

- Shopping
- Car expenses
- Banking
- Life insurance
- Real estate taxes
- Credit card fees

Let the saving begin ....

Buying Bulk Is a Great Investment

Buying in bulk, as in the example above, is a great way to save, provided that you keep it in perspective. Do you have to pile towels on the floor because the linen closet is filled with bargain toilet paper? Do you have to park your car outside because the garage is filled with discount tires? Don't laugh; we've seen it all! Just keep a couple of simple rules in mind and you'll be fine.

1. Are you taking advantage of a special sale at your local supermarket, or driving across town to a warehouse place like Sam's Club? If it's the latter, is there a membership fee, and how much? Remember, you have to mentally *amortize* (write off) the fee against your savings. Be sure to do this. As an example, the Sam's membership fee is $35 per year. Are you saving enough by making purchases there to make the $35 fee worthwhile? The fee may well be worth it for you, but be aware of it.

2. Try to limit your purchases to around a three-month supply as opposed to a year supply—unless you're planning on converting your home into a mini-supermarket, that is. And remember, prices can go down as well as up. So, if you buy a one-year

Investor's Idiom

To **amortize** means to write off a debt or fee over time. If you pay a fee of $240 a year to join a gym, for example, you might want to amortize that fee over the year by including $20 a month on your monthly income statement as your gym fee.

supply of chocolate chip cookies after a long period of price increases, you may have bought at the "top," with little or no savings to show.

3. Factor in transportation costs. We know people in New York City who drive to Vermont and Maine to shop at factory outlet stores, only they forget to factor in the cost of the gas they spend, not to mention their time. And sometimes the prices aren't much better than they are locally.

Your Car: Leasing vs. Ownership

There are two ways to look at this issue: first, from an aesthetic point of view, and second, from a financial point of view. If you simply like to drive around in a new car every two to three years, either because it makes you feel good or because you feel it is important for your business image, then lease. If, on the other hand, you want the least-expensive alternative, then buy (or take out a loan).

Advantages of Leasing

What are the advantages of leasing? Well, there's that thrill of driving a new car every two or three years. In addition, because the monthly payments are less, you are able to drive a more expensive car. Why are the payments less? Because you are not buying the car, you are simply paying for the *depreciation*, or the wear and tear, on the vehicle. When the lease is up, the dealer retains title to the car.

Investor's Idiom

Depreciation is the loss in value of an item over time due to wear and tear. Like amortization, the financial reflection of depreciation can be spread out over time. If you own a computer and use it in your home business, for example, the IRS allows you to deduct part of the computer's value each year as a depreciation expense.

You also have a little more flexibility: At the end of the lease, you can either walk away or purchase the car. Why is this important? Well, seen many Peugeot or British Sterling dealers lately? If you had purchased either car around 10 years ago, you would not be a happy camper; chalk up one for leasing. On the other hand, if you leased a Mazda Miata in 1990 for 36 months, your purchase-option price (the price you can buy the car for at the end of the lease) would have been 10 to 20 percent less than the then-current market value. So you could have purchased the car and immediately sold it at a profit. Finally, if you use the car in your business, you can deduct the rental payments on your business tax return.

Disadvantages of Leasing

Leasing sounds pretty good so far, right? Let's look at the negatives and how to reduce some of them.

1. *Capitalized Cost Deduction*. This is the leasing equivalent of a down payment. The larger this figure, the lower your monthly payments. You can usually negotiate this figure lower, sometimes a lot lower. Just make sure you do so without budging on the monthly payment.

2. *Disposition Fee*. This is a fee charged if you do not buy the car. Tell the dealer you don't want to pay this fee (or have the dealer deduct this cost from some other category).

3. *Excess Wear and Tear*. This is subjective and determined by each individual dealer at his or her discretion. What about parking lot "dingers," or a broken outside mirror or antenna? Are these excess or normal? Have the dealer define excess wear and tear for you—in writing.

4. *Annual Mileage Allowance*. This usually runs 10,000 to 15,000 miles per year. You get no credit if you use less than the allowance and you pay a penalty (e.g., 20¢ per mile) if you run over the allowance. Be sure to determine your projected miles before making the lease decision. If you know your mileage will be greater than the allowance, you can usually "buy" additional miles (e.g., 10¢ per mile), but excess mileage can be an expensive proposition. Here's an extreme example: Jack's contract reads 10,000 miles per year on a 36-month lease, with excess miles charged at 20¢ per mile. His actual mileage turns out to be 60,000 (20,000 per year). His charge for excess miles of 30,000 (60,000 actual – 30,000 contractual) is $6,000 (30,000 × 20¢)! Ouch! Even if he'd bought an extra 10,000 miles per year for 10¢ per mile, he's still out $3,000! Moral of the story: If you are going to put a lot of miles on your car, don't lease.

The Bottom Line on Leasing

Every situation is different, but in general:

♦ The economics favor leasing if you plan to keep the car for less than two years.

♦ It's a toss-up for years three and four.

♦ The economics favor buying if you plan to keep your car for more than four years. Why? Because when you buy, you are financing something that will have some value when you stop making payments. All you are financing with a lease is depreciation. At the end of a lease period you have nothing. The costs of actually buying a car are simple and few in number: rate (in percent) and monthly financing charge, plus any paperwork fee. And, of course, how much you want, or have, to put down (down payment).

If you do go for the lease option, try to limit your search to cars on a lease "special." These are deals made when the manufacturer and/or dealer absorbs some of your cost and gives up some of their profit to promote a particular model. Why? Well, perhaps they have an excess inventory. For example, assume a Mazda Millenia is priced at $30,000 and the dealers are offering a "special" 36-month lease (no money down) of $325 per month. The upgraded S version, meanwhile, might be priced at $36,000, or 20 percent more. However, there is no special lease, and the best you can do is $475 per month for 36 months, or 46 percent more.

So, if you plan to put low mileage on your car and trade it in frequently, it pays for you to use a lease—but only go for cars on a special lease package. Otherwise, buy your car and bargain down everything and anything you can. It's your money! If you want additional information on leasing, check out www.leasesource.com, which has an online worksheet to determine leasing pluses and minuses.

For more general information on car pricing and leasing, call *Consumer Reports* at 1-800-205-2445 or visit their website at www.consumerreports.org.

Other great sources of info:

- *Edmund's Automobile Buyer's Guide*: www.edmund.com

- *Kelley Blue Book* (indispensable if you are going to sell your current car or trade it in on a new one): www.kbb.com

If You Buy a Car

If you can own your car for at least eight years, you will have maximized your investment. Before buying, don't forget to check the Internet for the lowest prices and read magazines like *Consumer Reports* for helpful tips. Above all, shop around for your financing; don't just accept the dealer's rate. Here again, the Internet can be a great source of helpful information, as can local banks.

Finally, if you live in an urban area, make sure you really need a car. If you do, don't forget to factor in the cost of parking. Good public transportation can be a great alternative, supplemented by rentals when you need a vehicle for vacations or specific trips. The savings can be substantial.

Choosing a Bank

Banks make money by taking in deposits from customers and lending it out to other customers. That's why banks pay you less interest on your savings account than they charge you when you want a loan. The difference is the bank's profit. If a bank pays you 4 percent on your savings account and lends money to a company for 12 percent, the bank has made 8 percent. Different banks pay different savings account and CD rates, however, so shop around before you choose a bank. Many local newspapers carry various bank-account fees in table format once a week; check in the financial section of yours.

Super Strategy

There are basically three types of insurance everyone needs to carry:

- ◆ Life insurance, which provides income for your family in the event of your death.
- ◆ Health insurance, including disability income insurance. Disability insurance should cover 50 to 75 percent of your salary. Make sure it's noncancellable and guaranteed renewable.
- ◆ Liability insurance, which covers you if anyone sues because they are injured on your property or by your car. You'll save a bundle in premiums if you look to cover only major losses, not minor ones.

If convenience is important to you, make a short list of banks near your home or workplace. Think about the types of bank accounts you want, and then comparison shop via telephone. Before you do, estimate roughly how many checks you write per month. Different banks have different fees and requirements. Some banks will require a minimum balance, but will waive check-writing fees if you keep that balance. Others allow you, say, five free checks a month. Others charge you for each check you write, no matter what. Some banks will allow you to combine balances from savings accounts, CDs, and checking accounts to meet a minimum balance. Then there are ATM fees to contend with. Some banks won't charge you if you use their machine, but will charge you upward of $1 for using a machine at another banking institution. Some banks charge you no matter whose ATM you use. These fees may not sound like much, but they really add up.

Another option is to forego a bank checking account altogether and use one that draws from your money market fund. We discussed that option in Chapter 3.

It's a good idea to choose a bank that offers overdraft protection as well. An overdraft is a bounced check. These can easily cost you $10 to $30 per pop and are usually the result of carelessness (when you don't keep your check register up-to-date) or poor communication (when you and your spouse don't update your individual entries in the joint checking account).

Life Insurance

If you have straight or ordinary life insurance, look into term insurance. Term insurance covers you for a specific term—say, 20 years—instead of your entire life. You can obtain the same dollar amount of insurance for much lower premiums with term life insurance. Many people set the term to cover them until the year their last child is expected to graduate from college. Also check with your employer to see if you are eligible for a group insurance rate.

Knocking Down Real Estate Taxes

Real estate taxes are established by a local board of assessors or a town assessor who estimates how much your home is worth. Basically, your home is assessed a certain value, and that value is multiplied by the property tax rate, for every $1,000 of value in your home. Schools are typically the highest consumer of tax dollars (up to around 70 percent or more), followed by municipal services, such as police and fire departments.

If your home is assessed at $245,000 and your tax rate for your town is $5 per $1,000, your tax bill is $245 × $5, or $1,225. It's always possible that your house has been overvalued by the assessor. Check to see if your home has been assessed in line with your neighbors' houses, making allowance for number of bedrooms and other features, such as a deck or pool. Also compare your house with similar homes in other parts of town. The town office or assessor's office will make this information available to you.

If you feel your assessment is too high, check with the assessor's office for the proper procedure. Nothing ventured, nothing gained. Be careful, however, not to start the process without a good case—assessments can be raised as well as lowered.

Credit Cards

In Chapter 7, we're going to really get down to business on how to dig yourself out of debt, but let's take a moment now to think about what a drag credit cards can be on your financial plan. Credit cards are a very expensive debt if you don't pay off the balance in full each month. Annual rates of 15 to 20 percent are common, plus many cards charge a membership fee. Look at it this way: Let's say you're carrying around a $2,000 balance on a credit card that has an 18 percent annual interest rate. Each month you pay them the minimum amount, which we'll say is $20. The yearly interest on that $2,000 balance ($2,000 × .18) is $360. Your minimum $20 a month payment you've been making adds up to $240 for a year. *You're not even paying off the interest!* A bad investment. Very bad.

If you're doing everything "right" financially and are earning a solid return on some solid investments, what's the point if you're paying out tons of interest on your credit cards? You may be earning 15 percent on $5,000 in a great stock mutual fund, but if you're paying 18 percent on $5,000 on a maxed-out credit card, well, you're not getting ahead, are you?

First, if you have more than one credit card, ditch the rest and get down to one. No one needs more than one credit card. Now, which one should you carry? If you have trouble paying off your balance in full each month, think about switching to a *charge card*, as opposed to a *credit card*, such as the American Express card. In other words, you are required to pay the balance off in full each month, so you won't be tempted to carry it (and you'll think twice about what you charge on it!).

If you do have the discipline to pay off your card every month, why not get one that works for you? If you travel frequently by air, think about a card that offers free mileage. If you drive, how about a card that earns free gas or dollars toward the purchase of a new car? Once you have your monthly balance under control, you'd be amazed at how many transactions (supermarkets, doctor/dentist bills, and so on) you can put on your card and how the bonuses pile up.

Investor's Idiom

The difference between a **credit card** and a **charge card** is that a credit card enables you to carry a debt indefinitely, as long as you pay interest. Any debt put on a charge card, in contrast, has to be paid for within a specified period, typically 30 days. If you don't pay off your charge card account during that period, you will have to pay penalties and interest.

Little Things That Add Up

Besides savings on big items like cars, taxes, and insurance, there are literally hundreds of little savings you can come up with on your own. Here are a few examples:

1. Think about alternatives: Does it cost more to pick up the paper on the way to work or have it delivered at home?

2. Make clothes last. What's the cost of a new shirt versus the cost of turning the collar and/or cuffs on an old shirt?

3. If you're a clotheshorse, try to buy for next season at the end of this season, when everything's marked down.

4. To save on entertainment expenses, think about cocktails at home and just the dinner meal out. Restaurants make much of their profit from the bar. If movies are your passion, don't forget to take advantage of special weekend matinee movie prices.

5. Plan ahead on vacation trips, keeping an eye out for off-season rates on both air tickets and hotels.

6. There are great deals on phone charges right now, but be sure to read the small print. Also, have your long-distance carrier check your usage to see if there's a plan that best fits your pattern of calling. It doesn't cost anything to ask.

These are just a few tips to get those creative saving juices flowing. You may be skeptical about saving $10 here and $20 there doing you much good, but in the end those few dollars that you've saved add up to a lot more than you think!

The Least You Need to Know

◆ You pay taxes on each additional dollar you earn on your job, but saving is free, so it's a lot easier to get ahead by saving than by working more.

◆ Get in the habit of preparing monthly income statements to keep track of your spending.

◆ You can earn a higher rate of return from buying in bulk than from many investments.

◆ If you plan to own a car for under two years, leasing may be a better deal than buying.

◆ Choose a bank that offers overdraft protection, as well as the convenience you need and the best rates in your area.

Chapter 7

Solving Debt and Credit Problems

In This Chapter

- ◆ Checking and repairing your credit history
- ◆ Building good credit
- ◆ Using, not abusing, credit cards
- ◆ Good debt vs. bad debt

Credit can be either a tremendous boon to your financial life or a dangerous drain, depending on how wisely you use it. Human beings have been struggling with its temptations for centuries.

Credit preceded the coining of money by more than 2,000 years. Coinage is dated from the first millennium B.C.E., but old Sumerian documents, circa 3000 B.C.E., reveal a systematic use of credit based on loans of grain by volume and loans of metal by weight. These loans often carried interest.

About 1800 B.C.E., Hammurabi, a king of the first dynasty of ancient Babylonia, gave his people the earliest known formal code of laws. A number of the chief provisions of this code regulated the relation of debtor to creditor. The maximum rate of interest was set at $33\frac{1}{3}$ percent per annum for loans of grain repayable in kind, and at 20 percent per annum for loans of silver by weight. All loans had to be accompanied by written contracts witnessed before officials. Land and other assets could be pledged against a debt. So could the creditor, as well as his wife, concubine, children, or slaves. And you thought you had it bad! Personal slavery for debt was limited to three years. (Source: Sidney Homer, *A History of Interest Rates*, Rutgers Univ. Press, 1977.)

Creditors may no longer be able to take your first born, but nothing can screw up your financial goals more than a whopping debt or a bad credit report. In this chapter, we're going to show you how to avoid and fix credit mishaps—and get into great investing shape.

What Does Your Credit Report Say About You?

Before a credit card company issues you a card or a bank lends you money, they will check out your credit report. There are credit-reporting agencies (CRAs) that do nothing but gather credit information about you from bankers and other creditors and sell that information to banks, stores, and other issuers of credit.

If you've ever defaulted on a student loan, failed to pay off a charge account at a department store, or forgotten to pay a bill because you moved, rest assured that these transgressions are on your credit report in black and white. In addition, your report carries your Social Security number, your past and present addresses, your salary, and any other details of your financial life the credit-reporting agency has been able to snag. Pretty creepy, huh?

Fiscal Facts

When you apply for a credit card, a bank loan, or any other form of credit, you typically sign something that gives permission to the creditor to obtain your credit history. The creditor subscribes to credit reporting agencies, which forward your credit report. The information on the credit report is based on what other creditors have reported about you.

CRA Horror Stories

Nothing can be more upsetting than to discover—the hard way—that you have a bad credit report. We've each had that experience. Ed was shocked when he was turned down for a credit card recently. He exercised his right to request a free copy of his credit report. (Whenever you are turned down for credit, you can contact the credit agency whose information was used to turn you down and get a copy of the report.)

Ed's report was clean as a whistle, except for one little detail: a state tax lien of $130, filed on June 10, 1997, for the transfer tax on a home sold back in 1991. The actual tax was a measly $25; the $105 was interest.

Ed made a slew of phone calls. Finally someone at the state tax department explained that the state had gone after both the buyer and seller of Ed's house, but the buyer never responded and the seller (Ed) did not have a current address in their system. So the state filed the lien. It's a good thing Ed and his wife found this out before they refinanced their mortgage several months later, because it took a month to clear up.

Investor's Idiom

A **lien** is a legal right to take someone's property and hold it until the owner pays a debt.

Debra was stunned when a mysterious "unpaid loan" for $2,000 showed up on her credit report. It took six months of persistent phone calls and letters before she determined that her alma mater had mistakenly assigned a single college loan two identification numbers. This made it look like she had actually had two college loans—and had failed to pay off one of them.

What about you? Do you have something like this lurking in your report? Are you sure you don't? Do you want to wait until you try to buy a car, a house, or a gym membership to find out?

How to Check Your Credit Reports

We recommend that you look at your credit reports from at least the top three CRAs every year. These are:

- ◆ Trans Union: 1-800-888-4213, www.transunion.com (you can order your report online; fees vary by state)

- ◆ Experian (formerly TRW): 1-866-200-6020 (866 is toll free), www.experian.com (you can order your report online but it'll cost you $9.00)

- ◆ Equifax: 1-800-685-1111, www.equifax.com ($9.00)

If you own a business, you will want to run a credit check on it periodically, too. You might also want to be able to check on your customers' credit. The top credit-reporting agencies in this field are:

◆ Dunn & Bradstreet: 1-800-234-3867, www.dnb.com

◆ Experian (formerly TRW): 1-866-200-6020 (866 is toll free), www.experian.com

Although you can also order your credit reports by mail, we recommend calling because you may or may not need to send a fee and you may also need to send things like a xerox of your social security cards. Call first or go online.

How do you get a copy of your report? Each CRA has slightly different policies, but basically they will have you send proof of your Social Security number and address. Our information is accurate as of July 2002 but you can always contact the Federal Trade Commission, Consumer Response Center-FCRA at 202-326-3761 for a specific agency's name and number. The FTC website is: www.ftc.gov. Also check out www.freecreditreport.com.

Your Credit Reporting Rights

FCRA stands for the Federal Fair Credit Reporting Act, which gives you specific rights regarding the privacy and accuracy of information in your credit report. Specifically:

◆ If a company denies you credit based on information supplied by a CRA, it must tell you and provide you with the name, address, and phone number of the CRA.

◆ You can request a free copy of your report if it has been less than 60 days since your credit request was denied. In some states (e.g., New Jersey), you are entitled to a free report the first time you request one, with or without credit denial. Otherwise, credit reports typically cost $8.

◆ You can dispute inaccurate information in your credit report, and each CRA will tell you exactly how to do that. For example, if you've refused to pay for your new washing machine because it's not working and the store has reported you as a bad credit risk, you can have your side of the story reported on your credit report and have the debt designated "disputed" instead of "unpaid."

◆ The CRA must remove or correct inaccurate information within 30 days of dispute.

Crash Alert

Credit reporting agencies can make mistakes, because they do not verify the information they receive—they just report it. So get reports for you and your spouse regularly and check them out carefully, so you can clear up any issues pronto.

♦ In most cases, a CRA may not report negative information that is more than seven years old (10 years for bankruptcies). If you have a good reason for having failed to pay a bill—maybe you failed to pay it because you moved and it was not forwarded to your new address, for example—you can pay the bill and have it erased from your report.

♦ You may request that your name be removed from CRA lists for unsolicited credit and insurance offers. Incidentally, you will be surprised at how many such offers show up as "inquiries" on your credit report! Now you know how to reduce your daily junk mail overload!

No Credit Is Not Good Credit

Don't make the mistake of thinking that because you've never used credit, you have good credit. What you have is no credit, and if you have no credit, you won't be approved for mortgages or auto loans. Many credit card companies won't approve you, either. You need to establish a personal credit history that shows you can make regular payments on a debt over time.

Although banks and credit card companies tend not to lend to people with no credit history, department stores are usually willing to let someone with no credit history open a charge card account. A charge account lets you buy something without paying cash for it at the time of purchase. You are expected to pay the purchase off by the end of the month. Some charge accounts let you pay off only a minimum balance monthly and charge you interest on the remaining balance.

When you get your first charge account, make a few purchases each month and pay for them by the end of the month. Never miss a payment or pay late.

Another way to establish a credit history is to buy something on layaway. With a layaway plan, you make a down payment on a piece of furniture, for example, and pay it off with regular monthly payments. You can't take the item home until all the payments have been made.

Investor's Idiom

A **charge card** allows you to "charge" an item, or buy it without paying cash at the time of purchase. You are expected to pay the purchase off within 30 days, whereas with a **credit card** you can make monthly minimum payments indefinitely. Another way to buy without paying at the time of purchase is to use a layaway plan, which allows you to make a down payment and monthly payments. When you buy something on layaway you can't take it home until all payments have been made.

This is another way to prove that you can be trusted to make regular payments. But, you need to ask whether the creditor reports timely payments of items on layaway to credit reporting agencies. Not all of them do.

Finally, make sure your efforts to establish good credit are being reported to the CRAs. Check your reports six months after using a charge account or other credit regularly and if no positive information has been reported, ask the issuer of the credit you're using to send a report to the CRAs. Request a copy for yourself, also.

Credit Cards: You Only Need One

Some people collect credit cards as if they were baseball cards. Not only is this confusing (which one do you use when, and where?), but it can get expensive. Most cards charge an annual membership fee. And credit card rates are very high compared to other lending rates: 16–18 percent, for example, versus around 8–9 percent for auto loans.

We highly recommend that you have only one credit card. Pick the card with the lowest rate and no annual fee and transfer your balances from other cards to this one. That's step one toward effectively managing credit card debt.

Step two is to pay off the balance and continue to pay in full every month.

Finally, for step three, once you pay off the outstanding balance and consolidate down to one card, rates no longer matter. Why? Because you are going to pay off the balance outstanding, in full, each month. Now you can switch, before the next annual fee (if there is one) on your current card comes due, to the card you really want. Ask yourself these questions when choosing a credit card:

◆ What card do most of the stores I frequent take? American Express? Visa? MasterCard? Discover?

- ◆ Do I travel by air a lot? Would a card that earns frequent flyer miles benefit me?

- ◆ What other benefits would I like to earn by using a card? Free gas? Shopping discounts?

How to Really Get Your Act Together

Once you have your credit card debt under control and the best card in your wallet or pocketbook, you can take the offensive by using your card as a reporting device. Remember the advice we gave you in Chapter 4 about gathering and entering your expenses on a monthly income statement? Well, you can charge practically all your purchases—from getting your car washed to new shoes for the kids—on a credit card.

Now, here comes the cool part. Each month, you get an itemized listing of your charges for entry onto your monthly sheets. And, with some cards, you even get an annual report with all your purchases sorted into expense categories. Perfect! Your financial statements will practically write themselves.

A Checking Account? Who Needs It!

If you go this route, you might not even need a checking account. Most money market funds (more on those coming up) allow you to write checks against the money in your money market account. These checks usually have to be for at least $250.

Simply use your credit card to pay for almost every purchase you make and write one check a month, drawn from your money market account, to pay off your credit card, and a few others for rent or mortgage and car payments. No more balancing a checkbook, no more paying for checks, no more exorbitant bounced-check fees—plus you get that monthly list of exactly what you spent and on what from your credit card company. Is this smooth, or what?

Whip out your scissors and start cutting up all the credit cards you don't need. Get down to one card and you'll also be down to one easy-to-read financial statement. Now you're in control.

> **Super Strategy**
>
> Pay off your credit card every month and use it for every purchase you make. Not only will you avoid throwing away money on credit card interest, the credit card company will send you an annual list of everything you've bought, broken into categories, which you can use to create your annual balance sheet. Life doesn't get much easier than that!

Debit Cards—a Better Choice?

Debit cards enable you to make purchases with a direct deduction from your checking account rather than a charge to a credit card account. They are often packaged together now as a combination cash card (which can be used for deposits and withdrawals at bank cash or ATM machines) and debit card.

Debit cards are very convenient, and you do avoid interest charges by using them instead of credit cards, but they can make it even more of a hassle to balance your checking account. You have to keep track of every little purchase you make with your debit card and enter it into your check register. You can quickly lose control of your balance and run into overdraft and service charges.

To avoid the risk of overdraft charges or bounced checks, open up a line of credit with your checking account. There typically is no charge unless you actually use the line, whereupon the rate is around 11–12 percent. Guess what, though? If you apply for a line of credit, your bank will check your credit report. If there are any problems, you will be turned down for overdraft protection.

Investor's Idiom

A **debit card** can be presented like a credit card when you make a purchase, but the cost of the purchase is deducted at the time of purchase from your checking account.

Credit card, debit card—or one of each? The choice is yours. But if you opt for the debit card, keep close tabs on your checking account balance. This includes communication and coordination with your significant other!

How Much of Your Income Should Go Toward Reducing Debt?

"Okay," you're thinking, "this is just dandy to talk about having no credit card debt and using one credit card as my own private accountant, but I'm in debt up to my eyebrows! How do I dig myself out?" Every situation is different, but we do have a rule of thumb that should give you some guidance.

Some mortgage experts recommend that your mortgage payment should be no more than 25–30 percent of your gross income. So figure that a week's salary should cover it. Your gross income is what appears on your W-2 statement plus any other earned or unearned income (like income from a trust account). Consider earmarking an additional 5–10 percent of your gross income for reducing educational loans, auto loans, charge accounts, credit card debt, and anything else you're carrying like a load of rocks.

Good Debt vs. Bad Debt

What's "good" debt? Debt that represents a worthwhile investment with appreciation potential is good debt. Home mortgages and education loans are good debt. Plus, mortgage interest (and taxes) are deductible on your Form 1040 Schedule A. Bad debt is loans on depreciating assets such as cars, clothing, a new pair of skis, etc. Make every effort to pay off bad debt first.

The main reason to minimize your bad debt is to increase your financial flexibility and peace of mind. Most people borrow right up to their limit and have nothing in reserve. If they face some unexpected crisis, they have to borrow more (if possible) on existing assets. This means taking out a home equity loan or refinancing their home mortgage, or tapping into their 401(k) plan. If these measures don't do the trick, they're looking at a second mortgage and, ultimately, at selling off assets (the car, the home, etc.). It gets to the point where you're trying to put a size 10 foot into a size 9 shoe.

This is why the emergency fund we discussed in Chapter 3 is so important. It provides you with the freedom to make good decisions and the flexibility to pay for them.

> **Fiscal Facts**
>
> After World War II, credit of all sorts proliferated (especially consumer and mortgage credit) and there were some modifications to existing credit instruments. New federal agencies used "moral obligation" notes, mostly to promote the real estate mortgage market, and these new issues often exceeded in volume the new financing of the Treasury itself. (From **A History of Interest Rates**, pg. 334.)

How Much to Set Aside for Peace of Mind

We've talked before about having an emergency fund that represents 10 percent of your annual income or $10,000, whichever is greater, and we've talked before about how each individual's situation differs. But let's get into more detail. Sid Sod, for example, may participate in his employer's group health plan, short-term disability, and long-term disability plans. These are deductions from his pay slip. Nancy Nerd is self-employed; she either must try to obtain these health plans on her own (at considerably greater expense), or make sure she has enough in her emergency fund to cover broken arms and other nasty surprises. She'll need a significantly larger emergency fund than Sid Sod. In fact, she'll probably need more than she can really afford to put aside. Buying health insurance would be a wiser choice for her to make than for her to try to put aside enough to cover a medical catastrophe.

The 10 percent emergency fund is there to cover unanticipated expenses. So if you don't have insurance, get it! Don't plan to meet the need with the emergency fund. Similarly, saving for that new car or home should be built into the emergency fund so that you don't incur "bad debt" to buy these necessities.

If You Spend It, Replenish It

Above all, when you deplete your emergency fund, always replenish it before you invest or make any other financial allocations. And never, never use your credit card as an emergency fund. Far too many people get into terrible debt by making that mistake.

Examples of unanticipated expenses that should be covered by the emergency fund are:

- Damage claims not covered by insurance (whether health, auto, or home)
- Your daughter's wedding
- Major auto or appliance repairs, etc.
- Rent or mortgage payments if you lose your job

Whatever befalls you or any member of your immediate family, make it your goal to be able to deal with it via your emergency fund—without the need to tap your other investments or take on additional debt. Don't use the emergency fund for luxuries like a vacation in Tahiti or a sailboat.

The Least You Need to Know

- Nothing can screw up your financial goals more than a bad credit report.
- Check your credit history once a year to catch errors.
- No credit is not the same as good credit; you have to use credit to build a credit history.
- Get down to one credit card, then pay off its balance monthly.
- Use your credit card to make all your purchases. This is an easy way to keep track of your expenses.
- Statistics show that people "spend" more when they use credit cards. Remember, a credit card is debt, not money.
- If you want to use a debit card, get overdraft protection.

Chapter 8

Trim Your Taxes

In This Chapter

- Figuring out your taxable income
- Evaluating employer-provided health care and child care
- What you need to know about medical savings accounts
- Deduction strategies for your investments

This book is about putting your money to work so you can have the life you want. We've already talked about cutting expenses so you can meet your investment goals. An even more painless way to increase the amount of money you can put to work for you is to trim your taxes to the bone. We touched on this topic in Chapter 6, but here we'll explore every conceivable way you can keep more of what you earn at work with your investments. We'll also update you on the sweeping changes created by the Economic Growth and Tax Relief Reconciliation Act of 2001, which President George W. Bush signed into law. (See why we just call it the Tax Relief Act?)

What Are All Those Different "Incomes" Anyway?

Most of us view tax time like a shot: We just want to get it over with as quickly as possible. Fill out those forms and stick 'em in the mail. Boom, you're done and you don't have to think about it for another year. What a relief, right? Well, it may seem less painful this way, but you're really not doing yourself any favors. When it comes to the government and your money, ignorance is not the bliss it's cracked up to be. It's costly. So pay attention—we're going to save you some money here.

Fiscal Facts

Blame the Civil War for having to pay your federal income taxes: 140 years ago, the federal government authorized an income tax on individuals to help defray the cost of the War Between the States.

Before we can tackle your taxes, we need to define a few terms. It can be pretty confusing to look at your tax return and see phrases like taxable income, gross income, and adjusted gross income. What are all those incomes, anyway? Taxable income is the number that determines how much tax you pay, but where does it come from?

We'll answer this question in a few steps. Let's start with gross income. Gross income includes ...

♦ Wages, salaries, and tips—reported on your W-2.

♦ Dividend and interest income—reported on Schedule B of your income tax return.

♦ Taxable refunds (e.g., state tax refund).

♦ Alimony received.

♦ Business income—reported on Schedule C or C-EZ.

♦ *Capital gains*—reported on Schedule D.

♦ Taxable distributions from IRAs, pensions, and annuities.

♦ Rental income.

♦ Income from partnerships, corporations, and trusts—reported on Schedule E.

♦ Farm income—reported on Schedule F.

♦ Unemployment compensation.

♦ Taxable Social Security benefits.

The next step is to calculate your adjusted gross income (AGI). Adjusted gross income is gross income less ...

♦ IRA deductions.

♦ Student loan interest deductions.

- Archer MSA (Medical Savings Account) deductions (Form 8853).

- Moving expenses (Form 3903).

- One half of self-employment tax (Schedule SE).

- Self-employed health insurance deduction.

- Keogh (i.e., qualified) and SEP and SIMPLE plans.

- Any penalty of early withdrawal of savings (e.g., CDs).

- Any alimony paid.

Now that you have your adjusted gross income, you can take deductions and exemptions. Deductions from adjusted gross income are either itemized, meaning you list each and every one of them, or standard, meaning that you take a deduction for a specific amount allowed by the IRS. For 2001 the standard deductions were …

- $4,550 for a single person.

- $6,650 for the head of a household.

- $7,600 for married people filing jointly (or qualifying widow or widower).

- $3,800 for married people filing separately.

If you don't think your itemized deductions will add up to more than the standard deduction offered, take the standard deduction.

It will be worth your efforts to itemize your deductions if you have heavy expenses in the following categories:

- Medical and dental expenses not reimbursed by insurance

- Taxes (state, local, real estate, and personal property such as automobiles)

- Home mortgage interest and *points* (Form 1098)

- Gifts to charity

- Unreimbursed job expenses (Form 2106)

- Other expenses, such as safe-deposit box rental, etc.

Investor's Idiom

A **point** is 1 percent expressed in terms of the size of your mortgage. So one point on a $100,000 mortgage is $1,000; two points is $2,000; and so on.

If you itemize, you can deduct the full amount of your AGI: $66,475 or less for single filers and $132,950 for married filing jointly. Above these sums a decreasing percentage of your itemized expenses can be deducted. As an example, if your AGI were $330,000 and your itemized deductions were $40,000, only $34,000 could actually be deducted from your AGI.

Now you can subtract any exemptions you may have from your AGI.

As of 2001, the IRS says you can subtract $2,900 per household member for income up to $132,950 for a single filer ($199,450 if filing jointly). At higher income levels the exemptions are scaled down. Pick up a copy of *The Complete Idiot's Guide to Doing Your Income Taxes 1999* (Alpha Books) for more help in this area.

So here's the process to get to your taxable income:

> Gross income – adjustments = adjusted gross income – deductions and exemptions = taxable income

Now you've got your taxable income!

Spankin' New Tax Bracket and Lowered Tax Rates

The Tax Relief Act that President Bush signed into law created a brand-new tax bracket, lowered personal income tax rates, and increased certain credits and deductions. We'll get you up to speed on all of it, starting with the new brackets.

The Tax Relief Act delivers lower tax rates for the first time since 1986 and creates a new 10 percent bracket for income up to $6,000 for single people and $12,000 for married people filing jointly. For 2001, this new tax bracket was given to eligible taxpayers as a tax credit.

In addition, Congress reduced the higher tax brackets, although the 15 percent tax bracket stays the same. The tax cuts will be phased in over time, and look like this for a single person.

Taxable Income	2002	2004	2006
$1–$6,000	10.0%	10.0%	10.0%
$6,000–$27,050	15.0	15.0	15.0
$27,050–$65,550	27.0	26.0	25.0
$65,550–$136,750	30.0	29.0	28.0
$136,750–$297,350	35.0	34.0	33.0
$297,350+	38.6	37.6	35.0

Here's a lovely thought: If you're having trouble saving the magic 10 percent figure we recommend in Chapter 1, why not let these lower tax rates help you out? Just don't spend the kickback. In effect, the IRS is reimbursing you for your savings!

Uncle Sammie and Your Marginal Income Tax Rate

As you learned in Chapter 6, your marginal income tax rate is the tax rate Uncle Sam will apply to your next dollar of income. Specifically, if you look at the instruction booklet for IRS Form 1040, you will see near the back a page titled "Tax Rate Schedules." There is a schedule for each of four status categories:

1. Single

2. Married filing jointly

3. Married filing separately

4. Head of household

You will probably be in the first or second category. For each status, there is a schedule or table. There are five different taxable rates that are applied to your income.

So if you are single and your taxable income is $65,551 for 2002, what is your tax and what is your marginal tax rate for 2002? Well, the first $6,000 you earn is taxed at 10 percent and the next $21,050 is taxed at 15 percent. Whatever you earn between $27,050 and $65,551 is taxed at 27 percent. Your salary is $65,550, so that last dollar you earn is taxed at the next rate, which is 30 percent.

Let's figure out your total tax. Simply multiply each level of income by the tax rate.

$6,000 × .10 = $600.00

$21,050 × .15 = $3,157.50

$38,500 × .27 = $10,395

$1 × .30 = $0.30

These are the taxes due on each tier of income. Adding them together, we get your total income tax due on $65,551—$14,152.80.

In this example, the marginal tax rate is .30, or 30 percent. This is the rate at which your next dollar of taxable income will be taxed. But note that your average tax rate is $14,152.80 ÷ $65,551, or 21.6 percent!

Super Strategy

Your employer may offer group health plans (medical and/or dental) and a 401(k) plan. If you subscribe to either, a sum is deducted from your regular pay. Although this comes out of your pay envelope, it is deducted before your W-2 reportable income is determined. In other words, you do not pay taxes on that portion of your salary that goes toward health benefits and 401(k) contributions. All the more reason to maximize your 401(k) contributions and fully participate in employer group health plans. Just check to make sure your premiums do come out pretax.

Employer-Based Health- and Child-Care Funds

Some employers offer a third type of deduction from your income: nonreimbursed health-care and dependent-care expenses. Examples of the former would include medical and dental deductibles and co-payments, plus other expenses not normally covered (e.g., eyeglasses).

There is a catch, however: The difference between legitimate expenses claimed and the total deduction is forfeited. For example, if you arrange to have $3,000 deducted from your pay at the beginning of the year but only file claims totaling $2,500, you are out the $500. In other words, use it or lose it! So estimate carefully.

Medical Savings Accounts: Are They a Good Deal?

In 1997, for the first time, the IRS allowed for a medical savings account deduction (Form 8853) for the first time. Medical savings accounts (now called Archer MSAs) are designed for self-employed individuals and small companies, for whom the cost of health insurance can be prohibitively expensive. The individual (or the company) buys health insurance with a high deductible (e.g., $2,000–$3,000 for an individual, $3,000–$5,000 for a family). But how do you come up with the "scratch" to cover that high deductible, if you need to do so? This is where the medical account comes in.

With an Archer MSA, you split the money you would normally spend for complete health insurance into two parts:

1. Money spent to purchase a cheaper and less comprehensive medical insurance plan to cover big medical bills (typically above $4,950).

2. You put the rest of the money you would have spent on health insurance into a 100 percent tax-deductible savings account. You can pay your insurance deductibles and co-payments from this account. Or you can save it. What you don't spend,

you can keep (and invest!) tax free. Because this is such a nice tax break, the law limits your tax-exempt savings to 75 percent of your one-year deductible (65 percent if you're single).

This is still a pilot program, so changes may be made from time to time, but the basic outline is in place. On March 8, 2002, President George W. Bush signed into law a one-year extension of the program, so at least we know MSAs will be around until December 31, 2003. If you are self-employed or work for a small business, this could be an important deduction. And remember, all deductions reduce the amount of tax you have to pay.

How the Archer MSA Works

As stated, you can keep up to 65 percent of the deductible for yourself alone, or up to 75 percent if you have a family, in a medical savings account. You can also deduct the full amount of your contribution to the account (it's on Line 25 of Form 1040).

Let's say Charlie Cheap has bought insurance with a $2,000 *deductible*. He can contribute 65 percent of $2,000, or $1,300, to his medical account every year. The sums in the account grow tax deferred to age 65. If Charlie taps into the account in the interim for medical reasons, there is no tax due. If he digs into it for nonmedical reasons before age 65, there is both income tax due and a 15 percent penalty. After age 65, if he withdraws for nonmedical reasons, he does not incur the 15 percent penalty.

> **Investor's Idiom**
>
> The **deductible** is the amount of expense you agree to cover before your insurance kicks in.

Is this a good deal? Well, it puts a large premium on staying healthy up to the point where the account exceeds the deductible. And can you afford to both put aside the deductible and pay the premium? It seems like a good deal for the "healthy and wealthy." But for the rest of us, we're not so sure. Remember, you can also buy health insurance at group rates even if you're self-employed by joining certain professional groups or fraternal organizations.

As for MSAs, keep your eyes open for any modifications announced via your local newspaper or television station. Check with local banks as well as mutual fund companies to see if they participate. They will also be up-to-date as modifications unfold.

Buying Your Own Health Insurance May Be a Better Deal

If you are self-employed or employed by a small business, buying your health insurance may be a better deal for you than a medical savings account. Under the Taxpayer Relief Act of 1997, and as modified in 2001, the deductions for health insurance expenses of self-employed individuals (and their family members) were to steadily rise to 100 percent in 2007. The tax law President Bush signed in 2002 accelerated the schedule, raising the amount you can deduct for 2002 to 70 percent, and to 100 percent after 2002. That's a pretty hefty potential deduction; and the more you can deduct, the less you pay in taxes.

Bush Gets Busy

The new bill also offers some relief for the "marriage penalty" by increasing the standard deduction for married people filing jointly and increasing the 15 percent tax bracket to include more of married people's income. These changes will be phased in 2005.

Other changes created by Bush's sweeping tax reforms include:

◆ The child credit will double over the next 10 years to $1,000 per child. Expenses eligible for child-care credits and adoption credits are increased.

◆ Starting in 2002, limits on how much you can contribute to an educational IRA to save for your children's education increase. And you can begin to use those savings not just for college, but also for primary and secondary school costs.

◆ The amount you can contribute to your retirement IRAs will gradually increase from $2,000 to $5,000 by 2008. The limit on 401(k) plan contributions will gradually increase to $15,000 by 2006, with "catch-up" provisions that let taxpayers over 50 contribute more.

Gains and Losses on Securities Transactions

Now let's take a look at some other deduction strategies you can apply to trim your taxes. There are four broad deduction strategies that can help put more of your money to work for you. The first one we'll tackle concerns gains and losses on securities transactions (securities being stocks and bonds, of course).

What you paid for a security is the *cost*, and what the security is currently worth is its *current market value*.

♦ If the market value is higher than the price you paid, you have an *unrealized gain*.

♦ If it is lower, you have an *unrealized loss*.

♦ If you actually sell the security, you create a *realized gain* or *loss*.

♦ This gain or loss is called short-term if you held the security for up to 12 months before you sold it. If you held it for more than 12 months, you've realized a long-term gain or loss.

Save Big Bucks by Holding Out for Capital Gains

This is a very important distinction, because short-term gains are taxed at ordinary income tax rates. Long-term gains, on the other hand, are taxed at capital gains rates, which are significantly lower.

Tax Rates (2001)

Ordinary	Capital Gains
15%	10% (this rate drops to 8% for a gain on an investment held over 5 years)
27.5%	20% (this rate will come down to 18% for securities purchased after Dec. 31, 2000, and held for at least 5 years)
30.5%	20% (" ")
35.5%	20% (" ")
39.1%	20% (" ")

So if you sell a security after holding it for 12 months or less and realize a gain of $5,000, and you're in the 30.5 percent tax bracket, you will owe $1,525 ($5,000 × .305) in tax. This realized short-term gain might also bump you up to a higher marginal tax rate, i.e., 35.5 percent. Ouch!

If you hold the security for 12 months and one day before selling it, your tax will only be $1,000 ($5,000 × .20). Clearly, you can hang on for another 24 hours to save that chunk of change, can't you? It'll be more than worth it to hold profitable securities for at least the 12 months required to qualify for a long-term capital gain and avoid Uncle Sammie getting a larger helping of your profits.

Using a Loss to Offset a Gain

What if you have realized a gain on one security and have an unrealized loss on another security? You can realize the loss (by selling the security) and use it to offset some or all of the gain.

If the realized loss exceeds the realized gain, you can apply the difference, up to $3,000 in any given year, to reduce your ordinary income, which—yes, you guessed it—reduces your tax bill. If your loss exceeds the $3,000 limit, you can "carry" the difference over to the next year(s).

Be careful with what you do with the proceeds, however! There's a catch: If you buy the same security back within 30 days, this is referred to as a "wash sale," and you won't be allowed to take the loss. The rule refers to "substantially" the same security. You can buy a similar security (e.g., Growth Mutual Fund A vs. Growth Mutual Fund B, or ABC Drug stock vs. XYZ Drug stock). Or just wait 31 days and buy the original stock back if you wish.

All these transactions are entered on IRS Form 1040, Schedule D.

Super Strategy

With securities, your decision should always be driven by investment merits, not tax merits. All things being equal, however, take full advantage of the tax laws. Just apply these three rules:

1. Try to hold securities longer than 12 months so you can realize long-term gains and your profit is only subject to capital gains tax, not income tax.

2. Offset gains with losses wherever possible.

3. Beware the 30-day "wash sale" rule!

Did You Say Tax-Free Interest Income?

Investing in bonds that generate tax-free interest is another cool tax strategy. The interest paid by municipal bonds is, with a few exceptions, not taxed by the federal government. A municipal bond is a bond issued by a municipality, like your city, town, or county. A municipality is basically any self-governing region.

By the same token, interest income from direct obligations of the U.S. government is not taxed by the individual states. The feds don't go after the interest income generated by state and local bonds and, in return, the states don't tax interest income generated by bonds issued by the federal government, like U.S. savings bonds or treasuries.

Municipal-bond interest income from a municipality in your state of residence is also free of state tax. Bonds like this are referred to as double-tax free.

Types of Muni Bonds

Municipal bonds fall within two broad categories:

1. *General obligation (GO) bonds* issued by the state or a city, town, or county within the state are backed by the tax-raising ability of the state or municipality. The issuer can't print money to get itself out of trouble like the federal government, but it does have the power to raise taxes when it needs money.

2. *Revenue bonds* are issued by an agency of a city, county, or state for a specific purpose. Revenues from that agency pay the interest on bonds that are out-standing. Revenue bonds are issued to build toll roads, bridges and tunnels, water and sewer systems, and the like. If the agency that issues the bonds gets into financial trouble, it can raise its tolls or rates, but cannot expect to be bailed out by the local or state government.

Fiscal Facts

The progressive income tax created the strong demand for tax-exempt state and municipal bonds. This put pressure on bonds issued by corporations and the federal government to offer higher inter-est rates to attract buyers.

Investor's Idiom

If you buy a municipal bond, you won't have to pay federal income tax on the interest. There are two main kinds of municipal bonds: **general obligation bonds,** which are issued by a state or city and are backed by the taxing power of the issuer, and **revenue bonds,** which are issued by the agencies that build infrastructures for municipalities. These agencies can't tax, but do have the power to raise tolls or rates to cover debts.

Why Not Load Up on Munis?

If you can avoid federal taxes by owning municipal bonds instead of U.S. Treasury securities, for example, why wouldn't everyone do this? There are two reasons:

1. The municipal bond is not backed by the "full faith and credit" of the federal government the way Treasury bonds are. There is a risk that you could lose your

principal. You can modify this risk (but not eliminate it entirely) by limiting your holdings to municipalities with the two highest credit ratings (AAA and AA). Credit ratings are issued by Standard & Poor's and Moody's, among others.

2. Municipal bonds typically yield less than Treasury securities. The issue is, how much less? To answer this question, investors translate municipal bond yields into tax-equivalent yields. This means they adjust the municipal bond yield upward to reflect the tax savings, and then compare that number to the current yield on a U.S. Treasury security.

Use the table below to calculate tax-equivalent yield. The bold numbers across the top represent the municipal bond yield percentages; the bold numbers in the left-most column represent the year 2000 marginal tax rate.

Tax-Equivalent Yields Chart

	3.75%	4.00%	4.25%	4.50%	4.75%	5.00%	5.25%
10%	4.16	4.44	4.72	5.00	5.27	5.55	5.83
15%	4.41	4.71	5.00	5.29	5.59	5.88	6.18
28%	5.21	5.56	5.90	6.25	6.60	6.94	7.29
31%	5.43	5.80	6.16	6.52	6.88	7.25	7.61
36%	5.86	6.25	6.64	7.03	7.42	7.81	8.20
39.6%	6.21	6.62	7.04	7.45	7.86	8.28	8.69

How did we get these numbers? Well, if a muni bond is yielding 3.75 percent and your marginal tax rate is 15 percent, you want to know how much a non-tax-free bond would have to yield for it to be worth as much to you as the muni bond, right? So for the taxable bond to be attractive it would have to yield at least as much as the muni, plus enough to cover the tax bill.

To figure this out, just divide 3.75 percent by .85 (1.00 – the marginal tax rate of .15 = .85), which equals 4.41 percent tax equivalent yield.

How do we use this table? If a 20-year AAA or AA municipal bond today yields 5.00 percent, look on the table and you'll see that the tax-equivalent yield is 7.25 percent (at a 31 percent marginal tax rate). How does it compare to a 20-year U.S. Treasury yield?

The Treasury is yielding 5.54 percent (at the time of this writing), while the tax-equivalent yield on the muni is 7.25 percent. The muni looks like the better deal! You get a considerable pickup in yield (1.71 percent) by buying the municipal bond.

Here's another calculation investors run to decide whether or not to buy a municipal bond instead of a super-safe comparable Treasury bond. Compute the tax-free yield as a percent of the taxable yield; the closer to 100 percent, the more attractive the municipal. In the above example, 5.00 percent ÷ 5.54 percent = 90 percent, which is historically quite high. Remember that interest income is entered on IRS Form 1040, Schedule B.

Home Equity Loans Are Deductible

For individuals, interest-expense deductions are now essentially limited to home ownership. This means that you cannot deduct interest on auto loans, credit cards, and other debts from your adjusted gross income. You can deduct interest, however, on your home mortgage and on a home equity loan.

What's a home equity loan? Essentially, it's a revolving line of credit with your home serving as *collateral*. A revolving line of credit puts an upper limit on what you can borrow. You can borrow up to that amount, and you only pay interest on what you actually use. If a bank gives you a $20,000 line of credit, for example, and you only use $10,000 of it, you'll only be charged interest on $10,000. A credit card is essentially a revolving line of credit.

If you qualify, it may make sense to pool all your nondeductible loans and pay them off with a home equity loan. Interest payments on credit card debt, for example, are not tax deductible, but mortgage payments are. Rates are reasonable (e.g., 5 to 6 percent), especially compared

Crash Alert _____

Approval of a home equity loan application will depend on how the lender views your ability to repay. You can be sure the lender will dig up your credit history and will also want to check out your income and cash flow. This is another good reason to check your credit reports for errors and problems once a year. Definitely check them months before you plan to apply for mortgages or any other important loans, to give yourself time to clear up any messes.

to credit card debt. However, there are some qualifications you'll have to meet before a bank or mortgage company will issue you a home equity loan.

Your maximum credit will be based on the appraised value of your home times a "margin of safety" of typically 75 percent less the current mortgage outstanding. As an example:

Appraised value	$100,000
Percent	0.75
Base	$ 75,000
Less mortgage outstanding	$ 60,000
Potential credit line	$ 15,000

This borrower would be approved for a $15,000 line of credit.

Home Equity Loan vs. Second Mortgage

Home equity loans typically have variable rates, meaning the rate can change over the course of the loan. You may wish to consider a second mortgage with a fixed rate as an alternative. The differences are fairly straightforward: The home equity loan has a variable rate with a variable loan (up to the maximum approved), whereas the second mortgage has a fixed rate with a fixed loan amount. It differs from a revolving line of credit in that you pay interest on the entire loan amount.

Taking on a home equity loan or a second mortgage is not a transaction to be entered into lightly, but it may make sense if you have a lot of high-interest, nondeductible loans outstanding, such as credit card debt, and the costs are reasonable versus the amount of the credit line.

Timing Can Make a Big Difference

All the tax strategies in this chapter are delved into in much greater depth and detail in *The Complete Idiot's Guide to Doing Your Taxes 1999.* We just want to get you thinking about these ideas.

Our final suggestion is that each year, usually around Thanksgiving, you look at your prospective tax returns for the current and following year. Did you get a big bonus this year that you don't think will be duplicated next year? Did you not get a bonus this year, but expect one next year? Try to postpone receiving any income that you can until the following year so you don't have to pay taxes on it this year.

Similarly, try to chalk up as many expenses as possible before the end of the year. If you have a big medical bill to pay, for example, pay it before December 31 and you can deduct it. Need a new computer for your business? Buy it before the end of the year, taking advantage of both Christmas sales and a tax deduction.

By reacting to actual or prospective changes in your income, you may be able to accelerate or defer certain deductible expenses to reduce your taxes. Specific areas to look at are medical and dental expenses, taxes, and mortgage payments. Moving payments from December to January or vice versa can make a difference.

The Least You Need to Know

- ◆ "Taxable income" is the number on your tax return that determines how much income tax you owe.

- ◆ Taking the maximum deductions from your paycheck for group health plans and your 401(k) is a good tax strategy, but if your employer also offers pretax deductions for nonreimbursed health care and child care, you'll need to estimate your expenses very carefully to avoid getting burned.

- ◆ For many self-employed people, taking the full deduction for health-insurance expenses may be a better deal than a medical savings account.

- ◆ Short-term gains on investments are taxed at ordinary income tax rates; better to hold onto an investment for at least a year so that any gains are taxed at the lower capital gains rate.

- ◆ Offset capital gains with losses wherever possible.

- ◆ The interest on municipal bonds is tax free.

- ◆ It may make sense to pool all your nondeductible loans and pay them off with a home equity loan because the rates on a home equity loan are usually reasonable, and the interest is deductible.

Part

Investing 101

The stock market is volatile, meaning it goes up and down a lot in reaction to all kinds of news. This doesn't mean it's a bad investment. As you learned in Part 1, its volatility is partly why it's a good investment. Remember, over time the ups and downs of the stock market tend to cancel each other out, leaving a historical return of around 11 percent. That certainly beats parking your cash in the bank for 4 percent.

In Part 3, you'll learn how to pick up the phone and order research material that'll make sense to you. You'll know how to contact and use a broker. You'll be ready to start designing an investment portfolio tailored to your investment objectives. But first we discuss how to clean up your debt. Because if you are paying 18 percent on thousands of dollars in debt, how are you ever going to get ahead, even with the best investments? As Will Rogers might say, that dog don't hunt.

What Are They Up to on Wall Street, Anyway?

In This Chapter

- How commissions on stock trades work
- Bull and bear baiting
- Making sense of a stock table
- Coping with market ups and downs

Fifty-odd years ago, the then-head of General Motors Corporation, "Choo Choo Charlie" Wilson, reportedly harrumphed: "What's good for General Motors is good for America."

At the time, his statement may have seemed rather arrogant and self-serving, but to those with shares in the company, his words hit home. In financial terms, the translation goes something like this: Corporate America is not only a key employer of many of the citizens of this country, but it is owned by them. The stock market represents this ownership of corporate America, and, as we were reminded by the market's reaction to the wave of corporate scandals in 2002, when corporations go bad, that's bad for America.

Investors watched billions of dollars in stock market holdings collapse as Enron imploded, WorldCom filed for bankruptcy, and Global Crossing, Adelphia Communications, and Tyco scandals came to light, followed by SEC inquiries into stalwarts like Johnson & Johnson.

Congress promptly passed a corporate-oversight bill designed to discourage "creative" bookkeeping, diminish conflicts of interest, and crack down on financial abuses. Some folks called it watershed legislation—the most important since the 1930s laws enacted after the Great Depression that brought much-needed regulation to the stock market. Others questioned whether it would really have much impact.

The nerves of investors were understandably frayed by the wild swings in the stock market. The losses were certainly painful. Nonetheless, we live (and hope to prosper) in a capitalist society, and the capital is largely provided by the stock market. Historically, the market has recovered from worse times and has gone on to make investors in it wealthy. If you learn how it works, you'll learn how to protect yourself from its volatility and still earn great returns on your investments.

A Little Background Music, Please

The stock market in this country consists of a number of exchanges, plus the NASDAQ over-the-counter market. The exchanges include …

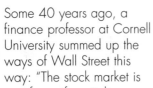

Fiscal Facts

Some 40 years ago, a finance professor at Cornell University summed up the ways of Wall Street this way: "The stock market is the purest form of capitalism. What other mechanism offers the individual the opportunity to secure abundant wealth irrespective of race, color, creed, age, gender, social standing, or inheritance? All you need is a grub stake and the right combination of luck and skill."

- Philadelphia Stock Exchange.

- New York Stock Exchange.

- American Stock Exchange (owned by the National Association of Securities Dealers, or NASD for short).

- Pacific Stock Exchange.

- Boston Stock Exchange.

- Cincinnati Stock Exchange.

- Chicago Board Options Exchange.

Philadelphia is the oldest exchange, organized in 1790. The New York Stock Exchange, also known as "the Big Board," is by far the largest and the best known. The organization that became the NYSE began trading stocks under a buttonwood tree at what is now 68 Wall Street on May 17, 1792. On March 8, 1817, the traders wrote a constitution and the name "New York Stock Exchange Board" was adopted. The name was changed to "New York Stock Exchange" on January 29, 1863.

Some years later, a rival exchange, the New York Curb Exchange, was founded. While NYSE members had moved indoors, "the Curb" literally traded outdoors until 1921. In 1953, the New York Curb Exchange changed its name to the American Stock Exchange. Although the short name is "the Amex," old-timers still refer to it as "the Curb."

The NASDAQ is basically an automated information network that provides quotes (prices) on stocks for brokers registered with the National Association of Securities Dealers (NASD). Trades are done by phone or computer, with traders (members of the NASD) profiting from the spread between a stock's bid and asked prices, rather than adding a commission, as they do with exchange-listed stocks.

Investor's Idiom

The **asked price** is the price that someone who owns a stock and wants to sell it is asking for it in the market. The **bid** is the price a buyer is willing to pay for the stock. The **spread** is the difference between the asked price and the bid price. If a NASDAQ trader has a seller who is willing to sell a stock for 30 and the trader can get a buyer to bid 30¼, the trader can keep the ¼ as his profit. That quarter point is the spread.

In rough numbers, there are about 3,200 stocks listed on the New York Stock Exchange, compared to about 900 on the Amex. The number for the NASDAQ is huge, probably approaching 40,000.

Fiscal Facts

How the broker who handles a securities trade is compensated can vary. On the New York Stock Exchange, for example, the system is "plus commission," while on the NASDAQ over-the-counter market, it's "ex-commission." If you buy 100 shares of ABC stock via NYSE for $90 each, you will pay $9,000 for the shares plus a commission of $25. Your total transaction price is $9,025. If that stock were traded on the NASDAQ, the stock would be priced at $90.25, with the commission built in. You'd still pay a total transaction price of $9,025, but you wouldn't be aware that the extra $25 is commission.

What's with All the Animal References?

There's an old saying on Wall Street: "Bulls make money, bears make money, but pigs never do." But what's a "bull" and what's a "bear?" Bulls are people who believe a stock or the stock market is going up in price. Bears believe the price of a stock and/or the stock market is going down.

Of course, the question still left to answer is where did these particular names come from, anyway? There are two explanations that are usually bandied about. The first is based on how each animal attacks: the bear by raking down with his large sharp claws, the bull by tossing up his large sharp horns. The second explanation comes from *The Wall Street Journal Guide to Understanding Money and Markets* (by Kenneth M. Morris, Fireside, 1999)and is a little fancier. According to the *Journal*, the term *bear* comes from sellers of bearskin who had a penchant for selling the bearskins before the bears were caught. Later on, the term morphed to represent speculators who, on a hunch that the price would drop, agreed to sell shares they didn't own. Their next move would be to quickly buy the low-priced stock and sell it for the previously agreed higher price.

Fiscal Facts

New York Stock Exchange volume:

December 15, 1886: First million share day (1.2 million shares)

October 29, 1929: 16.4 million shares traded as the stock market crashed

August 18, 1982: First 100 million share day (132,681,120 shares)

October 28, 1997: First billion share day (1,202,550,000 shares)

January 4, 2001: First 2 billion share day (2,129,445,637 shares)

Because bull and bear baiting were once popular sports, bulls came to mean the opposite of bears. Bulls were those who bought heavily, expecting a stock price to go up.

Whatever explanation floats your boat, the words have carried down through the years, and people to this day describe themselves as bullish or bearish, depending on how they feel about a given stock or the market.

But What Do All Those Numbers Mean?

Have you ever ventured onto the stock pages of *The Wall Street Journal* or your local paper and been utterly overwhelmed and confused? Well, we're here to prep you so you can dive back in with total confidence. Those rows and rows of tiny numbers are called stock tables and are loaded with useful information, if you know how to read them.

Stock tables vary slightly from publication to publication. We have included the explanation for the daily table from *The Wall Street Journal*. The first stock listed in the August 2, 2002, table was AAR. Reading from left to right, here's an explanation for each figure:

52-Week

YTD % CHG	Hi	Lo	Stock	SYM	DIV	YLD%	PE	Vol 100s	Close	Net Chg
-8.2	17.45	6.96	AAR	AIR	.10	1.2	dd	570	8.27	-0.47

◆ **-8.2.** This is the year-to-date percentage change in the stock price.

◆ **17.45 6.96.** The number on the left is the highest price at which this stock has traded for the last 52 weeks, excluding the last day of trading. The number on the right is the lowest price the stock has sunk to during the last 52 weeks. If there is a triangle symbol pointing up or triangle pointing down in this column, it indicates that there was a new 52-week high or low on the last day of trading.

An S before the price change would indicate that there was a stock *split* or stock dividend amounting to 10 percent or more.

◆ **AAR.** This is the name of the stock. It's usually abbreviated so it can fit into these minuscule rows; e.g., AutDataProc is Automatic Data Processing.

◆ **AIR.** This is the stock or "ticker" symbol. When you enter an order to buy or sell AAR, you would say, for example, "Buy 100 AIR." Stock tickers were first introduced on the NYSE back on November 15, 1867.

Investor's Idiom

If you own a share of stock priced at $100 and the company that issued it **splits** it in two, you'll own two shares of the same stock after the split worth $50 each. A stock split increases the number of shares outstanding and decreases share price of the stock. This is typically done when the share price has become very expensive, making the stock difficult to buy and sell. The stock split increases the marketability of the stock.

♦ **.10.** This is the annual cash dividend (10¢), based on the most recent quarterly declaration. For every share of this stock you owned, therefore, you would get 2.5¢ as a dividend payment every quarter (every three months).

♦ **1.2.** This is the yield. Yield is derived from dividing the cash dividend of 10¢ by the closing stock price, which the table tells us farther down is $8.27.

♦ **dd.** This is where you would typically find the price/earnings ratio. It is the stock's market price divided by the company's earnings. It is a measure of the absolute and relative value of the company because it makes it easy to compare the company's performance to that of other companies with stock outstanding. In this case we see "dd," which is a note indicating that the company suffered loss in the most recent four quarters.

Although the company's earnings are not listed in this table, we can derive them from the P/E ratio and the price (P). P/E ratio is a key concept to master because it tells you whether a stock is over- or undervalued. Remember, a stock that is undervalued will probably rise in price to its proper value, so when it's undervalued it could be a good buy.

♦ **570.** This is the volume, or number of 100 share (round lot) trades. So 570 means 57,000 shares traded that day.

♦ **8.27.** This is the closing price for the last trading day. This is the price used in the P/E ratio.

♦ **-0.47.** This is the net change in price for the last trading day (net change from the previous day).

Now you are ready to dazzle your friends and neighbors by whipping open the financial pages and commenting intelligently on the performance of Coca-Cola (abbreviated in the stock tables as KO) or Microsoft (MSFT) stock.

The Key to Your Stock Knowledge: Price-Earnings Ratios

As we said, the Price-Earnings—or P/E—ratio is a key concept to master. So let's do just that. The P/E ratio is price divided by earnings; the resulting number indicates how much or how little investors think of the earnings performance of the company, or:

$$\frac{\text{Price of stock per share}}{\text{Annual earnings per share}} = \text{Price Earnings Ratio}$$

The P/E ratio is probably the most popular and useful measure of a stock's value. You can use it to compare the performance of a particular stock to the performance of the market as a whole, or to the stock of other companies in the same industry. Or you can compare current P/E to historical P/Es. It's like today's temperature: You can compare it to yesterday's temperature, the temperature on the same day last year, or the highest and lowest temperatures on record. There are two caveats or adjustments that need to be made to the *E* part of it:

♦ Some companies experience big swings in earnings. During a year of low earnings, the stock will have a very high P/E ratio. For example, assume a stock with $.10 in earnings is selling at $20 per share. This stock would have a P/E of 200! ($20 × .10 = 200.) Anyone looking at the P/E ratio might conclude that this is a greatly overvalued (or overpriced) stock. But what if this represented the low in the company's business cycle, or the company just suffered a long strike? For this reason, analysts will "adjust" the earnings, either by using normalized earnings (what the company should earn in an average or normal year), or by estimating prestrike earnings. Let's assume that in either case, these normalized earnings amount to $2.00 per share. Now the P/E ratio is a more realistic 10 ($20 ÷ $2 = 10).

♦ Some companies experience earnings during a year or quarter that will never happen again. Let's say the company above, for example, sells one of its divisions and reports earnings of $4.00. If we didn't adjust for these one-time earnings, the resulting P/E ratio of 5 ($20 ÷ $4 = 5) might mislead investors to assume the stock was very underpriced and a really good buy.

Look into My P/E Crystal Ball

P/E ratios are very useful because they allow us to examine how a company has performed over time and make intelligent decisions about whether to buy or sell its stock. For instance, we can compare current to historical P/E ratios. We can also compare a company's current P/E ratio to the performance of the market as a whole (using the S&P 500's P/E, for example). This comparison is called the relative P/E. All of this information is listed in the newspaper.

Let's look at a simple example: Scooby Inc. makes Scoobies, and although the demand for Scoobies ebbs and flows (it's especially high just before Christmas), it doesn't fluctuate enough to require us to make an adjustment or normalize earnings.

Scooby Inc.

10-Year P/E Range	10-Year Relative P/E Range
20–10	1.2–0.8
Current P/E	**Current Relative P/E**
12	1.0

Take a look at the first column. Over 10 years, the P/E for Scooby Inc. has varied from 20 to 10. The current P/E is 12. So we can conclude that Scooby is selling close to its historical low P/E of 10. Hmm … this might be a good time to buy, because we can expect that Scooby stock will bounce back from this low.

The second column, however, tells us that the relative P/E of 1.0 is smack in the middle of the historical relative P/E range of 1.2 and 0.8. Hmm … maybe Scooby Inc. won't bounce back from this low. We'll have to do more research before deciding whether or not to buy this stock. We'll need to investigate whether earnings are increasing or decreasing, for example.

If you are going to get involved with trading individual stocks, an understanding of P/E ratios is crucial. The point is that the P/E is only useful when compared to other P/Es—be they historical or market figures. It's not a stand-alone number.

Should You Play with the Big Kids or Just Get a Piggyback Ride?

Before you dive headlong onto the trading floor, let's think for a moment about how much time you're willing to invest in, well, investing. Only you can decide how much time and energy you're willing to devote to it. The great thing is you have options. Let's take a look at them now.

Take the Easy Route

If you want to buy individual stocks, you'll be competing with full-time professionals who live and breathe P/E ratios and have the latest research and the finest analysts at their disposal. Just because you like to drive, does it make sense to drive in the Indy 500? Not only are you very unlikely to win, but you also could get hurt.

Owning a single stock or a limited number of stocks subjects you to an unhealthy degree of market risk (as the Enron employees who invested their retirement savings in company stock learned, sadly). When the stock market is at an all-time high, there is always at least one stock that is selling at a new low for the year. Can you guarantee that you will not own that stock?

Fiscal Facts

Prior to 1957, Standard & Poor's service used two indexes, a daily and a weekly index of 90 stocks. In 1957, S&P scrapped these indexes for a modern index of 500 stocks, calculated by a high-speed electronic computer. It is based on 425 industrials, 25 railroads, and 50 utilities. The index is carefully weighted according to the importance of the various stocks used. The 500 stocks represent the prices of shares making up from 90 to 95 percent of the value of New York Stock Exchange common stock issues held by investors.

The best way to minimize market risk is to own a broadly diversified list of common stocks, spreading the risk out over 25 to 50 stocks. One bad apple out of 50 is acceptable; one out of one is not.

So when it comes to your IRAs, 401(k)s, and other tax-deferred investments, stick with stock mutual funds. When you buy into a mutual fund you are buying shares in the fund, and the fund owns hundreds of stocks. Through the fund, you own those hundreds of stocks, too. Now, that's diversification. And you didn't have to do any of the hard work.

We'll dig into how to mix and match mutual funds in your portfolio to meet your investment needs in Chapter 12.

Creating Your Own Stock Index Fund

You can also consider buying and holding your own individual securities, with the emphasis on buying and holding. Remember, the more you trade your stock, the more taxable capital gains you could generate (go back to Chapter 8 to review how capital gains work if you need to). You could wind up owing a lot of tax and really eating into your profits.

Above all, keep in mind that if you want to own individual stocks, the idea is not to compete with professional traders. Trust us, if you try, you'll give yourself an ulcer. Most professional traders have ulcers, for that matter! Not to mention a pathological inability to sleep through the night without calling Tokyo.

Super Strategy

A better strategy might be to create your own personal index fund. An index fund is a mutual fund that mimics an index, such as the S&P 500, by buying the same stock in the same proportion as the index. The fund requires very little management: You simply buy the stock and hold it. No trades, no capital gains tax. You could purchase all 30 stocks in the Dow Jones Industrials index, for example, or the Dow Jones composite of 65 stocks (30 industrials, 20 transportation stocks, and 15 utilities). These appear in *The Wall Street Journal*, C Section, usually on page C2 or C4, under the heading "The Dow Jones Averages."

Just Buy Large-Cap Stocks

Similarly, you could select the 25 or 50 largest stocks in the S&P 500 index. By largest, we mean the stocks of companies with the most amount of money circulating in the stock market. This amount is called the market capitalization of a corporation. It equals the number of shares outstanding times the stock's market price. General Electric is currently the largest market capitalization stock (or large-cap stock) listed on the stock exchange, with over $302 billion of its stock outstanding (being bought and sold on the market). The company with the largest market capitalization listed on NASDAQ is Microsoft, which has about $261 billion of its stock circulating.

You would be surprised at how much of the S&P 500 index you could own by just owning the 25 or 50 largest stocks in the index. The top 50 stocks in the S&P 500 index account for over half of the index's total value. So to set up your own index, you could just buy those stocks—rather than all 500 in the index.

Alternatively, you could buy the 25 to 50 largest stocks in the S&P Barra Growth Index. This index represents the most rapidly growing stocks in the S&P 500. This index currently contains 164 names. You would be surprised at how much of each index you can capture just by owning the 25 or 50 largest stocks.

	Top 25 Stocks as % of the Index	Top 50 Stocks as % of the Index
S&P 500	39.8%	54.4%
S&P Barra Growth	59.1	79.9

Here are lists of the top 25 and 50 stocks held by the S&P Index and the S&P Barra Growth Index at the time this book was written. To get a current list, contact Standard & Poor's at 1-800-852-1641.

S&P 500 Index (500 Members)

Top 25	Top 50
(1) General Electric Co.	(26) Abbott Laboratories
(2) Microsoft Corp.	(27) Eli Lilly & Co.
(3) Exxon Mobil Corp.	(28) Viacom Inc.
(4) Wal-Mart Stores Inc.	(29) Amgen Inc.
(5) Pfizer Inc.	(30) Pharamcia Corp.
(6) American International Group	(31) Oracle Corp.
(7) Johnson & Johnson	(32) Wyeth
(8) Citigroup Inc.	(33) Bell South Corp.
(9) Coca-Cola Co.	(34) Wachovia Corp.
(10) International Business Machines Corp.	(35) Medtronic Inc.
(11) Procter & Gamble Co.	(36) 3M Co.
(12) Intel Corp.	(37) Anheuser-Busch Cos. Inc.
(13) Merck & Co. Inc.	(38) AOL Time Warner Inc.
(14) Philip Morris Cos. Inc.	(39) JP Morgan Chase & Co.
(15) Bank of America Corp.	(40) Bristol-Myers Squibb Co.
(16) SBC Communications Inc.	(41) Freddie Mac
(17) Cisco Systems Inc.	(42) American Express Co.
(18) Verizon Communications Inc.	(43) Bank One Corp.
(19) Wells Fargo & Co.	(44) Morgan Stanley
(20) Chevron Texaco Corp.	(45) DuPont (E.I.) deNemours & Co.
(21) Fannie Mae	(46) US Bancorp
(22) PepsiCo Inc.	(47) Hewlett-Packard Co.
(23) United Parcel Service Inc.	(48) Fifth Third Bancorp
(24) Home Depot Inc.	(49) Washington Mutual Inc.
(25) Dell Computer Corp.	(50) Walgreen Co.

S&P Barra Growth Index (148 members)

Top 25	Top 50
(1) General Electric Co.	(26) Bristol-Myers Squibb Co.
(2) Microsoft Corp.	(27) American Express Co.
(3) Wal-Mart Stores Inc.	(28) Fifth Third Bancorp

continues

S&P Barra Growth Index (148 members)   (continued)

Top 25	Top 50
(4) Pfizer Inc.	(29) Walgreen Co.
(5) Johnson & Johnson	(30) Gillette Co.
(6) Coca-Cola Co.	(31) Schering–Plough
(7) Procter & Gamble Co.	(32) Texas Instruments
(8) International Business Machines Corp.	(33) Kimberly-Clark
(9) Intel Corp.	(34) McDonald's Corp.
(10) Merck & Co. Inc.	(35) Target Corp.
(11) Philip Morris Cos. Inc.	(36) Colgate-Palmolive
(12) Cisco Systems Inc.	(37) Lowe's Cos.
(13) PepsiCo Inc.	(38) United Health Group Inc.
(14) United Parcel Service Inc.	(39) First Data
(15) Home Depot Inc.	(40) Marsh & McLennan
(16) Dell Computer Corp.	(41) HCA Inc.
(17) Abbott Laboratories	(42) Cardinal Health, Inc.
(18) Eli Lilly & Co.	(43) Tenat Healthcare Corp.
(19) Amgen Inc.	(44) Bank of New York
(20) Pharmacia Corp.	(45) Automatic Data Processing Inc.
(21) Oracle Corp.	(46) Baxter International Inc.
(22) Wyeth	(47) MBNA Corp.
(23) Medtronic Inc.	(48) Kohl's Corp.
(24) 3M Co.	(49) Qualcomm Inc.
(25) Anheuser-Busch Cos. Inc.	(50) Sysco Corp.

How to Manage Your Index Fund: Leave It Alone!

Once you've created your personal index, what do you do? Nothing. Absolutely nothing. Don't execute a single trade. Just collect the dividends and invest them in a taxable or tax-free money market fund. One caution: This strategy only works if you are investing a large sum at one time. If you are investing $100 to $400 per month, you can't really buy 25 to 50 stocks at a time. If that is your situation, you can still participate in an index by buying an index mutual fund or ETF (exchange-traded fund). More on those in Chapter 12.

The Best Ways to React to Blips

If you believe the newspapers, we should hold our collective breath every time the stock market takes a plunge and breathe a collective sigh of relief the minute the Dow Jones average heads back up.

As a long-term investor, though, you should have absolutely no interest in and no concern for short-term blips in the market. Just keep breathing, no matter what! Whether the market is up or down today, last week, or next month is irrelevant to your long-term game plan. In fact, ignore the financial section of the newspapers entirely (once you have shown everybody how you can read it).

By the same token, don't torture yourself following the daily ups and downs of your mutual funds. Just check on them once every three months. Each calendar quarter the papers publish quarterly mutual fund results. And you will most likely be able to assess each of your fund's quarterly reports.

 **Fiscal Facts**

There's a very complicated principle behind dollar cost averaging that we call K.I.S.S.—Keep It Simple, Stupid!

The most important thing you can do with this quarterly information is not react to it. Remember, you are in this for the long haul, and over time quarterly ups and downs mean nada.

Asset Allocation/Rebalancing

Rebalancing is a handy concept to help you keep your investments on target. When you invest, you allocate your money among various types of ventures according to percentages that you set as goals.

For instance, assume that last year you had a $100,000 portfolio and you decided to invest 50 percent in stocks and 50 percent in bonds. Obviously, you end up with $50,000 in both stocks and bonds. Let's say last year was a very good year for stocks, but not so good for bonds. Let's say that by now your investment in stocks has grown to $72,000, but you took a bit of a loss in bonds, and are left with $48,000 there. Your total portfolio is $72,000 + $48,000, or $120,000.

Crash Alert

Applying rebalancing to your portfolio is only an effective strategy for tax-deferred accounts. If your portfolio is not tax-sheltered, cashing in some of your stock to buy bonds and rebalancing your portfolio could cause you to owe a lot of capital gains tax.

It's great that you've made money, but now your portfolio is a little out of whack. You definitely have more than 50 percent invested in stock and less than 50 percent invested in bonds. Time to rebalance. In this case, you need to sell some stock and buy some bonds in order to split your $120,000 50/50 between stocks and bonds. You should rebalance so you have $60,000 in stocks and $60,000 in bonds. You've figured out where the scales tipped and rebalanced your investments so you stay on track. Once a year, on your birthday (there's that day again), check to see if your stock or bond portion is out of balance and needs to be rebalanced.

How Much Stock Should Be in Your Portfolio?

According to Ibbotson Associates[1] (a firm specializing in financial statistics), common stocks have provided an average return of 10.7 percent over the last 76 years. This is more than twice the return for long-term Treasury bonds (5.3 percent average) and three times the average 3.81 percent return for T-bills. It's also over three times the average inflation rate of 3.1 percent for the same period.

(1) Source: Calculated using data presented in Stocks, Bonds, Bills and Inflation® 2002 Yearbook, ©Ibbotson Associates, Inc. Based on copyrighted works by Ibbotson and Sinquefield. All rights reserved. Used with permission.

So the evidence is overwhelming that you should keep a significant portion of your assets in common stocks—if you are at least 10 years from your planned retirement age. The simple rule is the longer time you have until you retire, the more you should have in common stocks. Here are some guides for how you should consider allocating your assets at different ages.

	Age 17–35	Age 36–45	Age 46–55
Stocks	100%	70%	50%
Bonds	0	30	50
Bills	0	0	0

Another easy rule is: Multiply the number of years until you retire by two to get the percentage of your assets you should keep in stock.

Age	Years to Retirement × 2 =	Stock %
up to 25	40 × 2	80%
30	35 × 2	70
35	30 × 2	60
40	25 × 2	50

Age	Years to Retirement × 2 =	Stock %
45	20 × 2	40
50	15 × 2	30
55	10 × 2	20

Here's another good rule: Subtract your age (e.g., 60) from 100, and use that figure (40) for your stock percent. Just pick one of these rules and stick with it.

Each of these rules of thumb reflects two principles that should be the guiding light behind all of your retirement investing:

♦ The further you are from retirement, the more of your assets should be invested in stock.

♦ Change your stock/bond ratio no more frequently than every five years. You're not a professional investor, so you shouldn't be reacting to every zig and zag in the markets. Stay the course and you'll do fine.

What if you're starting to invest just before a "change point"—at age 44, for example? Start with the allocation recommendations for the next closest age bracket—45 to 50, in this case.

If You're Over 55

If you are over 55 or fewer than 10 years from retirement, you're dealing with the biggest risk in stocks, which is their volatility. Although over the long run stocks do very well, a dip right before you need your money can trash your retirement. You can only reduce this risk by reducing the percentage of your assets in stocks. On the other hand, only stocks offer some protection against inflation. And they can really grow. Therefore, it's wise to keep some equity in your portfolio even after you retire. How much? That's up to you. At least 10 to 20 percent is great, if you can swing it and are comfortable with that level of risk.

Dollar Cost Averaging, or How to Own Stocks and Stay Happy

But how do you avoid the emotional roller coaster that is so much a part of the stock market? By staying well diversified and remembering that over the long haul, market ups are great and market downs are buying opportunities—so they're great, too.

Ignore the histrionic reports in newspapers and on TV when the Dow Jones takes a dive. It will recover; it just may take awhile. As long as you have the time to ride it out, your portfolio will be fine.

After all, market drops are great buying opportunities. Assume you invest $300 per month in stock mutual funds. Market goes up? Great, you're worth more. Market goes down? Great, you can buy more shares with the same amount of money (think of this as the financial equivalent of a white sale). Let's say you bought $300 of a $10 fund last month, or 30 shares.

The fund declines 10 percent: Cool, $300 buys you 33 shares this month ($300 × $10 × .9 = $9 = 33). Is this a great game or what? 10% of $10 = 1; $10 – $1 = $9; $300 ÷ 9 = 33 shares.

You now have under your belt two of the great secrets to successful investing:

◆ Rebalance your portfolio from time to time.

◆ Don't sweat the stock market's ups and downs. Use dollar-cost averaging to navigate these sometimes-treacherous waters.

Super Strategy

What if you reach a five-year mark and the table calls for you to cut back on stocks, but the market is weak and you are concerned that you won't get a good price for them? Because you're not a professional investor, go ahead and sell the stock anyway. If you're truly convinced that stocks have declined substantially and you wish to wait a year, go ahead, but don't defer your decision more than a year.

Here's how you can "marry" these two great investment secrets: Assume you are adding monthly sums to a taxable portfolio and it's time to rebalance. Simply divert all your monthly sums to the now-underweighted asset class (e.g., stocks or bonds) until the proper balance is regained. No tax consequences! What could be simpler?

And the hits just keep coming! If you're still frothing at the mouth to get into buying individual stocks, read the next chapter.

The Least You Need to Know

♦ Bulls believe stock prices are going to rise; bears think stock prices are going to fall. You can ignore both by using dollar cost averaging.

♦ Stock investors try to find and buy undervalued stocks, because the stock price should eventually rise to more accurately reflect its value.

♦ Unless you have a lot of money to invest in a wide range of individual stocks, stick with stock mutual funds because they provide greater diversification.

♦ Set percentages for how you want to allocate your assets and rebalance your portfolio once a year. And only change your stock/bond ratio every five years.

♦ The further you are from retirement, the more of your assets should be invested in stock.

Chapter 10

So You Want to Play with Stocks

In This Chapter

- Tips for trading like a pro
- What makes a stock worth buying
- How to glean the gold from annual reports
- Using a broker to place a trade

If you are an amateur investor, there are only three reasons to own individual stocks:

1. Your employer is a publicly traded company, and you want to own a few shares so you can keep current on company developments. If this is the case, see if your employer offers a stock purchase plan (which usually sells the stock at a discount price). Buy the minimum number of shares.

2. A relative passed away, leaving you shares of ABC Corporation with this admonition: "Whatever you do, don't sell ABC Corporation." If your conscience won't let you sell, give the shares to your favorite charity and take the tax deduction.

3. You love the action. Some people play the horses, some people play roulette or poker, some people play the office pool, and you play the stock market. Okay, we all have our vices; admit it to yourself (and your spouse), control it as best you can, and get on with your life. Just don't call what you're doing investing. It's entertainment—pay for it out of your entertainment budget.

You might also buy individual stocks for the reason we discussed in the previous chapter: to invest a lump sum in a taxable portfolio for retirement purposes. But this won't satisfy a desire to tangle with the pros in the stock market, as you're not supposed to trade these stocks. Remember …?

Still not persuaded? Still want to trade like a pro? Okay, here we go!

Tips for Trading Like a Pro

Do:

♦ Use your broker to execute your trades, not to do your research. After all, paying full commission to a broker is like paying list price for a car.

♦ Negotiate your broker's commission before, not after, placing the order.

♦ Choose carefully between a full-service broker versus a discount/deep discount broker. If you feel you are getting your money's worth from a full-service broker, God bless, but you probably don't need or want his/her suggestions and reports. At least, not enough to pay for 'em.

♦ Avoid speculative securities. Initial public offerings (IPOs), *penny stocks*, and "hot tip" stocks aren't worth the risk. Even the best traders don't buy all their stocks at what turn out to be low prices; mistakes are part of the business. But good quality stocks recover and eventually go on to new highs; losers just curl up and die. IPO's are simple to deal with: The "hot" ones go to large institutional customers; the little person might get a few shares if he/she is lucky. If you are offered a good chunk of an IPO, odds are the broker was unable to unload all the shares to institutional customers and is calling with a "hot tip" because he's got to get rid of them somehow. Penny stocks are a speculator's dream. A $40 stock that goes up an eighth equals a yawn, but a $1 stock up $\frac{1}{8}$ equals a 12.5 percent gain! There's also the ego boost of saying "I just put away 10,000 shares of X." But "up $\frac{1}{8}$" can quickly become "down $\frac{1}{8}$." And wait until you see the commission on 10,000 shares! Temptation, get thee hence!

Investor's Idiom

Penny stocks are stocks that are selling for a very low price—typically one, two, or three dollars.

Regarding hot tips in general, please face facts: You're a small player, and when the hot tip gets all the way down the chain to you, it'll be lukewarm at best. The rule of thumb is: If an investment seems too good to be true, it *is* too good to be true.

If You Buy It, You'd Better Love It

Ideally, you should buy stocks that you never have to sell. We say this because you must pay taxes every time you sell a stock for a profit.

If you paid $10,000 for a stock, held it for a year and sold it for $15,000, you would have $14,000 to reinvest—not $15,000. The difference is the long-term capital gains tax (e.g. 20 percent) on your $5,000 profit. If you had sold it before a year was up, you'd have a short-term capital gains tax (up to 39.1 percent). Depending on your tax bracket that can be a huge bite out of your profit. In addition, there are commission costs for both the sale and the subsequent purchase. Not to mention state and local taxes.

> **Super Strategy**
>
> Obviously, there are good reasons sometimes to sell a stock. Maybe you made a mistake in the first place, or the company has fallen apart. But your best bet is to buy the stocks of stable, high-quality companies that you'll feel comfortable owning for a long time. If they pay a modest but growing cash dividend, so much the better.

The Biggest "Do" of All

Here's the "Big Daddy Do" for amateur investors: Limit your investments to quality companies. What's a quality company? Below are the characteristics that make a company worthy of your precious investment dollars:

- **Market leadership.** If you want to buy stock in a certain industry, buy the market leader—buying number two or number three is not worth the aggravation. How can you tell if a company is the market leader? When size, marketing power, and cost control make it the most profitable company in its industry; when its new products or services are more readily accepted in the marketplace than the competition's; when it's the name investors buy when they want to participate

> **Fiscal Facts**
>
> The top ten NASDAQ stocks, as of August 6, 2002 are Microsoft, Intel, Cisco, Dell, Oracle, Amgen, Fifth Third Bancorp, Applied Materials, Qualcomm, and Comcast. They represent nearly 40 percent (38.6 percent) of the total NASDAQ weighting.

in the industry; and when it's the last stock to be sold (if it ever is sold) when investors look to reduce industry exposure.

♦ **A strong balance sheet.** Professional investors don't like to be blindsided by a company that suddenly develops credit problems. A strong balance sheet (more assets than liabilities) ensures a high credit rating, which in turn ensures that the company pays low interest rates when it does borrow. A strong balance sheet also enables the company to quickly take advantage of acquisition opportunities.

Ideally, an industrial company would have no debt, but this is a rarity. To evaluate a company's debt position, take a look at its debt to total capitalization ratio. This ratio is found in the annual report and should be between 25–30 percent. To figure it out for yourself, use this formula:

$$\frac{\text{long-term debt}}{\text{long-term debt + preferred stock + common stock + retained earnings}}$$

♦ **A consistent and seasoned track record.** Any company whose stock you seek to own should have at least a 10-year public (not private) record to analyze. Look for how well or poorly the company did in previous industry and/or general economic downturns. Do revenues and earnings increase each and every year? Nine years out of ten? At least four years out of five?

Be careful of companies with above-average earnings growth (+10–20 percent) but only average or below average (+3–5 percent) revenue growth. This may indicate that management is trying to improve the bottom line by raising prices or cutting costs. This will only keep the company profitable for so long if revenues aren't increasing.

Here's a neat rule: Look for companies where unit sales (e.g., the number of widgets sold per year) are growing at least 50 percent faster than the real, or inflation-adjusted, gross domestic product (GDP) in this country. The GDP is reported quarterly in newspapers and on TV newscasts.

Crash Alert

Be leery of corporations that buy back shares each year, irrespective of stock price levels. In some cases, they even borrow money to make the purchases. This is just a maneuver to improve the stock price.

♦ **A high reinvestment rate.** What does the company do with the money it makes? Does it pay out a significant sum to shareholders in the form of cash dividends? Companies that pay out a high percent of earnings to stockholders as cash dividends are telling you, by their actions, they do not view the future of the company with much favor. If they did, they would reinvest those dollars back into the business. Does it buy back a significant number of shares, or does it reinvest a significant portion back into the business? When a company buys back its own shares, it's artificially forcing up the stock price by decreasing the amount of stock outstanding. Sometimes management will do this to protect a stock that has been pummeled by investors for what management believes to be short-term or transitory reasons.

Researching Individual Stocks

There are good research resources available to the individual investor, many at your local library. In addition, if you hire a full-service broker, you can indirectly avail yourself of his or her research department.

In our opinion, the two most basic, cost-effective, and objective research tools are the *Value Line Investment Survey* and *Standard & Poor's Stock Guides*. Both may be available at your local library, but if not, or if you wish to have your own personal copies, we have provided subscriber numbers below (aren't we nice?).

The Invaluable Value Line

The basic Value Line service covers approximately 1,700 stocks. For each stock, Value Line provides two rankings: timeliness and safety. Of the two, pay particular attention to safety. Stocks are ranked on a 1–5 basis, with 1 being the safest. Don't consider any stock with less than a 2 rating.

Value Line also provides scores for four other key indicators:

- ◆ Financial strength
- ◆ Stock price stability
- ◆ Stock price growth persistence
- ◆ Earnings predictability

Value Line includes, in addition to the rankings and key indicators cited above, a great deal of relevant statistical and narrative information. Value Line reports are updated regularly. The individual company write-ups will take some getting used to, but after a while, you will find that you can easily determine a company's earnings growth rate and the consistency of that growth rate.

Use Value Line to help you select at least 25 stocks that:

◆ Are safe or very safe (remember, that means a ranking of 1 or 2)

◆ Are growing at an above-average rate

◆ Are growing consistently and steadily

What does "above average" mean? We suggest you look for a minimum of 8 percent and, ideally, 10 percent growth. And keep an eye on consistency. For a 10 percent grower, 10 percent a year is perfect but rarely achieved. A range of 8–12 percent is very consistent. From 6–14 percent is acceptable. But if the company's earnings swing between 0 percent and 30 percent, for example, it's too volatile to be in your portfolio.

To subscribe to Value Line, call 1-800-634-3583. A one-year subscription costs $598, but you can get a 3-month trial subscription for $65!

S&P Stock Guides: Another Great Tool

Standard & Poor's Stock Guides (Bond Guides are also available) are an excellent research tool. The guides come out monthly and cover approximately 6,000 stocks, as well as mutual funds and variable annuity/life investments. Annual subscription prices are $195 for the Stock Guide and $363 for the Bond Guide. Special year-end editions are $24.64 (Stock) and $33.00 (Bond) (all prices here do not include shipping and handling). You can order by calling 1-800-852-1641, option 5, or visit their website at www.standardpoor.com/ProductsandServices/InvestmentServices.

The Best Newspapers for Stock Info

Finally, two newspapers, *Investors Business Daily* and *The Wall Street Journal*, do an excellent job of tracking the stock market and individual stocks. Either may be available at your local library. To order a subscription to the *Journal*, call 1-800-831-2525 and ask for source key 9MJW11, or subscribe online at services.wsj.com. To subscribe to *IBD*, call 1-800-547-1919 or visit www.investors.com.

If you simply must follow the market during the day, both CNBC and Bloomberg Information TV do a good job of keeping you current. For a nightly wrap-up, check out PBS's Nightly Business Report.

Investor's Idiom

A corporation is expected to issue an **annual report** once a year that includes the company's financial statements—income statement, balance sheet, cash flow statement, etc. The company is also required to file a **10-K report** with the Securities and Exchange Commission (SEC). The 10-K is the same information in the annual report, minus pictures and narrative. A company must also file an **8-K report** with the SEC within 30 days regarding any event that could affect the company's performance. The **SEC** is an agency that was founded by Congress in 1933 after the 1929 stock market crash to regulate the stock market and protect investors.

All the News That's Fit to Print: Company Annual Reports

The most valuable research you can get your hands on is provided by the companies themselves. Once you purchase individual equities, the company (or your brokerage firm) will begin stuffing your mailbox with quarterly and annual reports.

If you want those reports before you purchase a stock, check the stock tables in *The Wall Street Journal*'s Section C. You will find a three-leaf clover–type symbol next to those companies that provide a free annual and free current quarterly report. To obtain these reports, call *The Wall Street Journal*'s Annual Reports Club at 1-800-654-2582, fax your request to 1-800-965-5679, or order via the Internet at www.wsj.ar.wilink.com.

Annual reports and quarterly reports are like report cards. Avoid the verbiage and the pretty pictures, and you'll be able to tease out trends from the financial statements. The *10-K* is the annual report equivalent filed with the *SEC*. It's sometimes more revealing than the corporate reports to shareholders and comes without the rosy verbiage.

Finally, the *8-K* form is a report that a corporation's managers must file with the SEC within 30 days of any event that might affect the financial status or share price of the company.

Analyzing a Company's Annual Report

When that annual report arrives in the mail, skip all the narrative and pictures and turn straight to the Income Statement near the back (also called the Profit/Loss

Statement). Below is a guide for how to analyze each item of the Income Statement—'cause there's gold in them thar hills! (While you're at it, take a quick gander again at the personal income statement you developed in Chapter 4. It's basically the same.)

- **Gross or Total Revenues.** For quarterly reports, how do revenues compare with the previous quarter and the same quarter in the previous year? For annual reports, how do they compare to last year, five years ago, 10 years ago? You are looking for changes or breaks in the normal patterns, up or down. If you find any, scan the text for explanations. If you aren't satisfied with them, call the company, ask for the investor relations officer (IRO) and introduce yourself as a shareholder with questions. If there is no IRO, or you are still not satisfied, go progressively up the line: treasurer, financial vice president, president. Remember, you are a shareholder, an owner; act like one.

- **Gross Profit.** This figure is the result of subtracting the cost of goods from the actual revenues. Cost of goods sold is the cost of making each additional unit of whatever's being sold. Gross profit is an indication of manufacturing efficiency: Is it improving or deteriorating? Again, compare the numbers for previous years and quarters. If you really want to get fancy, divide gross profit into revenue and multiply by 100 to get a percentage called "gross profit margin." You can analyze every item on the income statement this way—by dividing it into revenue. This way you can see how each item looks as a percentage of revenue. If gross profit is only 5 percent of revenue, for example, where's all the revenue money going? Why isn't gross profit higher?

- **Selling, General, and Administrative Expense (SG&A).** Again, compare to past periods. Any big changes? Divide this expense (SG&A) into revenue.

  If the resulting percentage is very high, maybe that's your answer for why gross profit is low—because the company has very high expenses.

- **Research & Development (R&D).** Sometimes this item is included in SG&A; sometimes it's broken out separately. For some companies (such as technology companies), this is a critical expenditure; it could make or break future growth opportunities. Look to see if R&D is rising in line with revenues; if not, the company may be shortchanging its future to keep its current earnings looking attractive.

- **Earnings Before Interest, Depreciation, and Amortization** (referred to as EBIDA and pronounced "E-bah-dah"). the current trendy figure used to measure a company's profitability and efficiency.

- **Pre-Tax Earnings.** Earnings before taxes; again, divide into revenues to obtain pre-tax margins.

◆ **Tax Rate.** Is the tax rate rising or falling? If falling, management may have manipulated it to cover up declining revenues.

◆ **Net Income.** Income after taxes. Any cash dividends on common stock will be paid from this sum.

There you go. You're now your own security analyst! It's kind of like being a detective: looking for clues in all the right (or wrong) places. As you go through this exercise for the first time, think how each of these categories relate to your personal income statement.

Analyzing the Balance Sheet

Just like your personal balance sheet, a corporate balance sheet in an annual report is broken down between assets and liabilities, and each of these categories, in turn, are divided into short- (or current) and long-term assets and liabilities. Like so:

Assets	Liabilities
Current Assets	*Current Liabilities*
Cash & Marketable Securities	Accounts Payable
Accounts Receivable	Debt due w/in 12 mos.
Long-Term Assets	*Long-Term Debt*
Plant	Mortgages
Equipment	Debentures
Other	*Shareholders Equity*
Goodwill	Preferred Stock
	Common:
	Par Value
	Paid in Capital
	Retained Earnings
Total Assets	Total Liabilities and Shareholder's Equity

The balance sheet contains all the information you need (i.e., is the company carrying lots of debt? What kind of cash is available?) to analyze a company's financial strength and financing strategies. Analysts look at several ratios when examining a balance sheet. These ratios indicate the amount of long-term debt the company is carrying and how it relates to the amount of equity outstanding.

Debt-to-Equity ratio: Total Debt/Total Equity

Debt ratio: Total Debt/Total Assets

Current ratio: Current Assets/Current Liabilities

Analysts also watch for increases or decreases in cash, accounts receivable, and accounts payable.

How to Use a Broker to Place a Trade

Once you've decided what stocks you want to buy, you'll need a broker. *Broker* is a generic name for the person in the middle who facilitates trades between buyers and sellers. Many brokerage firms have created more impressive titles such as "registered representative" (because the brokers are registered with the Securities and Exchange Commission and represent their firm), sometimes shortened to "RR." "Account executive" (AE) is another popular title.

Find a *full-service, discount,* or *deep discount broker* the same way you would find an insurance agent—by asking friends and relatives to recommend someone or by looking in the Yellow Pages under Stock and Bond Brokers. However, this still may seem like too much work for you. If these options don't pan out for you, you might want to contact your local bank, as banks increasingly offer a wide variety of investment services.

Investor's Idiom

A **broker** will act as an intermediary between you and the stock market. He or she will seek out buyers for stock you want to sell and find sellers of stock you want to buy. **Full-service brokers** also provide research and make recommendations. **Discount** and **deep-discount brokers** are services that simply execute trades.

A full-service broker's tasks are the following:

1. To broker a trade.

2. To serve as an investment resource for the customer—calling the customer with stock or bond recommendations, for example.

3. To move stock "off the shelves" that his or her firm has brought to market for a corporation. There have been cases where brokers push bad products in exchange for bonuses from the company, or just to earn a fat commission.

Sometimes #3 is the only reason for #2! Discount, and especially deep discount, brokers perform only role #1.

Placing an Order with Your Broker

Think of the order you give to your broker as falling within one of three forms:

◆ **The Market Order.** This instructs the broker to buy or sell at whatever the current market price is, no matter where it goes before your order is filled. You can expect that your broker will complete trades of 1,000 shares or less at or very close to the last trading price recorded. Such orders are typically executed electronically. You can usually get your price confirmed before you hang up after placing the order with your broker. Larger orders of 25,000+ shares may have to be "worked." For example, if ABC stock is moving up and you place an order to buy 50,000 shares of that stock, which was trading at 45, you may receive a report from your broker that you purchased:

10,000 shares at $45^1/_8$

15,000 shares at $45^1/_4$

10,000 shares at $45^3/_8$

At this point, your broker may say: "I can fill the balance at $45^3/_4$." Now it's your decision: Do you want to fill at that price or step aside and see if the price declines? If you go ahead, your broker would most likely report the balance of the trade as:

100 shares at $45^1/_2$

100 shares at $45^5/_8$

14,800 shares at $45^3/_4$

Your average stock price (before commissions) would be $45.40.

◆ **The Limit Order to Buy or Sell.** Using the above example, you might conclude that ABC stock will settle down in price and instruct your broker to "buy 50,000 shares of ABC with a 45 limit." Next, you must tell the broker if this is a day order (i.e., either filled that day or canceled) or "good 'til canceled" (referred to as GTC). That means the order will stay open until the broker fills it or you cancel it.

The problem with GTCs is you can forget you placed them. Maybe a few weeks later you'll buy alternative stock XYZ only to receive a follow-up call from your broker stating that "we just filled your GTC on ABC." Whoops, a little short on money? It's easier to stay on top of things if you cancel and reenter your order each day, although your broker won't appreciate the extra work.

♦ **The Stop or Stop Loss Order.** Let's say you bought ABC stock at 30, saw it shoot up to 45³/₄, and it has now backed down to 42. At this point, you may be more willing to lock in a gain rather than roll the dice to see if it crests the 45³/₄ high again. So you instruct your broker to place a stop loss order to sell at $40. If the stock goes up, great; if it goes down, you're "out" at 40.

Unless you are a professional investor dealing with large orders, our advice would be to use market orders. Of the three, there isn't the margin of error that exists in the latter two choices. You're still getting in on the action, but you're letting a professional do most of the work.

Discount Brokers

Discount/deep-discount brokers perform a single task: They execute your order, be it market, limit, or whatever. In some cases, you don't even talk to a human being. If you know what you want to do and don't have a large or otherwise difficult order, go the discount route. There's one caveat, though: Once you choose a discount broker, stick with him or her. Otherwise, you'll be reconciling statements from at least two different brokerage firms, and that's just no fun. You want to keep things as simple as possible, right? Right!

The advantage of a discount broker is a lower commission rate. Period. No free toasters, no hand-holding, no "hot tips." If this is all you want from a broker, go for it.

When Should You Buy Stock?

It depends on how much money you have and how much time you want to devote to managing your individual stock holdings. We're going to assume your answer to both questions is: "Not much."

Super Strategy

If you set aside an additional sum each year to purchase stocks, or if you plan to reinvest your dividends, pick an annual portfolio anniversary date. Avoid vacation months, holiday months, or January, which is generally a strong month for stock prices because institutions are buying stocks for their pension and profit-sharing plans that month. Pick your birthday month, or, if your birthday clashes with any of the above stipulations, an "interim" time like late October—early November.

If you have selected your stocks but can only afford to purchase a round lot (100 shares) of each, go ahead and buy. If you can buy, say, 200 shares of each, buy 100 now and the rest:

♦ On your anniversary date—usually your birthday

♦ Or if the stock declines 10 percent from your purchase price, whichever comes first

Rebalancing Your Stock Holdings

If you look at the stocks you've purchased, they probably fall into a few different categories. For instance, some might be "energy" (i.e., oil, gas, and utility companies) or "technology" (i.e., software manufacturers). These categories are called sectors. A *sector* is a particular segment of the economy. Now, when your portfolio anniversary comes up, take a look at how each stock you hold in each sector has performed.

Now, stick with us here. We're going to tell you to do something that might not seem like the obvious choice: If you plan to purchase more stocks, put more money into the stocks that did poorly. Why? So that you maintain positions for each sector that are comparable. This is another example of dollar cost averaging.

Let's say you started with $10,000 and split it evenly, buying $2,500 worth of stock in each of four different sectors: technology, health care, energy, and finance. By the end of the first year, maybe your technology stocks are now worth $3,000, health care stocks dropped to $2,000, energy shot up to $4,000, and your finance stocks held steady at $2,500. Your portfolio is now worth $12,000, but you no longer own an even 25 percent in each sector.

$3,000	(technology)
+ $2,000	(health care)
+ $4,500	(energy)
+ $2,500	(finance)
= $12,000	

We're suggesting that you rebalance your portfolio so that you again own 25 percent in each sector. With a $12,000 portfolio, that would mean holding $12,000 × .25, or $3,000, in each sector. You'll have to sell off some of your energy stocks to beef up your holdings in health care and finance.

Professionals might disagree with this approach, arguing that you should pour money into your "winners" and less into your "losers." This is fine for professionals whose job it is to carefully research their holdings. Right now, you're a rookie and your one big asset is (yes, you guessed it) time. As long as you stick with top quality investments, the time you invest in them is more than likely to pay off. You may not have as many big winners, but, by the same token, you should have fewer (and maybe no) losers.

Diversifying Your Stock Portfolio: How Many Holdings Are Enough?

We mentioned in a previous chapter that you need at least 25 stocks to achieve an acceptable degree of diversification. That doesn't mean that owning 25 drug stocks will give you diversification, however! You need diversification by number (25+), and by sector or type.

Let's look at how the S&P 500 is weighted by sector, and compare this to four tax-advantaged portfolios we've set up:

Diversification

Sector Weighting	S&P 500	S&P 500 Top 25(1)	S&P 500 Top 50(1)	S&P Barra Growth Top 25(1)	S&P Barra Growth Top 50(1)
1. Basic Materials	2.9%	0	4	4	2
2. Industrials	11.0	8	4	8	4
3. Consumer Disc.	13.5	8	6	8	14
4. Consumer Staples	9.2	16	10	20	18
5. Energy	6.8	8	4	0	0
6. Finance	18.7	20	28	0	10
7. Health care	14.2	12	20	36	32
8. Technology	16.1	20	14	24	20
9. Communication Serv.	4.6	8	10	0	0
10. Utilities	3.1	0	0	0	0
Total	100.0	100.0	100.0	100.0	100.0

(1) Equal weighted

As you can see, our four model portfolios own stock in at least 6 of the 10 sectors that are available in the market. This is so we won't be zigging when the market is zagging.

If you select individual securities for your portfolios, be sure to line them up by sector as shown above to make sure you have good diversification. Keep in mind the following rule of thumb: For each of the five biggest sectors of the S&P 500, try not to own more than two times the percentage amount of stock that the S&P 500 owns. And make sure you don't own less than half of what the S&P 500 owns in each of those same five sectors.

Okay, if you want to play with stocks, at least we've done our best to goof-proof you!

The Least You Need to Know

- Save bucks by using a discount broker to execute your trades, not to research them.

- Avoid IPOs, penny stock, "hot tips," and other speculative trades.

- Only buy quality stocks that you feel comfortable owning for a long time.

- The best research tools are Value Line, *S&P Stock Guides*, *Investor's Business Daily*, *The Wall Street Journal*, and company annual reports.

- In general, stick with market orders when having your broker execute a trade.

- Rebalance your portfolio once a year.

Chapter 11

Slow and Steady Wins the Race: Fixed-Income Securities

In This Chapter

- ◆ What are fixed-income securities?
- ◆ Using fixed-income securities to protect your portfolio
- ◆ The lowdown on bonds
- ◆ How to buy Treasury bonds
- ◆ What to buy and what to avoid

Maybe you're not the type that likes to take big chances. You like to know what's coming around the corner, and, if you can't, you at least like to have a back-up plan to deal with life's little boomerangs. If this is you, there are two words you need to remember: fixed income. A fixed-income security entitles you to regular fixed payments of interest income on your investments. If the stock market gives you the heebie jeebies, fixed-income securities are a fine alternative investment. If you do have designs on the stock market, they're a great way to balance out your portfolio. In this chapter, we're going to give you the lowdown on fixed-income securities and how they can benefit you.

What Are Fixed-Income Securities For?

Bonds and notes are fixed-income securities that corporations and governments issue in order to borrow money. When you buy a bond or note, you are agreeing to lend the company issuing the bond or note a sum of money. In return the company gives you a fixed-income security and promises to make specified interest payments to you and return the full amount borrowed when the security matures. The amount of income, the timing of the payments, and the maturity date are all spelled out.

When corporations raise money using fixed-income securities, it's called *debt financing*. When they issue stock to raise money, it's called *equity financing*.

Investor's Idiom

Bonds, notes, and **bills** are all IOUs that corporations and governments issue when they want to borrow money. The IOU promises to pay interest and the amount borrowed on a specified date. In the case of the US government, these IOUs are called bonds when the specified date is longer than 10 years from the date the bond is issued. When the maturity date is between one and ten years from issuance, the IOU is a note. When it's one year or less from issuance, the IOU is called a bill.

Bonds and other fixed-income securities really balance out the risk of carrying stocks in your portfolio. Unless you lend money to a borrower with lousy credit, you can count on getting your money back when the fixed-income security matures. Plus, you earn all that interest income.

When the stock market is tanking, it can be a great relief to know that you have some of your money in nice, safe bonds. Even better, when the stock market is performing miserably, the bond market tends to do really well, and vice versa. This seesaw effect keeps your portfolio on an even keel when you own both stocks and bonds. What's happened in 2001 and 2002 is a good example.

Since fixed-income investments play such an important balancing role in your portfolio, let's take a closer look at them.

When Do You Get That Groovy Interest Income?

Most, but not all, fixed-income securities pay interest twice a year (on the annual anniversary of the original issue date, and again six months later). For example, five-year U.S. Treasury notes yielding 6.625 percent and due May 2007, pay interest in May and November each year. Plus, the Treasury will pay you back the amount you lent it (your principal) on the maturity date, May 2007.

Beware the Call Feature

Some fixed-income investments include a "call" feature. What is this? Well, let's say you have a home mortgage. This is essentially a fixed-income security you sold to your bank. You, as the borrower, agreed to make fixed monthly payments and to pay off the principal by a final maturity date. You have, however, the right to pay off your mortgage in advance and to refinance your mortgage to take advantage of declining interest rates. This right is the "call" feature. You can "call" your mortgage anytime and pay it off. Some U.S. Government bond issues and the vast majority of corporate and municipal issues also have call features. These give the issuer/borrower the right to pay off ("redeem") the bonds issued.

Why would the borrower want this right? Well, let's go back to our example of Treasury notes paying 6.625 percent interest and maturing in 2007, and pretend the issue is callable. Now, what if interest rates declined to 3 percent? The Treasury would love to be able to pay off the note at 6.625 percent and issue a new note. It would save so much interest!

This would be a drag for you, though, because now you no longer have a 6.625 percent note. Sure you got your principal back, but now if you want to re-invest it, the best you'll do is a new Treasury note at 3 percent. Your interest income has been drastically reduced by this swift move and there's not one thing you can do about it. Boo hoo!

> **Crash Alert**
>
> Call features only benefit the original issuer; they never benefit the purchaser or owner. Therefore, either don't buy any issues with a call feature, or be very careful about incorporating them into your bond portfolio.

Now, let's assume that rates increase to 8 percent. You would be very pleased if the Treasury would call your note so you can reinvest at 8 percent, but the Treasury sure doesn't want to pay 8 percent when it's got you locked in at 6.625 percent.

In this case, the Treasury would not exercise the call right.

Sinkers

Now, let's return to the example of a mortgage. Your monthly payments may stay the same over the life of the mortgage, but as you get closer to maturity less of the monthly payment is interest and more of it reduces the principal balance. The amount of interest income going to the bank is declining. Some corporations issue bonds that do the same thing—the part of the payment that is devoted to interest gets smaller and smaller as the bond gets closer to maturity. These are called sinking fund payments, or "sinkers."

Here's an example of what you receive each six months for a $100,000 purchase of a 6 percent corporate bond due in 10 years with a mandatory sinking fund starting in year 5.

Year		Interest	Principal	Total
4/30/02	1A	(Issue Date)		
	1B	$ 3,000		$ 3,000
4/30/03	2A	3,000		3,000
	2B	3,000		3,000
4/30/04	3A	3,000		3,000
	3B	3,000		3,000
4/30/05	4A	3,000		3,000
	4B	3,000		3,000
4/30/06	5A	3,000		3,000
	5B	3,000		3,000
4/30/07	6A	3,000	$10,000	13,000
	6B	3,000		3,000
4/30/08	7A	3,000	10,000	13,000
	7B	3,000		3,000
4/30/09	8A	3,000	10,000	13,000
	8B	3,000		3,000
4/30/10	9A	3,000	10,000	13,000
	9B	3,000		3,000
4/30/11	10A	3,000	10,000	13,000
	10B	3,000		3,000
4/30/12	11A	3,000	50,000	53,000
		$60,000	$100,000	$160,000

Is this a good deal for you? Well, because you are getting some of your principal paid back before maturity, you are faced with the reinvestment rate issue. Unless you are living off the principal and interest, you have to reinvest your interest and sinking fund payments back into the bond market. If rates go down, it's a bad deal for you. If rates go up, it's a good deal for you.

Super Strategy

To paraphrase Will Rogers, "It's not the return *on* your principal, it's the return *of* your principal ...." When buying fixed-income securities, don't just look for notes and bonds with the highest interest rates. If a borrower is willing to pay high interest rates, its credit must not be very good. "Junk" bonds, for example, are high-yielding bonds from corporations with lousy credit ratings. They may pay a lot of interest but the risk that you will never be paid back part or all of your principal is also very high—too high to risk. The highest yield, per se, cannot be your objective; it must be the highest yield on the highest quality bonds.

The Wonderful World of Bond (No, Not James)

The bond is a popular form of fixed-income security. But in the world of finance, you've probably heard the term tossed around with stocks as if they're one and the same: "Stocksnbonds, stocksnbonds." Well, obviously, they're not.

For one, when you buy a stock you are buying equity—ownership in the company that issued the stock. You are now an owner, entitled to share in the profits and to suffer the losses of the company. The company may or may not pay you dividends, depending on whether or not profits rise. The price of the stock you own may or may not rise. If it does, you could sell it and get your investment back many times over. But when you buy a bond, you are buying debt. You are not an owner; you are lending money to the company (or government) and it has agreed to pay you interest and to pay you back at a certain date. You are promised a specific return (the interest) on your investment, as well as the eventual return of your investment. Because you are not an owner, you are not entitled to a share of the company's profits, nor are you expected to suffer its losses. No matter how bad things get, the company is expected to honor its promise to pay you interest and return your principal at maturity.

Unlike bondholders, stockholders are not guaranteed a specific rate of return or that they will even get their investment back. On the other hand, a stockholder might make a huge return on investment if the company in which he or she owns stock starts to take off. A bondholder will never share in that possibility. Stocks are riskier investments than bonds, but offer the possibility of higher returns.

How Inflation Erodes Bonds

One more thing: We mentioned in Chapter 1 that inflation is a general rise in prices. When prices rise, it costs more money to buy the same thing. It's no fun when it costs $100 to buy the same bag of groceries you bought last year for $75—especially if you didn't get a raise.

Fiscal Facts

Here's a handy chart illustrating the differences between stocks and bonds:

Stock

Equity—investor is owner
Entitles investor to share in the company's profits—if there are any
Unlimited upside/downside
Value not eroded by inflation

Bond

Debt—investor is lender
Return of principal
Limited upside/downside
Value eroded by inflation

Stock prices typically rise with inflation, so the value of stock you own is somewhat protected from inflation. Bonds, on the other hand, offer no protection against inflation because a $1,000 bond bought today will only pay the bondholder $1,000 at maturity. If that $1,000 only buys $750 worth of groceries due to inflation, the value of the bond has been eroded by inflation. This is why bond prices typically decline when investors hear economic news that causes them to worry about inflation.

When Do You Want Bonds in Your Portfolio?

There are three reasons to own bonds:

◆ To meet current income needs. Bonds provide high current income. This is why, as you approach and eventually reach retirement, bonds will play an increasingly important role in your portfolio. You should be able to live off the income they generate when you no longer earn a salary.

Fiscal Facts

Each of the two world wars occurred just before a major turning point in the history of bond yields. World War I was accompanied by high and rising yields, and so was every earlier great war of modern times. World War II, in contrast, was accompanied by low and declining bond yields. World War II ended one year before bond yields reached their lowest point this century. In 1946, one issue of the long government bond sold yielding only 1.93 percent. (Source: **A History of Interest Rates,** pg. 335)

◆ To reduce the volatility or risk in your portfolio.

◆ In the unlikely event of another depression like the one that decimated stock prices between 1929 and 1932, having bonds in your portfolio can cushion the blow when your stocks take a hit.

Let's look an example. Let's say there are two portfolios: One is invested 100 percent in equities, and the other has 20 percent in bonds that pay 6 percent annual interest and 80 percent in stocks.

Portfolio One (100% Equities)				Portfolio Two (20% Bonds/80% Equities)			
Bond Return	Equity Return	Total Return	Index Nos.	Bond Return	Equity Return	Total Return	Index Nos.
-	+10	+10	+1.010	+6	+10	+9.2	+1.092
-	0	0	+1.10	+6	0	+1.2	+1.105
-	+20	+20	+1.32	+6	+20	+17.2	+1.295
-	–10	-10	+1.188	+6	–10	–6.8	+1.207
-	+30	+30	+1.544	+6	+30	+25.2	+1.511
Total Return		+50				+46	
Average		+10.0%				+9.2%	
Compound Annual		+9.1%				+8.6%	

The portfolio with bonds returns 8.6 percent. The portfolio invested exclusively in stock earns 0.5 percent more (9.1 percent) but it is much more volatile. Is it worth that small 0.5 percent difference to invest in bonds and have a more stable portfolio—especially as you get closer to retirement age?

How to Read a Bond Table

Like stocks, bonds are also listed in tables in the financial section of newspapers. Bond tables are useful for two reasons:

♦ If you own a bond and want to sell it, chances are the price is going to be different than what you paid for it. You need to know how different.

♦ Most bonds are already outstanding. Therefore, most of your bond purchases will be of bonds that have already been issued and are trading on the bond market. If you are going to buy an outstanding bond, you need to know its price and current yield.

A bond table is a handy way to adjust to changes in bond yields and/or prices. When bonds are first issued, they are priced to sell at *par*, or 100. As they trade, their price moves above or below 100, depending on the demand for the bonds. If a bond's price falls below 100, it is considered to be selling at a discount. If it rises above 100, it is selling at a premium. Bonds trade in "32nds"; 1/32, 2/32 price movements. For example, in May of 2002, the Treasury sold five-year notes that mature in May, 2007 and pay 4.375 percent interest. By August 1, 2002, the notes were trading at a premium price of 104 12/32 bid/13/32 asked, with a yield of 3.37 percent. Bid is what a dealer is willing to pay for your bond; asked is the price a dealer is willing to sell the bond for.

Investor's Idiom

Par is the original price of a bond, note or bill. It is also the amount that the security will pay back at maturity and is referred to as 100. Between issuance and maturity, a fixed-income security may be bought and sold, with its price rising or falling depending on interest rates and other factors. If a bond's price is over 100, the bond is said to be trading at a **premium**. If the price falls below 100, the bond is trading at a **discount**.

If the yield fell 30 basis points (.30 percent), what would the price of the bond be? Looking in a bond yield book (your broker or banker will have one), you would look down the yield scale to 3.07 percent and then over to 4 years 10 months to maturity to read a price of 105.87. Alternatively, if the yield rose 30 basis points, you would look up to find the price of 103.12. Know the price but want to find the yield? Just reverse the process!

Corporate Debt—An Unwise Choice for Small Investors

Corporations issue bonds and notes, but these are not wise investments for individual investors like you. Why not? Well, since you asked so nicely …

◆ Because corporate debt typically includes call features and/or sinking fund provisions—musts to avoid. Some corporations also issue a hybrid security called a
convertible debenture. A convertible claims to give you participation in both the
bond market and the stock market. Unfortunately, you just get two watered-
down products: (1) a coupon that pays less interest income than a plain old bond
and (2) a chance to buy the company's stock that doesn't kick in unless the stock
price rises at least 20–25 percent. Avoid convertibles and leave the field to the
experts who specialize in this product.

◆ Because most corporations have fluctuating credit ratings. You might buy bonds
from a company with a triple AAA rating, only to find that a few years later the
company has made some bad business decisions and has had its credit rating
downgraded to A or even BBB. Yikes, now you have to worry about whether the
company will be able to honor its promise to give you back your principal at
maturity.

◆ Outstanding corporate debt typically sells in individual units of 100 bonds
($100,000). Do you want to sink that kind of money into one company's bonds?
Not unless you have millions to invest, in which case you don't need this book,
you need your own private financial advisor.

◆ Corporate debt is primarily traded over the counter instead of on the New York
Stock Exchange or American Stock Exchange, which are more accessible to
individual investors. The NYSE might trade around $10 million in bonds on
any given day. Amex only does around $750,000. Meanwhile, roughly $100 million a day in corporate bonds is traded in the over-the-counter market. That's a
market that small investors don't really have access to, and those bonds aren't
quoted in the newspaper bond tables, either.

For all these reasons, corporate bonds are not a good choice for individual investors—
meaning you.

Here is a very rough approximation of the spreads between debt issued by the
Treasury, federal government-sponsored agencies like the Federal National Mortgage
Association (FNMA) and the Government National Mortgage Association (GNMA),
and some investment-grade corporate debt. As you can see, you can make more
money buying corporate bonds but you take on a lot more risk and aggravation. Stick
with Treasury and government agency paper.

Spread (Basis Point Difference)

Issuer	Issue	Yield V. T-Notes	
U.S. Treasury	4.375%, 5/2007	3.37	
FNMA	5.25%, 4/2007	3.81,	+44
IBM	5.38%, 4/2009	5.40,	+203
U.S. Treasury	4.875%, 2/2112	4.41	
FNMA	6.13%, 3/2112	5.01	+60
SBC Communications	5.875%, 8/2012	6.08%	+167

Okay, Corporate Debt Is Out—What Should I Buy?

Don't feel too bad about staying away from the tantalizing array of corporate debt out there. The U.S. Government issues plenty of options that are much healthier for your portfolio.

U.S. Government debt is issued by:

◆ The Treasury Department

◆ Government and Quasi-Government Agencies

U.S. Treasury debt takes one of three forms:

◆ Treasury bills (out to one-year maturity)

◆ Treasury notes (two- to 10-year maturities)

◆ Treasury bonds (maturities beyond 10 years)

Best of all, U.S. Treasury debt is backed by the "full faith and credit" of the U.S. Government. In other words, it's super safe!

There are also two other forms of Treasury debt:

◆ Treasury STRIPs—you met these in Chapter 5. STRIPs are Treasury notes and bonds "stripped" down to their individual coupons and maturity. These are sold at a discount like Treasury bills, and are very useful if you know you will need a sum of money by a certain date (college tuition, for example).

◆ Treasury debt also appears as inflation-indexed notes and bonds. These include an inflation adjustment, which you get when the bond matures. So if you buy a

$10,000 inflation-indexed bond and inflation has risen by 10 percent by the time the bond matures, you'll get your $10,000 principal back plus a $1000 inflation adjustment.

How to Buy Treasuries

Treasury securities are easy to purchase at regular Treasury auctions. You can partici-pate online via Treasury Direct (www.publicdebt.treas.gov/sec/sectrdir.htm). There are weekly T-bill auctions, monthly one-year T-bill auctions and quarterly Treasury note and bond auctions. Check your local newspaper or *The Wall Street Journal* for advance notices, which usually appear five to seven days before an auction. You can also deal directly with your nearest Federal Reserve Bank or ask your banker or bro-ker to make purchases for you for a small service fee of around $25. The minimum purchase is $1,000 and all bids must be made in $1,000 lots.

Buying Outstanding Treasuries

Besides buying Treasuries at auction, you can also buy outstanding Treasuries on the market. They will be trading either at a discount or a premium. Currently, most Treasury notes and bonds are selling at a premium, because interest rates have been declining for a long time (when interest rates fall, bond prices rise).

What does this mean to you? Well, a bond or note is selling at a premium because it pays a higher interest rate than current new notes or bonds. So if you buy an out-standing Treasury at a premium, you will get higher interest income than you would from the new Treasuries being auctioned. On the other hand, you don't get all of your principal back when you buy a Treasury that is trading at a premium. Remem-ber, the principal is the amount that the borrower originally borrowed. If you buy a $10,000 Treasury note at a premium, it'll cost more than $10,000, but $10,000 is all you get paid back at maturity.

A discount bond works in just the opposite manner. Let's say you purchase a Treasury bond trading at 96, or $9,600. You'll receive $10,000 at maturity, for a gain of $400. However, you'll get interest income from this note for around $400–$600 less than the current rate. Is it worth it to receive less income in return for greater principal return? That depends on what's more important to you—some people want income, some want a greater return in the long run.

If the answer to either question is no, just buy at the auctions.

Savings Bonds

The Treasury also issues savings bonds, which use to take only one of two forms: *EE* or *HH*. The Treasury has introduced a new series called I Bonds, as well.

Series EE bonds are purchased at half-price and their value eventually rises to par. You'd pay $5,000 for a $10,000 EE bond, for example. Its value will eventually rise to $10,000. When it gets to that point, however, depends on interest rates. Instead of receiving interest income from an EE bond, the interest income is added to the value of the bond, causing it to rise until you redeem it. If rates are high, the bond's value will increase quickly. If rates are low, it will grow more slowly. You do have to hold the bond for at least five years to avoid paying a three-month interest penalty. There are now also inflation-indexed savings bonds. A primary difference between savings bonds and Treasury bonds is that the owner of a Treasury bond can sell it prior to maturity, but the owner of a savings Bond cannot transfer it to someone else.

Series HH bonds are issued at face value (in other words, if the bond is for $10,000, you pay the full $10,000 for it) and earn interest by a pre-stated formula.

Investor's Idiom

Starting in September 1998, the Treasury began selling **Series I savings bonds,** which are inflation adjusted.

EE savings bonds are a good choice for college savings accounts, provided you purchase them at least five years before redeeming them. Unlike regular bonds, you don't have to report any income for tax purposes until you cash them in. This makes EE savings bonds great for taxable portfolios, like college funds. EE savings bonds are also a great gift for kids from relatives and can be purchased in denominations as low as $5.

Plus, EE savings bonds are no-brainers because you don't have to reinvest interest income every six months, as you do with Treasury notes and bonds.

The New I Bonds

Series I bonds are new bonds first issued by the Treasury in September of 1998 that provide built-in inflation protection (remember our discussion about how inflation can erode a bond's value?). The earnings rate of an I bond is a combination of two separate rates: *a fixed rate of return* and a variable *semiannual inflation rate*. The fixed rate remains the same throughout the life of the I bond, while the semiannual inflation rate is adjusted every six months based on changes in the Consumer Price Index. The semiannual inflation rate is combined with the fixed rate of an I bond to determine the I bond's earnings rate for the next six months. As of this writing the interest on I bonds is 4.4%, comprised of a 2.00% interest rate and a 2.38% variable semi-annual inflation rate.

You must hold I bonds for at least six months to get your original investment and earnings, however if you cash out before five years, you'll lose three months of interest. With 6-month CDs offering their lowest rates in almost 20 years, however, I bonds are not a bad parking spot for your savings.

Agency-O-Rama

The Treasury is not the only government agency that issues debt. There are a host of government agency and quasi-agencies (agencies created by an act of Congress, like FNMA) out there borrowing money including:

◆ The Federal National Mortgage Association (known as "Fannie Mae"). FNMA is a quasi-agency. Its debt is an implied (but not a guaranteed) obligation of the federal government. The agency's stock trades publicly on the New York Stock Exchange under the ticker symbol FNM.

◆ Federal Home Loan Mortgage Corp. ("Freddie Mac"). Like Fannie Mae, Freddie Mac is a quasi-agency/private corporation with stock listed on the New York Stock Exchange (symbol FRE).

◆ Student Loan Marketing Association ("Sallie Mae"). Sallie Mae is the third and last of the three public/private corporations. Its ticker symbol is STU, but the name changed recently to SLM Holding.

◆ Government National Mortgage Association ("Ginnie Mae") issues bonds that return both principal and interest, just as you pay your monthly mortgage in a single sum to cover both principal and interest. GNMAs are federally guaranteed. This is the only quasi-agency that enjoys this privilege. "Ginnie Mae" bonds are an example of a class of bonds called mortgage-backed securities (MBS). The MBS is a debt instrument with a pool of real estate loans (perhaps your mortgage included) representing the underlying collateral. As principal and interest payments are paid into the pool, they, in turn, are paid out to GNMA bondholders. Mortgage-backed certificates are issued by banks and insured by private mortgage insurance companies.

◆ Resolution Funding Corporation (RFC). These bonds are guaranteed as to principal, but not interest, and were issued to help resolve the Savings & Loan crisis of the late 1980s/early 1990s.

And a host of others!

CDs: A Viable Alternative to Government Debt

If you do want the guarantee of the federal government and aren't willing to venture into buying Treasuries, consider your old pal the CD again for the fixed-income segment of your portfolio. After all, CDs can be purchased in maturities up to 10 years, and for specific sums once you clear the minimum (usually $1,000). And the first $100,000 is completely guaranteed by the federal government.

As we mentioned earlier, though, CD rates are currently quite low, so this might be a good time to screw up your courage and visit the Treasury online and learn how to buy Treasury notes. It's really not that tough, we promise!

Nonetheless, CDs offer an interesting alternative to shorter-maturing government securities. And, if you buy at your local bank, you have the added convenience factor. CD rates tend to be competitive with government paper, especially Treasury bills, but you may need to shop around to determine which bank offers the best deal. The only problem with CDs is the penalty you incur (usually three to six months of interest, depending upon maturity) if you sell prior to maturity. And, unlike the new I bonds, they don't offer any protection against inflation.

The Least You Need to Know

♦ A fixed-income security pays you interest income when you lend a sum to a borrower, who promises to pay back the loan on a specific date called the "maturity date."

♦ When stock prices are falling, bond prices tend to rise, so having bonds in your portfolio can help to counteract declines in the value of your stock.

♦ Avoid call features, sinkers, and corporate debt.

♦ Buy Treasury bills, notes, and bonds and government agency paper for the fixed-income segment of your portfolio. Consider the new I bonds as alternatives to CDs.

Chapter 12

Navigating the Mutual Fund Universe

In This Chapter

- ◆ Picking winning funds
- ◆ How to avoid unnecessary fees
- ◆ Contact numbers for some excellent funds
- ◆ Managing several funds at a time

If you were to make a list of growth businesses for the 1990s, you'd have to place the mutual funds business at or close to the top. Although the first mutual funds were created before the 1929 stock market crash, mutual funds have truly exploded in popularity in the last 15 years.

Why did mutual funds become so popular? There are a few reasons:

- ◆ Mutual funds have become the product of choice for 401(k) plans, and both asset growth and dollars for those plans now exceed every other type of retirement plan.

- ◆ Some mutual fund firms have developed enough critical mass to justify advertising on—gasp—television during prime time, reaching all those Must-See-TV *Friends-* and *Frasier-*watching folks who probably have a little extra cash to burn.

♦ Some mutual fund managers actually have become cult figures who are frequently quoted and interviewed in major publications nationwide.

♦ With the downturn in the stock market in the late 1990s and the more recent turmoil, individual investors who got burned by holding only a few stocks are realizing that mutual funds offer much wider diversification than they could achieve on their own. Such diversification reduces the risk of investing in just one or several stocks. In addition, investors are discovering the merits of bond funds, which offer diversification plus an alternative to the stock market!

Still don't see why mutual funds are the hot ticket? Let's delve a little deeper. In this chapter, we're going to show you what mutual funds are and (more important) what they can do for you.

What Exactly Are Mutual Funds?

A mutual fund is a company that invests on behalf of customers who deposit money with it. The "customers" may be individual investors like you, or even big companies. Either way, the mutual fund company pools the money it collects and manages it with investment objectives that are carefully spelled out.

For example, one fund might invest only in technology stocks. Another might invest in small, emerging companies; another in government securities, or in corporate bonds. There are funds that mimic the S&P 500 index or other indexes. As you learned in Chapter 9, a fund that mimics an index is called an index fund. It is passively, not actively, managed—meaning that the fund's managers do very little except make sure the fund's holdings stay in proportion to the index it mimics. When you buy "shares" in a mutual fund, you own a piece of its investments proportional to the amount you've invested. Because the mutual fund is investing millions of dollars, it can develop a very diversified portfolio. By investing in a mutual fund, you achieve a level of diversification for your own portfolio that you could never afford to create by yourself.

Open-End and Closed-End Funds

All mutual funds are collective investment funds or portfolios registered with the Securities & Exchange Commission (SEC) under the Investment Advisers Act of

1940 ("The 40 Act"). Most mutual funds are open end. This means that they are always open to accepting more deposits from more customers and can continue to grow in size with no upper limit. Some funds are closed, meaning they accept no more deposits after their initial offering. Closed-end funds only sell a fixed number of shares—like a corporation does when it makes an offering. And, like many corporations' shares, closed-end funds are primarily listed and traded on the New York Stock Exchange or the American Stock Exchange. Closed-end funds only hold around 2 to 3 percent of the total assets invested in mutual funds.

You can buy shares in a mutual fund by contacting its distributor. (We provide some contact numbers later in this chapter.) The price you'll pay for shares is based on the net asset value that day, provided your order is received and accepted before the close of business (currently 4 P.M.). Orders received after 4 P.M. are priced at the next day's *net asset value* (*NAV*) figure.

With a closed-end fund, though, differences can develop between a share's net asset value and its market price because shareholders are competing to buy a fixed number of shares.

If the shares are selling above the net asset value, they are selling at a "premium." In contrast, shares trading below NAV are said to be selling at a "discount." Some closed-end funds sell at a discount of 20 percent or greater.

If you buy shares in a fund that's selling at a hefty discount and later the fund's share price bounces back, you could make a tidy profit. So if you are interested in closed-end funds ...

♦ Stick with discounts.

♦ Study the historical discount range to determine whether the current price is at the top, middle, or low end.

Investor's Idiom

Net asset value (NAV) is the dollar value of all the marketable securities (stocks, for example) owned by a mutual fund, less expenses, and divided by the number of the fund's shares outstanding. When you want to buy shares in an open-end mutual fund, the price you will pay is based on the net asset value. Because the shares of a closed-end fund trade on the market, however, its share price may differ from its NAV.

Crash Alert

Sometimes closed-end funds become open-end funds, thereby eliminating the discount that may have made them an attractive buy in the first place. You can check the current premium or discount by looking in the Monday *Wall Street Journal* (Section C near the back), and also in the Sunday *New York Times* "Money & Business" section (again, near the back).

Why would a fund choose to be closed rather than open? Fund managers are concerned with sell-offs that could be triggered by bad news or other events. For this reason, emerging market equity funds, specialized equity funds, and municipal bond (especially state-specific) funds tend to be set up as closed-end funds—because these types of funds are highly specialized and, therefore, vulnerable to bad news. With a closed fund, holders of the shares who wish to sell don't turn to the fund, but to the market. This protects the fund managers from having to raise the money to buy back shares in the event of a sell-off.

Avoid Load Funds

Do you simply pay the NAV times the number of shares you want to purchase when you buy shares in an open-end mutual fund? Not always. Some funds deduct a sales charge from your principal; this is referred to as a "front-end load." Funds that charge this fee are called "load" funds. Loads currently make up 5.0 to 5.5 percent of your investment and go to whomever sold you the fund (your broker, for example); they do not go to the fund itself.

Funds that do not charge this fee are called "no load" funds—and they are a much better deal. Here is a simple example of how front-end load can hurt your investment. Let's say you purchase $10,000 of a fund with a NAV of $10.00 and a 5 percent load:

	Load Fund	No Load Fund
Principal Amount	$10,000	$10,000
Less Sales Commission	$500	$0
Net Available	$9,500	$10,000
Net Asset Value	$10	$10
Number of Shares	$950	$1,000

If you buy the load fund, you lose $500 or 5 percent of your principal before it even has a chance to work for you! Think twice before buying a load fund.

Back-End Loads and 12b-1 Fees

Some funds also charge you when you redeem (sell) your shares. This charge is referred to as back-end or back-door load. It is also called a deferred sales charge. The intent here is to penalize investors who make frequent fund purchases and sales.

Back-end load may run as high as 6 to 7 percent of the amount you sell in the first year, scaling down to zero by, say, the seventh year. This charge, if applicable, is deducted from your gross proceeds when you make the sale. Again, these charges do not go to the fund company, but to whomever makes the transaction for you.

Finally, many funds charge a shareholding servicing fee, often referred to as a 12b-1 fee. This fee, limited to .25 percent, is used as an inducement to brokers who have helped or may help sell fund shares. It is vital that you learn before purchasing shares in a fund whether it charges front- or back-end load, and/or a 12b-1 fee. It's your money, after all! Simply ask your broker, call the fund company, or request a *prospectus*.

Investor's Idiom

A **prospectus** is a legal document prepared by a mutual fund and sent out to potential investors that describes the fund and its operations.

Index and Tax-Advantaged Funds

If you can shelter all the dollars you want to invest in IRAs and 401(k)s, great. But if you put some of your money directly into equity mutual funds, without the shelter of an IRA, you will have to pay taxes on any gains the fund makes. Even if you immediately reinvest any dividends or gains from the fund, you will have to pay taxes to Uncle Sam on them. Bummer. To avoid this situation, you can limit your mutual fund holdings to one of two types of stock funds—index funds and tax-advantaged funds:

♦ Index funds mimic the behavior of stocks in a particular index (such as the S&P 500). The fund just buys the stocks in the index in the same proportion as they appear in the index and holds them. Since there are few trades, few capital gains are generated for you to pay taxes on. The oldest, largest, and least-expensive fund is the Vanguard Index 500, which mimics the S&P 500 Index. Vanguard is at 1-800-662-7447.

♦ Tax-advantaged funds make a conscious effort to minimize taxes by minimizing trading. The fund managers don't completely ignore opportunities to improve the portfolio by buying and selling, but they do it as little as possible to avoid generating taxable capital gains. The fund managers will also attempt to offset gains with losses whenever possible—again, to reduce taxes.

Super Strategy

There are only a handful of tax-advantaged funds available at this time, but they could be useful for your portfolio if you can't shelter all your investment income in 401(k)s and IRAs. Keep an eye on the financial pages for further developments.

Exchange-Traded Funds

In addition to index mutual funds, you can now purchase and hold index funds that trade on an exchange (like closed-end funds, but without the discount or premium). ETFs have grown like crazy since their introduction several years ago. In 1998, total ETF assets were $10 billion; today, the combined assets of just the top 30 of the 125 ETFs is $82 billion. The largest, SPDR Trust (short for S&P 500 Index Fund), has assets of $28.5 billion. The next largest, NASDAQ-100 Trust (which holds the 100 largest-market-cap NASDAQ stocks) has over $19 billion in assets.

All but two of the ETFs trade on the American Stock Exchange and can be found in *The Wall Street Journal*, Section C, next to the American Stock Exchange listings.

Are ETFs for real? Definitely. Fund expenses are low, if not lower, than those for index mutual funds, and you can buy or sell at any time during normal trading hours. In contrast, regular mutual fund shares can only be traded after closing prices are in. They work best, however, in a buy-and-hold mode because you do incur commission costs every time you make a trade. If you can minimize commissions and are not a compulsive trader, however, ETFs are an excellent choice.

What's Out There in the Fund Universe?

There are over 9,000 open-end funds currently operating. Morningstar recently broke them down as follows:

Domestic Equity Funds	4,048
International Equity Funds	1,259
Taxable Bond Funds	1,924
Municipal Bond Funds	1,818
Index Funds & Others	252
TOTAL	9,301

Open-end funds are listed by the National Association of Securities Dealers (NASD) once they have at least 1,000 shareholders or net assets of $25 million. Money market funds, which we discussed in Chapter 3, number about 1,300, of which 875 are taxable and 425 are tax free (either general or state specific). There is a listing each Thursday in *The Wall Street Journal* (Section C near the back) which tells you the average maturity of the fund, its seven-day yield, and total assets of the fund. The *Journal*, *Barron's*, Yahoo! Finance, and CBS MarketWatch also carry the Fund Info

Service, which is indicated by a "club" symbol that accompanies mutual fund listings. The symbol directs investors to a Web site or toll-free number to quickly obtain prospectuses, information kits, and applications for participating funds. The financial information can be downloaded instantly or hard-copy versions can be mailed within 24 hours.

Why Funds Are a Great Investment Option

There are several key reasons why you should consider mutual funds:

♦ **Professional Management.** The manager of a given mutual fund may not be more intelligent or luckier than you, but he or she can devote full-time attention to what you can, at best, only give a portion of your time. In addition, professional investment management has access to research and to market information that would either not be available to you at all or only after a time delay—and timing is crucial when making investment decisions. In addition, corporate "road shows" stop off at various professional management offices to bring them up-to-date, but don't expect them to come knocking on your door. Finally, influential Wall Street professionals share their opinions first with large, commission-generating customers—like mutual fund managers.

♦ **Instant Diversification.** We've shared with you the importance of diversification. To achieve even bare-bone diversification, you would need 25 sector-diversified equities and at least 10 different bond issues (unless you limit your bond portion to governments), at $100,000 each. Want to add some international stock? Prepare to add at least 50 more. Get the picture?

♦ **Low Costs.** We've pointed out layered fund expenses such as front- and back-end loads and 12b-1 fees. Funds also charge management expense fees that approximate 50 to 75 *basis points* (.50 to .75 percent), and go as high as 75 to 150 basis points for some equity funds. If you stick to no-load funds that keep expenses low, however, you'll find that investing in mutual funds is a great deal cheaper than investing in stocks on your own and paying commissions and transaction costs. Some index mutual funds have expenses as low as 12 basis points (.12 percent). Try topping that!

> **Super Strategy**
>
> The ultimate diversified portfolio is the index fund. This is a mutual fund set up to mimic an index, such as our old pal the S&P 500 or other indexes like the Russell 2000 Small Cap Index and the Wilshire 5000 Index. Can you afford to buy all 500 stocks in the S&P 500? Probably not, but a mutual fund can. And by buying shares in that fund, now you can, too.

- **Terrific Variety.** Whatever you want, the fund industry offers. Want to invest in Japanese companies? Health care? New Jersey municipal bonds? Indonesian utilities? There's a fund somewhere doing just that.

- **Ease and Convenience.** Usually, you can complete your transaction with one phone call and a minimum of paperwork. And if you stay within a particular fund family, you can switch funds with no—or at the very least, minimal—expense, over the phone.

Investor's Idiom

There are 100 **basis points** in one percentage point. So 100 basis points = 1 percent.

These are some of the more significant reasons why mutual funds have reached unparalleled popularity in this country (other than those prime-time TV ads). You just have to use your head (and our advice) in making your selections. Start by requesting annual and quarterly reports and prospectuses from funds that interest you. And actually read them before you buy!

How to Pick a Winning Fund

How do you pick a fund? Well, for starters, don't read those glossy financial magazines with the eye-catching headlines screaming from the newsstand about can't-lose mutual funds. Okay, read them if you must, but take a look at who's buying the ads that keep these mags afloat. That's right: mutual funds.

We have a better suggestion. Simply apply the following criteria, and you'll make excellent choices.

- **Performance.** Is the fund rate of return above average for its category for the latest one, three, and five years? Notice that we are not recommending that you buy the funds with the highest return or even the ones in the top 10 percent. We prefer to sacrifice some historical returns for consistency. Don't run out and buy a fund that just hit a home run; it might strike out the year after you buy it. Better to seek funds that consistently hit singles and doubles. If you get consistent above-average returns, you'll get superior results over the long haul.

- **Management.** Make sure that the same team has been managing the fund for at least the last five years. When a fund changes managers, you simply don't know whether the new management will do better or worse. You also may not be able to find out the track record of the new manager. Just stick with funds that have retained the same management for at least five years.

◆ **Size.** With index funds, go for the largest size fund because it would (or should) have the lowest expenses. But with actively managed funds, avoid unproven funds of small size, as well as very large, ponderous funds that may lack the flexibility to move from stock to stock or industry to industry as conditions warrant. Just for you, we've arbitrarily selected a range of $250 million to $5 billion. Minimum asset size per category is over $2 billion for the large-cap stock funds, $2.0 billion for most bond funds, and $500 million for small-cap stock funds.

◆ **No Load.** You know our feelings on this. We want to start with $1 working for us, not 95¢.

◆ **Expense Ratios.** We expect the administrator and the investment adviser for the fund to make a profit. But we don't want that green monster called greed to rear its ugly head. Stick with funds that keep expenses under

1.25% for equity funds

0.75% for fixed-income funds

0.50% for lower-yielding fixed-income funds (municipal bond funds and intermediate-term taxable bonds)

For our selection process, we relaxed or tightened the expense figure based on the fund category: less than 1.0 percent for large-cap stock funds, 1.25 percent for small-cap and international stock funds, and 0.50 percent for most bond funds.

Check Out These Funds

We applied the above criteria to Morningstar software to develop the following list of funds that we like. All funds meet the prestated criteria for performance, management tenure, no load, and retail customer availability.

We have included the telephone number so you can contact the fund directly for literature. We have excluded short-term bond funds, along with emerging country funds (which should only be purchased in closed-end format, as discussed previously). Finally, we have eliminated any funds that you, as a retail investor, would not be eligible to purchase.

Large-Cap Growth: Asset size $2.0 billion +, expense ratio ≤ 1.0%

American Century Ultra   1-800-345-2021

Fidelity Blue Chip Growth   1-800-544-8888

Fidelity Independence   (same as above)

Harbor Capital Appreciation   1-800-422-1050

Janus Growth & Income   1-800-525-8983

T. Rowe Price Blue Chip Growth   1-800-638-5660

Vanguard Growth Index   1-800-662-7447

Large Value: Asset size $2.0 billion, expense ratio max. 0.75%

Dodge & Cox Stock   1-800–621-3979

Fidelity Equity-Income   1-800-544-8888

Vanguard Equity-Income   1-800-662-7447

Vanguard Windsor II   (same as above)

Large Blend: Asset size $2.0 billion +, expense ratio max. 0.75%

Elfun Trusts   1-800-242-0134

Fidelity Asset Manager: Growth   1-800-544-8888

Fidelity Growth & Income   (same as above)

Schwab 1000   1-800-435-4000

State Farm Growth   1-800-447-0740

Vanguard 500 Index   1-800-662-7447

Mid-Cap Growth: Asset size $1.0 billion +, expense ratio max. 1.25%

Hartford Mid-Cap HLS   1-888-843-7824

T. Rowe Price Mid-Cap Growth   1-800-638-5660

Brandywine   1-800-656-3017

Mid-Cap Value: Asset size $1.0 billion +, expense ratio max. 1.25%

American Century Equity Income   1-800-345-2021

Longleaf Partners   1-800-445-9469

Oakmark Select 1   1-800-625-6275

Mid-Cap Blend: Asset size $1.0 billion +, expense ratio max. 1.25%

Meridian Value   1-800-446-6662

Small Growth: Asset size $0.5 billion +, expense ratio max. 1.25%

Liberty Acorn Z   1-800-426-3750

Vanguard Explorer   1-800-662-7447

Small Value: Asset size $0.5 billion +, expense ratio max. 1.25%

Ariel   1-800-292-7435

Small Blend (Value and Growth): Asset size $0.5 billion +, expense ratio max. 1.25%

Royce Premier   1-800-221-4268

Foreign Stock: Asset size $1.0 billion +, expense ratio max. 1.25%

American Advantage Int'l Equity   1-800-967-9009

Artisan Intranational   1-800-344-1770

Bernstein Tax-Managed Int'l Value   212-756-4097

Harbor International   1-800-422-3750

Liberty Acorn International   1-800-426-3750

Long Government: Asset size $1.5 billion +, expense ratio max. 0.50%

Vanguard Long-Term U.S. Treasury   1-800-662-7447

Intermediate Government: $2.0 billion +, expense ratio max. 0.50%

Vanguard GNMA   1-800-662-7447

Vanguard Interm. U.S. Treasury   (same as above)

Long-Term Bond: Asset size $2.0 billion +, expense ratio max. 0.50%

Vanguard Long-Term Corporate Bond   1-800-662-7447

Intermediate-Term Bonds: $2.0 billion +, expense ratio max. 0.50%

Fidelity Investment Grade Bond   1-800-544-8888

Fidelity Spartan   (same as above)

PIMCO Total Return   1-800-927-4648

Vanguard Interm.-Term Corp.   1-800-662-7447

Vanguard Total Bond Market Index   (same as above)

Muni National Long: $2.0 billion +, expense ratio max 0.50%

Vanguard Insured Long-Term T/E   1-800-662-7447

Vanguard Long-Term Tax Exempt   (same as above)

Muni National Intermediate: $2.0 billion +, expense ratio max. 0.50%

Vanguard Intermediate-Term Tax-Exempt   1-800-662-7447

Source: Morningstar, Inc., 1-800-735-0700; Morningstar.com

Don't be concerned with the short list of fixed income (bond) funds we've provided. We like mutual funds for equities, but recommend that you buy individual government securities (or municipals) for the bond portion of your portfolio. There are two problems with bond funds:

1. Much of the yield is eaten up by management fees.

2. When you buy into a bond fund, you can't stagger interest income to meet your individual income needs the way you can when you buy individual bonds and you know their maturity dates. We really like the idea of buying bonds of different maturities so that after you retire, you have interest income coming in every month that matches up with your monthly expenses, as well as annual bond maturities to reinvest as you see fit.

At the end of each quarter, newspapers such as *The New York Times* and *The Wall Street Journal* publish a special supplement on mutual funds. These special supplements provide a wealth of information on many funds, including phone numbers, fund objectives, assets under management, sales charges (if any), expenses, and NAV and performance results. Use these supplements to do your own screening! Or, go online at www.morningstar.com and print out its six-page Quicktake reports on any funds that interest you.

Money Market Funds

With respect to both taxable and tax-free money market funds, we used a much simpler screening process: Qualified funds had expense ratios under 40 basis points (0.4 percent) and assets over $1 billion. This is a good list of retail funds you can use that are large and have low expense ratios. Each list is alphabetical.

Assets ($ millions)	Fund Name
U.S. Treasury Funds	
$4,708.0	Vanguard Treasury
U.S. Government & Agencies Funds	
$2,497.0	Fidelity U.S. Gov't Reserves
$1,698.5	SSgA U.S. Gov't MMF/Class A
$6,793.0	Vanguard Federal MMF
General Money Market Funds	
1,888.0	Aon Funds/MMF
57,989.0	Fidelity Cash Reserves
1,006.0	Harris Insight MF/Exchange
11,832.5	SSgA Money Market Fund/Class A
1,082.5	Strong Heritage MF/Inv. Class
50,741.8	Vanguard Prime MMF/Retail
Tax-Free Money Funds	
2,508.2	Excelsior T-E Money Fund
2,767.5	Fidelity Spartan Municipal MF
9,964.1	Vanguard Tax-Exempt MMF

(Source: iMoneyNet, Inc./imoneynet.com/508-616-6600)

Space does not permit us to list state-specific funds, which may well be the first choice for those in higher tax brackets and high-tax states. But the above list at least provides a starting point.

Variable Annuity: a Mutual Fund Wrapped Around an Insurance Contract

Approximately 50 insurance companies offer at least 900 different variable annuity funds. An annuity promises to provide a sum in an annual or other regular (e.g., monthly) interval. A fixed annuity is for a fixed amount. A variable annuity provides an undetermined amount that depends upon the return of the underlying mutual fund.

Since a variable annuity is a mutual fund wrapped around an insurance contract, the "variable" depends upon how well the fund performs. Are variable annuities a good deal?

Variable annuities are like traditional IRAs, in the sense that they are tax-deferred funds subject to ordinary income taxes (up to 38.6 percent currently) when funds are withdrawn. Until withdrawn, variable annuity funds grow uninhibited by taxes. Unlike the traditional IRA, however, there is no limit to how much you can contribute to a variable annuity each year. In addition, when you do retire, you can convert a variable annuity to a fixed annuity. Probably a majority of annuities are held in our old friend, the 403(b) plan. The biggest drawback, in our opinion, is that if you buy a variable annuity, you have to pay not only the underlying mutual fund expenses but an additional fee of typically 1.1 percent for the *death benefit*. The death benefit guarantees that the holder's heirs will receive at least the principal back in the event of a market meltdown. But is that worth 1.1 percent each and every year? We don't think so.

If you wish to follow variable annuities, check the Monday *Wall Street Journal* in near the back of Section C.

> **Fiscal Facts**
>
> According to Morningstar, there are more than 9,300 funds (excluding money market funds). That's greater than the number of stocks listed on the New York, American, and NASDAQ exchanges.

Lifestyle and Tax-Efficient Funds

Two other new types of funds deserve mention. One is the so-called lifestyle fund. This fund allows you to set a target retirement date, and, as you approach that date, the asset allocation automatically shifts to less equity exposure. Be aware that a generic stock/bond ratio might not be appropriate for most investors because the ratio makes assumptions that might not apply to your age or risk tolerance. Nevertheless, the automatic asset allocation rebalancing concept is appealing. Vanguard seems to be the leader at this point.

We are wholeheartedly enthusiastic about a new concept that we discussed earlier for individual investing: so-called tax-efficient (or tax-managed, tax-preferred, and so on) funds. The concept is only several years old, with no more than 40 funds available at present. Once again, Vanguard is the leader and should be contacted if you have further questions.

With actively managed equity funds posting such strong gains these days, tax-efficient funds could be a good choice for your taxable investments. Vanguard currently offers the Tax-Managed Growth and Income Fund, the Tax-Managed Capital Appreciation Fund, the T.M. Balanced Fund, the T.M. Small-Cap Fund, and the T.M. International Fund.

Pick a Date to Rebalance Your Mutual Fund Holdings Annually

Well, by now you know what date that is. That's right, your birthday (unless it falls in January or near a big holiday). But what are you going to rebalance, and which portfolio(s)?

For your tax-deferred accounts (IRAs, 401[k]s, etc.), any actions you take will not trigger a tax bite. So if you are in equity mutual funds, rebalance them back to your original targets or your revised targets. This should only be necessary if the stock market has gone up or down significantly in the previous 12 months. Of course, if you have hit one of those rebalancing years we discussed in Chapter 10 and it's time to reduce your equity exposure, make the move irrespective of what the market has done.

If you have just one equity mutual fund, this is a fairly simple procedure: Sell some of your equity fund and use the proceeds to buy Treasury notes or bonds or shares in a bond fund. But what if you have more than one equity fund? Then you have to rebalance these funds within the equity portion. Let's say your portfolio of equity mutual funds looks like this:

	Initial Target	Current
Large-Cap Growth	30%	33%
Large-Cap Value	30%	33%
Mid-Cap Growth	10%	10%
Mid-Cap Value	5%	5%
Small-Cap Growth	5%	4%
Small-Cap Value	5%	4%
International	10%	8%
Emerging Markets	5%	3%
Total	100%	100%

First and foremost, figure out how much the equity segment of your portfolio is worth in dollars, then rebalance the individual equity funds so the percentage invested in each corresponds to your original target.

Rebalancing Taxable Accounts

With taxable accounts, the goal is to generate as few capital gains as possible. That's why we recommend passive equity holdings and/or index funds, which minimize taxes—if nothing's being sold, no capital gains are being generated. You don't want to sell equities in a taxable account unless you are at a milestone year (you might be approaching first-year college expenses, for example). If the equities in your taxable accounts have declined significantly, however, you do want to rebalance upward. Use the proceeds from bond or bond fund sales, which should generate minimal capital gains. That's all there is to it!

The Least You Need to Know

◆ A mutual fund is a company that invests on behalf of customers who deposit money with it.

◆ Look for open-end funds that keep expenses low and don't charge load or 12b-1 fees.

◆ Mutual funds are great for the equity portion of your portfolio, but for the fixed-income portion skip bond funds and buy individual bonds.

◆ Keep an eye out for developments in lifestyle and tax-efficient funds; these could be good buys.

Part 4

Rolling with Life's Changes

Life is full of transitions, shocks, and assorted doozies. Our happiness, in fact, has little to do with avoiding life's changes and everything to do with being prepared to roll with them.

Properly managed investments can make transitions like buying a home or retiring a lot smoother. Knowing how to handle exciting developments that affect your investments, such as changing jobs or inheriting money, can ease the stress that even the most positive events can cause. And it's crucial to know how to protect your assets from potentially devastating events like divorce.

This part is a primer on how to manage your investments through all the biggies: marriage, divorce, buying a home, educating your kids, inheriting money, changing jobs, and, yep, even that final spooky transition we'd all rather pretend is never going to happen. At least not to us.

Work Smart, Not Just Hard: Getting the Max from Your Job

In This Chapter

- ◆ Five vital questions for a new employer
- ◆ When your Social Security benefits can be taxed
- ◆ The changing retirement age
- ◆ How Medicare works

Are you one of those people who ignore every memo and form about complicated-sounding things like 401(k)s and vesting that come across your desk? Do you figure that if you ignore them, maybe they'll go away? Well, what's going away is your opportunity to squeeze the most dollars possible out of your job.

Now that we've got your attention … think of this chapter as your personal machete. Use it to cut through the thickets of paper and nonsense that many corporate human resource departments love to erect between you and simple answers about how to best handle the retirement benefits offered by your employer. And, if you're self-employed or thinking about becoming self-employed, we'll show you how to set up your own retirement account and get a major tax break in the process.

What to Ask a New Employer

There are five topics you must discuss with personnel immediately when you start a job at a new company. Make an appointment ASAP with a human resources person. You'll shock and amaze him or her if you walk in there with these questions under your hat:

1. "Do you have a pension plan, and, if so when am I eligible to participate?"

   Typically, each credited year requires 1,000 hours of work. If you start work before June 30, therefore, you will probably be eligible that year. If your hire date is much later than that, you will probably not be eligible until the following year. Find out if you will qualify in year one of your employment. How long will you have to work at the company until you are fully vested? Five years is typical.

2. "Can I transfer the money in my existing 401(k) plan to your 401(k)plan? How exactly do I do that? When can I start to participate in your plan? What are the investment choices offered by your 401(k) plan? Does the employer contribute and to what degree?"

   Get very specific answers here so you don't risk leaving the assets in your current 401(k) plan unsheltered. As we discussed in Chapter 5, you typically only have 60 days to get this together before the IRS can swoop in. You usually will be able to participate in your new employer's 401(k) plan after you've been there one year.

3. "Is there a bonus or incentive plan? How general or specific is it? Is it tied to my job performance or the performance of the company or my department as a whole? When will I be informed of the amount? When is it paid to me? Do I have to be a full-time employee when the checks are passed out?"

   It's better to have a bonus that's tied directly to your own performance, not to the performance of others. That way you control your own destiny. Bear in mind, also, that you don't want to screw yourself out of a big bonus or incentive check at your current job by leaving to take a new one. Before you leave, check out any pertinent dates. If waiting a few weeks to start your new job will keep you from losing money, you could either arrange that or negotiate a sign-on bonus with your new employer.

4. "Are there stock options? Am I eligible for them?"

   If the answer to both questions is yes, get the details. Normally, if you are eligible, stock options would have already been dangled as incentive to get you on board in the first place and would have been included in your hiring agreement.

5. "Does the company have a health plan? When do I and my family become eligible? Is there a choice of plans, or just one?"

   You want to know what kind of choice you have. There may be just one HMO, several alternative HMOs, or a traditional plan. There may be some variation that allows you to opt in or out of your HMO. Typically, you are eligible on the first of each month.

Super Strategy

When you start a new job, meet with your human resources contact right away to ask about the company's ...

- ◆ Pension plan.
- ◆ 401(k) plan and whether you can transfer money from your existing 401(k) into it.
- ◆ Bonus or incentive plans.
- ◆ Stock options.
- ◆ Health plan.

Also check with HR at your old job to make sure that you aren't forfeiting a bonus or incentive check by leaving. Sometimes just postponing your departure a few weeks can make a big difference.

Transferring Retirement Accounts

As we mentioned in Chapter 5, you have three options with your 401(k) plan when you change jobs:

1. Keep it with your previous employer, if it will allow you to do so (and many do).

2. Transfer it to your new employer, provided that it is willing to take your assets (almost all will).

3. Create an IRA rollover with a bank or broker.

If you choose option #2 or #3, remember that you have only 60 days to get this done; otherwise, the Feds will assume you are taking a distribution and hit you with taxes and, potentially, penalties. Given the choice, most people are most comfortable with option #2; when people leave a firm, they like it to be a clean break. Option #3 is really for those who can't do #2 or #1.

So You're Your Own Boss

If you are self-employed, you have to provide for yourself benefits that employers normally provide, such as retirement planning and health insurance. You should also carefully research all aspects of working from home. You'll want to maximize your business tax deductions to offset the fringe benefits lost when you leave an employer to set up your own business, such as health insurance, pension plan, sick leave, and vacations.

Setting Up Your Own Retirement Plan

One great way to both reduce your taxes and provide an important employment benefit for yourself is to set up your own retirement plan. As we discussed in Chapter 5, you can choose from the following plans:

- SEP-IRA

- SIMPLE-IRA

- Keogh (which will probably be referred to by your banker simply as a defined contribution plan, or D.C.)

- Owner-only 401(k)

Fiscal Facts

When you work for a company that provides health insurance, retirement plans, and other benefits, these fringe benefits are worth between 25 percent to 50 percent of your salary. If your salary is $40,000, for example, your benefits are worth between $10,000 and $20,000.

(Source: Paul and Sarah Edwards, authors of Working from Home, *G.P. Putnam's Sons, 1994)*

Any bank, mutual fund or brokerage firm, or insurance company will be delighted to provide you with the forms you need to open these plans—especially if you are thinking of keeping your assets with their institution. SEPs and SIMPLEs are very easy to open yourself, but you'll need help with the rather complicated paperwork required to set up a Keogh. For the owner-only 401(k) plans, contact Pioneer or Merrill Lynch and ask about the Uni-K.

If you've been self-employed for a while but haven't gotten around to setting up your retirement plan, boy, have you been missing out on a major deduction on your federal income tax!

Let's look at each of these plans individually, and with the ramifications of the 2001 tax law in mind.

SEP-IRAs are for small businesses and self-employed people. For 2001, the maximum contribution was $25,500. For 2002, the maximum contribution jumps to $40,000; however, only $30,000 is tax-deductible (pending a redecision or clarification in Congress).

SIMPLE-IRAs are another option for small-business workers and their employers. Here is the scheme for tax-deductible contributions through 2006:

Year	Under Age 50	Over Age 50
2002	$7,000	$7,500
2003	8,000	9,000
2004	9,000	10,500
2005	10,000	12,000
2006+	10,000	12,500

Keoghs, for self-employed people, rise from $35,000 to $40,000 in 2002.

For 401(k) plans, used by corporate employees; 403(b) plans, used by employees working for nonprofits and educational institutions; and 457 plans, used by state and local government employees, the scheme is as follows:

Year	Under Age 50	Over Age 50
2002	$11,000	$12,000
2003	12,000	14,000
2004	13,000	16,000
2005	14,000	18,000
2006+	15,000	20,000

The owner-only 401(k) is, as the name implies, ideal for the sole owner/employee of a business and his/her spouse. Like regular 401(k)s, it has two pieces: the employee contribution and the employer contribution, only in this case the employee and the employer are the same person! The employee contributions are the same as those in the previous chart for 401(k)s. In other words, the maximum contribution for 2002 from the employee would be $11,000. The maximum contribution from the employer is up to 25 percent of compensation (maxing out at $200,000). The limit of the two contributions—employee and employer—is $40,000 for 2002, which is equal to or greater than that of any other plan for sole proprietors. And the total sum, of course, is tax deductible. It's a good deal for toiling entrepreneurs.

We believe the Uni-K Plan to be the superior owner-only 401(k) plan presently available. Pioneer Investment Management USA Inc. is the trustee. Pioneer is an old-line firm, founded in Boston in 1928 at the birth of the mutual fund concept. If you are a sole proprietor interested in this plan, you can contact Pioneer directly but must work with a financial adviser, such as Merrill Lynch.

Mutual funds are the only products you can select for your Uni-K plan and they can be chosen individually from a selection of Pioneer, Merrill, AIM, Oppenhemier, and Alliance funds, or via portfolio groups (e.g., Aggressive Growth, Growth, Income, and so on).

We can't emphasize enough the importance of the Economic Growth and Tax Relief Reconciliation Act of 2001 for investors. You can now keep more of the income you earn and further reduce your taxes by contributing more and more to retirement plans over the next four years. What more incentive do you need to save and invest for your retirement? Get going already!

Investor's Idiom

Net earnings from self-employment are the amount of income on which you pay self-employment tax, minus the tax itself. Self-employment taxes are what self-employed people have to pay into Social Security because they don't have an employer contributing on their behalf.

People who hit the magic age 70½ trigger for required IRA distribution are often confused by the IRS distribution tables. Now the IRS comes to the rescue: Starting January 31, 2003, your financial institution will have to report to you exactly how much, at minimum, you must withdraw each year.

Anyway, if you take advantage of this situation, you can slice your taxes and build a strong retirement account at the same time. Let's say your *net earnings* on self-employment—after you deduct business and home-office deductions and the self-employment tax—are $25,000 and your federal income tax rate is 27 percent. Your federal income tax will be $25,000 × .27, or $6,750.

Now, what if you invest 15 percent of that $25,000 in a SEP-IRA? You would invest $25,000 × .15, or $3,750. And you can deduct that $3,750 from the $25,000 you earned, so now you owe federal income tax on just $21,250. Gosh, your tax rate just dropped from 27 percent to 15 percent because that deduction dropped you into a lower tax bracket. Now the amount of federal income tax you owe is only $21,250 × .15, or $3,187.50. That's a lot easier to fork over to Uncle Sam than $6,750, plus you've tucked away $3,750 to grow tax-deferred until you retire.

Super Strategy
If you are self-employed and haven't opened a SEP or SIMPLE account yet, get thee to a bank immediately! You are missing out on a huge opportunity to shelter your hard-earned bucks from Uncle Sam. If you invest the maximum allowable percentage of your earnings in a SEP-IRA, for example, you can deduct your entire investment from your income. This swift move will slice your income tax, plus that precious money is now sheltered under an IRA where it can grow peacefully tax-deferred until you retire.

Retirement ... at Last!

Whether you work for a big corporation or yourself, if you're doing well, you may be tempted to consider retiring early. Should you retire early? It sounds great, but remember:

1. Your benefits from Social Security and your employer's retirement plan will be reduced or even become nonexistent, depending on when you decide to retire. This means your own retirement portfolio will have to be that much larger.

2. Retiring early means your retirement dollars will have to last longer. Again, this means you'll need to accumulate more assets that will generate retirement income.

Fiscal Facts

Where do your Social Security tax dollars go? Out of every $1 ...

 ◆ 70¢ goes to a trust fund to pay retirees.

 ◆ 19¢ goes to a trust fund to pay Medicare beneficiaries.

 ◆ 11¢ goes to a trust fund to pay benefits to qualified disabled people.

How the Retirement Age You Choose Affects Social Security

Let's look specifically at Social Security. The earliest you can start receiving benefits is age 62. And, at age 62, you will only receive about 80 percent of what you would have received had you waited until age 65 to retire.

Starting in 2003, the full retirement age will be increased in steps until it reaches age 67. Full retirement age is the age at which you can expect to get full (but not necessarily maximum) benefits. Those born in 1937 or earlier will not be affected by the increase in the full retirement age.

Those born in 1938 will have full retirement age defined as 65 years and 2 months. Add two months for each year after 1938 that you were born. For those born in 1960 and later, 67 will be the full retirement age. If you were born in 1960 and want to take early retirement at age 62, your benefit will only be 70 percent of the age 67 full benefit. Find yourself on the following table, compliments of the Social Security Administration.

Age to Receive Full Social Security Benefits

Year of Birth	Full Retirement Age
1937 or earlier	65
1938	65 and 2 months
1939	65 and 4 months
1940	65 and 6 months
1941	65 and 8 months
1942	65 and 10 months
1943–1954	66
1955	66 and 2 months
1956	66 and 4 months
1957	66 and 6 months
1958	66 and 8 months
1959	66 and 10 months
1960 and later	67

Pay Tax on Social Security Benefits? Sad, but True

Are your Social Security benefits taxable? In some cases they are. Here's the gist of it:

If you file your federal tax return as an individual and your combined income is between $25,000 and $34,000, you may have to pay taxes on 50 percent of your Social Security benefits. If your *combined income* is above $34,000, up to 85 percent of your Social Security benefits are subject to tax. If you file a joint return, the numbers are between $32,000 and $44,000 (up to 50 percent) and over $44,000 (up to 85 percent).

About 20 percent of the people receiving Social Security pay taxes on their benefits. Each year recipients receive a Social Security Benefit Statement (Form SSA-1099). Use this form when filling out your federal income tax to determine if any of your benefits are subject to tax.

Investor's Idiom

Combined income is adjusted gross income (remember that?) plus nontaxable interest (interest on municipal bonds, for example) plus half of your Social Security benefits. It's just another way to hit up the fat cats!

Can You Work and Still Collect Social Security?

Can you work and still get all your Social Security benefits? It depends on your age and the amount. If you are under 65, the earnings limit is $11,280. And "earnings" are limited to wages and self-employment income. Income from investments and other sources is excluded.

What happens if you earn more than that? Your Social Security check will be cut by one dollar for every two dollars you earn over the limit. Another reason to think twice about retiring early! For those who have attained full retirement age (FRA), there is no retirement earnings test, thanks to the Senior Citizens' Freedom to Work Act of 2000! This means that your social security check amount is not reduced. You may still have to pay taxes, however, on the amount.

Advantages to Delaying Retirement

What if you choose to delay retirement? There are some advantages. Depending on when you were born, your eventual annual Social Security benefits will be increased from 5 percent (for those born before 1933) to 8 percent (for those born in 1943 or later). But, if you do decide to retire after age 65, please sign up for Medicare anyway at age 65; otherwise, your medical insurance could cost more.

Your spouse is also eligible to receive benefits at his or her full retirement age, which is currently 65. How much? Either 50 percent of your benefits or his or her actual earned benefits, whichever is higher. Your spouse can begin collecting benefits as early as age 62, but they will be reduced roughly 4 percent per year before full retirement age.

When and How to Apply for Your S.S. Benefits

Apply for Social Security benefits three months before the date you want the benefits to start. The Social Security Administration recommends that you discuss your plans with one of their representatives the year before you plan to retire.

Remember, the rules are not simple or straightforward, and are subject to change. What do you need to apply for benefits? Plan on having to present the following:

◆ Your Social Security number

◆ Your birth certificate (original or certified copy)

◆ Your latest W-2 or self-employment tax return

◆ Your military discharge papers

◆ Your bank name and account number (if you want to arrange direct deposit of your benefits)

How Does Medicare Work?

We've mentioned Medicare a few times. What's that all about? Medicare is a federal health insurance plan for people 65 and older (plus people qualified as being disabled, regardless of age). Medicare is divided into two parts: Part A and Part B. Part A is hospital insurance and Part B is for medical insurance—it covers doctor visits and other nonhospital expenses.

Part A and a Hospital Stay

Part A is what a portion of the Social Security deductions from your paycheck were going to for all those years. So you have already paid for it. However, "it" does not cover all of your hospital room and board charge. The difference is covered by coinsurance payments that either you or your insurance company must pay. You will also have to cover an annual deductible. If you arrange for your Social Security benefits to begin at age 65, you are automatically enrolled in Medicare Part A. If you choose to retire after your 65th birthday, be sure to sign up for Medicare at age 65; otherwise you won't be enrolled in Medicare Part A.

How to Pay for the Expenses Medicare Doesn't Cover

Part B of Medicare is optional. "Optional" is a misleading word, however, because you will be automatically enrolled—and the premium deducted from your monthly Social Security benefit check—unless you proactively opt out. If you opt in, the premium will not cover all your expenses. What's missing?

First there is an annual deductible. Second, in many instances, there is an 80/20 split: Medicare pays 80 percent, and you (or your insurance company) pay the remaining 20 percent. The question becomes this: Do you want to pay for the necessary coinsurance, or do you want to select one of the 10 existing Medicare supplement policies? If you choose one of the latter, they basically cover your coinsurance for both parts A and B, but charge you a premium. But wait, there's a third option: You can go the HMO route. The HMOs are cheaper but restrict you to specific doctors and procedures.

Crash Alert

Retiree health insurance offered by your employer may be another option you can use to cover the gap in Medicare coverage. Carefully check to make sure, however, that your employer's retiree health insurance being offered will provide the same benefits and roughly the same coverage you enjoy now. If not, you could end up in a pickle, looking for insurance at age 70 to 75 with possible pre-existing conditions. This client profile does not appeal to insurance companies.

Medicare Is in Flux

Medicare is in the process of being restructured and refinanced, which for you will mean higher premiums, deductibles, coinsurance, and so on.

If you want more information on Medicare, call Social Security at 1-800-772-1213 and request Publication No. 05-10043 (Medicare), which explains Medicare hospital and medical insurance.

We also recommend an excellent article in the September 1998 issue of *Consumer Reports* entitled "Medicare: New Choices, New Worries." Reprints of this special report are available for $3 per copy. Call 1-800-766-9988 or visit *Consumer Reports* online at www.consumerreports.org.

What About Lump-Sum Retirement Benefits?

When you do announce your retirement, your employer may very well offer you the option of receiving your defined benefit annuity in a single lump-sum payment. Essentially, your employer will take an interest rate provided by the federal government and apply it to your monthly benefit. You can either reject the option, or take the lump sum and turn it over to an insurance company, or invest it yourself. Just remember to confirm that your monthly income is going to be noticeably increased by going the lump-sum route. If that's not the case, sit back, relax, and enjoy the monthly checks from your employer's plan administrator.

Taking Your Home as a "Lump Sum"

Much has been written about a strategy where a bank or mortgage company buys your home (freeing up capital for you), and you pay the equivalent of a lease or rental fee. In other words, you would free up equity in your home while still enjoying living there. Although this is a reasonable option, we think you should give at least equal weight to the idea of selling your home and "downsizing" into a residence that is less expensive to own and maintain. Check with your local realtor to see whether either of these options—or just staying put—makes the most sense (and dollars) to you.

The Least You Need to Know

- When you start a new job, ask right away about the company's pension and 401(k) plans, incentive plans, stock options, and health plans.

- If you're self-employed, any bank, mutual fund firm, brokerage, or insurance company will be happy to help you set up your own retirement plan.

- Starting in 2003, the full retirement age will be increased in steps until it reaches 67.

- If your combined income is over $34,000, up to 85 percent of your Social Security benefits may be taxed.

- You will need some form of health insurance after retirement to cover expenses not paid by Medicare.

Chapter 14

The Ramifications of Romance

In This Chapter

- ◆ Using a prenup to avoid financial disaster
- ◆ Should you keep bank accounts and investments separate?
- ◆ The marriage tax
- ◆ Untangling assets after divorce

It's hard to think about money and love at the same time—but both have the ability to make us either turn green and act nuts or feel very secure and happy. Money and love are inescapably intertwined once two people marry. Every financial move you make is affected by your marital status, from how you choose to bank and invest, to how you protect your assets and the amount of tax you pay. In this chapter, we will go over the financial ramifications of romance.

When You Need a Prenup

We've all been bombarded with tabloid tales about this or that wealthy celebrity who invokes a prenuptial agreement when the wedding of the year turns into the divorce of the decade. What is a prenup, exactly? A *prenuptial agreement* is a legal document, signed by both parties, stating "that is yours and this is mine." With roughly half of all marriages ending in divorce, and with roughly half of the assets usually going to each party, you can understand why a wealthy spouse whose mate is not exactly flush would demand a prenup.

> **Investor's Idiom**
>
> A **prenuptial** agreement is a legally binding document signed by two people before they get married. Most prenuptial agreements simply spell out who owns what and who will get what in the event the marriage ends in a divorce. A few prenuptial agreements that have made the news lately go into great detail, even specifying how often the couple will have sex or see their in-laws!

But what about you? You're going to tell us you're not wealthy, but are you bringing something into the marriage that could eventually represent substantial wealth? A patented idea? Shares in your business—which could grow to become a regional or national chain? The great American novel in your desk drawer that finally finds its way to a supportive publisher? And what about those personal items handed down from generation to generation in your family? Or how about stock options that have no particular value at the time of marriage but will be worth a great deal some years hence?

What Can Happen If You Don't Have a Prenup

Without a prenuptial agreement, you and your spouse will be subject to the property-settlement laws of the state in which you reside. In eight states (Arizona, California, Idaho, Louisiana, Nevada, New Mexico, Texas, and Washington) all assets ruled to be marital property by the court will be split 50-50—even if one partner earned all the money.

In the other states, marital property division is up to the judge. And, surprisingly, even assets acquired before the marriage, such as a house, stock, or even a business are thrown into the pot. In some states, even a professional degree earned during a marriage is included. If you become a doctor, lawyer, or accountant during the marriage, for example, your spouse might be able to claim half your earnings stemming from that degree.

We are not suggesting you turn to your spouse and say, "Honey, we need a prenup." That's a hard sell, and frankly, after you're married it's too late. It's even too late if you wait until just before the wedding. Many courts will throw out a prenup that one party can prove he or she was pressured to sign because the wedding was already planned.

But before your marriage, be it your first, third, or fifth, we suggest you talk seriously with your lawyer about a prenuptial agreement. This applies to women as well as men; if you and/or your soon-to-be spouse have or expect to earn a lot of money, hammer out a prenup before you say "I do." It could save a lot of pain and anguish later on.

The Marriage Tax

The tax code was drawn up back in the day when one spouse worked and the other (guess which one?) stayed home and took care of the kids. So marriage got a favorable treatment under the tax code. The numbers looked roughly like this:

Status	Taxable Income	Tax Due
Single	$50,000	$10,880
Married, Filing Jointly	$50,000	$8,787

Today, both spouses are much more likely to work, yet the marriage tax break persists—but it only works for families with one breadwinner. Working couples who get married get slammed. Take a look at how two people, both with taxable income of $50,000, will be affected if they get married and both continue to work:

Status	Income Total	Income/Income Tax
Two Single People	$50,000 + $50,000 =	$100,000/$20,752
Married, Filing Jointly	$100,000 =	$100,000/$21,864
Married, Filing Sep.	$50,000 + $50,000 =	$100,000/$21,864

A couple will be penalized $1,112 if they get married! Clearly, if you are both going to work, the tax code suggests that you don't get married. The Economic Growth & Tax Reconciliation Act of 2001 was touted as offering some relief from the "marriage penalty" by increasing the standard deduction for married filers and increasing the 15 percent tax bracket to include more married filers' income. But read the fine print: These changes won't be phased in until 2005, with the major impact held back until 2008. If this offends you (and it should), write to your congressional representatives.

Joint Bank Accounts

You may be penalized on your income tax if you get married, but at least it's cheaper to bank. Unless one of you is living a secret life or the two of you have trouble communicating, there is no reason to keep separate checking accounts.

The main advantage of one vs. several checking accounts is the savings on monthly service charges and fees. In addition, if you have the type of account that pays a minimum interest rate for minimum balances, it's obviously easier to meet the minimum balance requirement when you combine assets in one account. An exception needs to be made if you are a principal or sole proprietor of a business; in that case, a separate business checking account is a must.

Crash Alert

If you and your spouse decide to share a checking account, we can't stress enough the importance of communication. Make it a habit to go over checks written and deposits/withdrawals made on a daily basis to avoid messy and expensive overdraft charges. And if your marriage should fall on the rocks and you separate, immediately dissolve any joint checking accounts.

Super Strategy

If you and your spouse separate, make no changes in the joint ownership of your taxable accounts. You don't want to pay taxes if there is the slightest chance of a reconciliation. If you proceed to divorce, your assets will be separated as part of the terms of the divorce decree.

Should You Keep Separate Investment Portfolios?

Whether you keep separate or joint investment portfolios depends on the type of account. Some accounts, like IRAs, must be legally kept separate. The same applies to any 401(k) or 403(b) retirement plan, or a defined benefit (pension) plan: The employee is the sole legal owner.

For taxable accounts, however, a joint name is preferable, for three reasons.

1. Most investment advisors and planners charge a fee based on a percentage of your assets, and the greater the assets the lower the fee. An advisor may charge 2 percent to manage $500,000, and only 1 percent on $1 million, for example. Also, most, if not all, financial planners charge a minimum dollar fee, and you wouldn't want to pay two minimum fees.

2. Even if you don't use an investment advisor or counselor, it's still easier to balance and manage a single portfolio, rather than two or more. We strongly suggest you stick with one broker for the same reason. Less confusing!

3. One spouse is usually going to be less investment savvy than the other. The spouse who takes less naturally to investing is always going to be tempted to say, "Oh, I let Fred/Mary take care of that." But what happens to that spouse if financially astute Fred or Mary is no longer around? Far too many elderly widows have found themselves in exactly this vulnerable position, easy prey to the

con artists who unfortunately exist in the investment business. Joint ownership confers upon the other party both the right and the obligation to know what is going on with their investments.

Untangling Your Assets During Divorce

Suppose you have moved, gradually or precipitously, from blissful wedlock to separate padlocks. Who gets what and how? Generally, you (and your lawyer) will look to the laws of the state in which you plan to file for divorce. As we mentioned, eight states split all marital assets 50–50. Some states will favor the wife, especially if she is non-working and a mother.

Handling the House

How easy or difficult the division of property will be depends upon the complexity of the assets and the attitudes of the individuals getting divorced. But, as a general rule, estimate the value of each asset and assume that each party will get half.

For many couples, their home is their biggest asset. To divide this asset or give it to one party, you'll need to have it appraised. One of the first calls you should make, therefore, is to your realtor. And don't even bother with secrecy; everyone probably knows what's happened.

Divvying Up Other Assets

The most difficult types of assets to deal with are family heirlooms and compensation-related issues like stock options and family businesses.

♦ First, you should each make a list of your individual assets and place a fair market value on each (to the best of your ability).

♦ Next, you and your lawyer should sit down with your soon-to-be ex-spouse and his or her lawyer to reconcile any differences.

Family heirlooms that have been in your family will generally go to you; but you may or may not have to give up something in return. A lot depends on your spouse's attitude.

Stock options are a bear: What were they worth at the time of the marriage? What are they worth now? What could they be worth? Just give your lawyer the facts and let him or her deal with the issue. If it can be negotiated, great; if not, you may have to litigate. State laws vary on this specific asset, but best to assume that stock options are one of the marital assets subject to distribution in a divorce. If it turns out otherwise, lucky you.

Provide your lawyer with the date and amount of options granted, and the date and price at which they can be exercised. You'll also need to obtain, in writing, a statement from your employer regarding whether the options are a basic part of your compensation package, or an incentive for future efforts.

QDROs—How to Split Retirement Assets When You Split

QDRO stands for Qualified Domestic Relations Order and it spells out how the assets held in pension and 401(k), 403(b), and 457 plans will be split in a divorce. They do not cover IRAs.

If you and your soon-to-be-ex can agree on how to split retirement assets (in a dollar or percent split), check with your plan administrator to obtain the necessary forms. Once completed, these become an official part of the divorce agreement, so be sure the divorce judge gets a copy. QDROs were created by the Employment Retirement Income Security Act of 1974, which means they are federal law and trump any IRS ruling, any prenup, and even any local judicial ruling.

You don't have to resort to QDROs if you can come up with other means of fairly dividing assets (e.g. "You keep the house; I'll keep the pension"). But when that's not possible, a QDRO is a smart alternative. In a simple, straightforward fashion, a QDRO directs the plan administrator to distribute X dollars or Y percent to the other spouse. Ideally it would be used to create or add to an IRA Rollover Account. Without it the recipient of funds from a split of retirement plan assets would be subject to federal taxes and in some cases even an early withdrawal penalty. Forewarned is forearmed!

Negotiate with Your Head, Not Your Spleen

If you've seen the movie "The War of the Roses," you have some inkling of the dark side of divorce. Sometimes two people can be zipping through an amicable divorce until she decides she wants half of the Simon and Garfunkel collection and he insists on keeping the dog—with no visitation rights. And then comes that killer statement: "Well, if you're going to be that way …," and everything unravels.

The chances that you and your lawyer are going to pull the wool over the eyes of your spouse and his or her lawyer are pretty small. So, be reasonable and fair. Where there is an asset or issue that you feel quite strongly about, be firm but convey the firmness via your lawyer. The more obstreperous things become, the longer the process takes, and lawyers charge by the hour. It's your money.

Unless you have a very amicable divorce pending (whatever that is), move out of the house immediately. You can arrange to come back and do your inventory and obtain necessary clothing at a mutually agreed upon time and date. It's a good idea to agree on that time and date before leaving.

Super Strategy

Divorce between two working spouses without children is (or should be) straightforward. Add a child or children and emotional pain enters the equation. Change one spouse to nonworking, add children and a long marriage, and you have a really difficult situation. But our advice is the same in every divorce situation: Keep your cool, be fair, be firm when you feel strongly about an issue or asset, and keep it lawyer to lawyer.

Other Divorce Options

Before you go the divorce route, please try a separation (legal or informal). With a little time and a little space, along with a fuller understanding of the dollar and emotional costs involved, many marriages can be repaired. Joint therapy and/or marriage counseling can also help repair the torn fabric of a marriage.

If divorce is inevitable and feelings are amicable, think about "no-fault" divorce. The two of you simply go before the judge and say it was no one's fault that the marriage failed. This can save a lot in legal fees, and you'll be unhitched that much faster.

The Least You Need to Know

- You need a prenuptial agreement if you are bringing anything into a marriage that could eventually represent substantial wealth.

- If you don't have a prenup, you will be subject to the property settlement laws of your state if you get divorced.

- If both you and your intended work, the tax code will actually penalize you for getting married.

- Married couples should keep their tax-deferred retirement accounts separate but share taxable investment accounts jointly.

- Don't forget about QDROs!

Chapter 15

Home Ownership: What You Need to Know

In This Chapter

- ◆ Down payment do's and don'ts
- ◆ Timing the real estate market
- ◆ Owning vs. renting
- ◆ Choosing between fixed-rate and adjustable-rate mortgages

Most everyone starts adult life renting rather than owning. The reason is simple: It's cheaper! Initially, you may not even be able to afford to rent on your own, hence your roommates and their socks on the living room floor. But some 5 to 10 years after you enter the work force, with perhaps marriage and children either present or on the way, the subject of purchasing your own home needs to be reviewed. In this chapter we will run you through key questions to ask yourself before you make the big life change from lowly renter to king or queen of your castle.

The Down Payment

Do you have the down payment necessary to buy a home? You will need to put down at least 10 percent, and in some cases up to 20 percent, of the purchase price of the home in order to obtain mortgage approval. There are also some first-time home-buyer programs that don't require such high downpayments—for example, VA loans and HUD programs.

Here are the best sources for your down payment, in order of preference:

♦ Savings. You planned ahead by putting aside the savings for 10 percent down, and you're ready to go.

♦ A loan from good old Mom and Dad (or your spouse's mom and dad). "We can pay it back at our convenience? At 0 percent interest?" Or how 'bout: "It's a gift? We couldn't possibly … well, if you insist!"

> **Super Strategy**
>
> Consider moving through a series of steps toward owning your dream home. Most people end up doing this: rental to condo to town house to starter home to the big comfy house in the 'burbs. Skipping any of these steps may leave you financially strapped.

♦ Tapping your retirement plans (Roth IRA, 401(k), etc.). Borrowing from the Roth IRA is preferable. If you borrow from your 401(k), it's considered a loan that you must pay back.

Do not borrow the money for your down payment. The cost of carrying what amounts to a first and second mortgage will most likely overtax you financially. If you approach your mortgage banker already carrying a debt like that, you might be turned down for the mortgage, anyway.

Timing Is Everything

The next question to ask is: What's the real estate market like? Hot, medium, or cold? If it's hot, you run the risk of paying inflated prices, potentially coming in at the top of the market. This translates to a higher down payment and higher monthly payments (principal, interest, and, in many cases, real estate taxes). If you then have to move for any reason, you run the risk of having to sell at a loss.

If possible, follow your local real estate market for several years before even considering home ownership. Most local newspapers carry charts or tables that show you whether home sales in your area are trending up or down, and to what degree. You can also get a feel by going to open houses and requesting sales literature on around a dozen homes that might meet your needs.

Specifically, you'll want to observe two indicators:

♦ Has the asking price been reduced, and, if yes, how much and how many times?

♦ How many days has the house been on the market?

In a "hot" market, homes are gobbled up in a matter of days, and the buyer pays the asking price. In a really hot market, with two or more buyers vying for the same property, the "winner" ends up paying more than the asking price. You definitely do not want to make your first home purchase in this environment.

You should also check out mortgage interest rates, but home prices are a more important indicator of whether or not it's the right time to buy. High mortgage rates and high home prices often go hand-in-hand—but not always. Seven years ago the trend was higher mortgage rates and lower home prices. Starting around August 1998, on the other hand, we saw lower mortgage rates and higher home prices. That trend is still in place as of this writing, with 40-year lows in mortgage rates and historically high home prices.

Re-Fi Mania

With current mortgage rates so low, refinancing has become an effective way to reduce household expense. But when and how should you refinance? Here's how to figure that out:

1. Total all your closing costs (document fees, appraisal, Title, etc.). Exclude the one month interest you'll be charged (interest is paid in arrears), because you'll make that up with a one month "holiday" on the new mortgage.

2. Deduct the new proposed monthly principal and interest payments from the existing P&I.

3. Divide 2 into 1. If the number is 12 (one year) or less, go for it. If above 24, forget it (remember, the average person only lives in his/her home for five years).

> **Super Strategy**
>
> A good rule of thumb: If you can handle the monthly payments on the home you want and you think it's selling at a good price, don't concern yourself with mortgage rates. Just focus on home prices. Don't forget, you can always re-finance your mortgage if and when rates fall.

Evaluate Your Mortgage-Worthiness Before a Banker Does

Once you start to keep tabs on the real estate market, make it a point to sit down with a mortgage banker and determine what he or she looks for in a successful applicant, so you can compare that profile to your present situation. If you can't find a mortgage banker willing to do this, go to a knowledgeable and experienced real estate broker. Basically, if you present your personal balance sheet and income statement (which you learned how to create in Chapter 4), the expert can tell you if you could qualify for a mortgage and how large a mortgage you could handle. If you don't qualify, you can spend the next few years both following the local real estate market and getting in better financial shape.

Compare Renting to Owning

If you are thinking about buying a home, sit down and calculate the total cost of home ownership vs. renting. When you rent, you pay a monthly rental fee and utilities. You may also pay for parking and laundry. That's about it. Home ownership, on the other hand, is not just about a monthly mortgage payment and taxes. There are many expenses you may not have considered, such as:

- Outside maintenance—yard work, painting, and equipment such as a lawn mower and leaf and snow blowers.

- Inside maintenance—carpet cleaning, floor sanding and coating, appliance maintenance, plumbing repairs, painting, and papering.

- Major repairs and replacements. Retain an inspection service to ascertain the expected life of your hot water heater, roof, siding, deck, etc. People stay in one home an average of five years, so for anything that will probably need to be replaced within five years, determine the cost and divide it by 60. Add this cost to your monthly payments.

On the bright side, your interest and taxes on a home are tax deductible, and you are gradually building up equity (ownership!) in your home. In addition, you won't be hit with yearly rent increases.

Over Time, Owning Should Save You Money

It's hard to come up with a specific example that is applicable to everyone, so let's make some broad assumptions and compare renting to owning over a 60-month (five-year) time frame:

Per Month	Rent	Purchase
Rent: $2,000 x (4% annual increase ÷ 2) =	$2,217	
Parking	160	
Utilities	100	$200
Laundry	24	12
Principal and Interest*		1,231
Transportation	50	200
Maintenance		100
Homeowners Insurance		50
Repairs		250
Taxes		300
Tax/Interest Deductions = 1,300 + 300 × .31 = 496 × .12 =		−41
Totals	2,551	2,302

Assumptions: $225,000 purchase price, 10% down, the balance financed at 6¼% over 30 years.

In this example, we have a pretty clear-cut case favoring purchase. Your case may be different.

Renting Pluses

Although it's generally considered preferable to buy, continuing to rent is definitely preferable to buying the wrong home at the wrong price at the wrong time in the real estate market. That's why we suggest spending several years watching the market and getting a feel for what constitutes a bargain in your price range and your area.

Owning your own home has always been considered part of the American Dream, but for people who bought when the real estate market peaked in the 1980s and suffered huge losses when they needed to move, the American Dream turned into a nightmare. That may be the case right now.

Remember, you're in charge; you decide when the time is right, and another year or two in a rental is not the end of the world. Be cool.

Fiscal Facts

The Consumer Price Index (CPI) is a group of prices that are followed by economists in order to gauge whether inflation is on the rise or waning. The CPI is probably the most well-known and widely reported inflation number we have. What is not well-known is that housing prices for both rental and owned residences makes up 40 percent of the CPI.

How Much of Your Income Should You Spend on Housing?

Twenty-five percent of your gross income is a reasonable sum to spend on housing. Some experts use up to 33 percent or even 50 percent, but let's be conservative! Our recommendation means that someone earning $100,000 can afford roughly $2,000 per month for housing. Assuming a 6¼ percent mortgage rate and a 30-year mortgage, principal and interest would equate to roughly $1,539 per month on a $250,000 mortgage, leaving $461 per month for taxes. That feels about right. And with 10 percent down and closing costs, you're looking at a $275,000 purchase. Naturally, taxes vary, as do home prices and what you get for your money. That $275,000 probably buys you a lot in Nebraska or North Dakota, but little (if anything) in San Diego, Boston, Chicago or New York City.

Fixed Rate vs. Adjustable Rate Mortgage

Your mortgage banker may offer you a choice between the following:

- A fixed-rate mortgage that locks you into a given interest rate for the life of the mortgage, which is traditionally 30 years
- An adjustable rate mortgage.

How long you intend to stay in the house is the key to your decision. An adjustable rate mortgage can be a good deal if you plan to stay in your house for no more than five years, and if the rate is sufficiently below the rate for a 30-year fixed-rate mortgage. If the adjustable rate is not at least 200 basis points (2.0 percent) below the 30-year rate, it's not worth the risk of escalating interest rates to commit to it. Right now, for example, short-term and long-term interest rates are all very low and there's not much difference between them, so fewer new homeowners are taking out adjustable rate mortgages.

I.O. for U.?

I.O. (Interest only) mortgages are the latest product in home financing. As the name implies, the monthly payments are for interest only, with nothing going to pay down the mortgage. Here is a comparison of an I.O.U. vs. an ARM. In each case, the principal amount being financed is $200,000, the mortgage rate is 5⅛ percent, and the fixed term is five years.

	I.O.	ARM	Difference
Monthly payment	$854	$1,089	-$235
Five-year totals	$51,240	$65,338	-$14,098
Mortgage reduction	—	$16,019	+$16,019

Even if we assume that the $235 monthly difference is invested at e.g. 5 percent per annum, the total of approximately $15,900 is still slightly below the mortgage paydown of the ARM. So, are there any circumstances in which the I.O. would be preferable to an ARM? Yes, two:

◆ The I.O. allows you to qualify for a larger mortgage or a more expensive home. In some cases, it could be the only way you could qualify.

◆ If you have no other means to fully commit dollars to your 401(k), 403(b), or 457 plan, or your IRA or emergency fund, etc., then maybe this is a good option. But you risk just spending the difference. Be careful that the I.O. doesn't just become another I.O.U.

Investor's Idiom

An **adjustable-rate mortgage (ARM)** is priced off the yield for the 10-year Treasury note. Since the yield on the note changes every six-to-twelve months, so will the interest rate on your ARM. And when short-term rates are lower than long-term rates, you may get a better deal with an ARM than with a long-term fixed mortgage. How much the ARM rate fluctuates over the duration of your mortgage depends on interest rates in general and the product itself. Most ARMs have a lifetime cap, above which the rate cannot rise.

You can also get three-year, five-year, or seven-year ARM's that lock in a fixed rate for three, five, or seven years, and then revert to an ARM. If you think rates are at or near their lows, these are much better than the traditional ARM with a "teaser" 6-to-12 month low rate.

The Costs of Closing

When you buy your first home, be prepared to cover closing costs of around 3 percent of the price of the house before the keys are yours. Closing costs vary from state to state, depending on whether the state says attorneys are required to handle the closing and on real estate tax rates.

Following is a summary of a typical closing statement. As you can see, there are columns for the borrower (buyer) and seller. Looking just at the columns pertaining to the buyer, we see that the buyer ends up paying over $6,000 in closing/settlement costs.

Line:

Line		Amount	Description
101	Contract sales price	$252,000.00	The amount you agreed to pay for the home
103	Settlement charges	6,384.81	Detailed below
120	Gross amount due from buyer	258,384.81	Total of lines 101 and 103

Less:

Line		Amount	Description
201	Deposit of earnest money	25,300.00	Down payment
202	Principal amount of new loan	100,000.00	The buyer's new mortgage
220	Total paid by buyer	125,300.00	Total of lines 201 + 202
303	Additional cash from buyer	133,084.81	Sum buyer must come up with at closing Summary of Settlement Charges (Line 103)
802	Loan discount	2,000.00	Buyer paid "points" (two) to get lower mortgage rate
904	Three months real estate taxes	1,548.22	Three months real estate taxes
905		6.94	Property overlaps two municipalities
1107	Attorney's fees	950.00	For the "closing"
1108	Title insurance	1,708.00	Required
1201	Recording fees	70.00	Required
1204	Notice of settlement	16.00	Required
1303	Faxes	45.65	
1304	UPS	40.00	
1400	Total Settlement Charges	6,384.81	Lines 802–1304

Second Mortgages—Pros and Pitfalls

Once you own a home, you will be bombarded with offers to place a second mortgage on your home. Second mortgages are tax deductible, but they place you in a financial straight jacket. With a second mortgage, you sign for a fixed-rate loan for the full amount of equity in your home. You might not need or use all the money, but you sure are paying interest on it.

A home equity loan is a better deal because it is a revolving line of credit—you only pay for what you use (like a charge card), and you can still deduct the interest from your taxes. A second mortgage is either a desperation step for someone who wants to finance a dramatic career shift, or a short-term means of coming up with the down payment on your first (starter) home. Do not enter into it lightly.

Pluses to Paying Off Your Mortgage

Mortgage (or rent) represents the largest single expenditure for the average tax payer. It's wise, therefore, to try to retire your mortgage before you retire yourself. There are three ways to accomplish this:

1. Stay in your home for 15–30 years and pay off the mortgage.

2. Pay off half the mortgage, sell your home and buy a condo/town house at half the price of your former home.

3. Benefit from escalating home values. If your home rises in value 50 percent in five years, for example, sell your home and buy a condo/town house at half the price.

Should You Shorten Your Mortgage?

Moving from a 30-year to a 15-year mortgage can make a big difference. Here's an example, using a 60-month occupancy assumption and a $200,000 mortgage. The figures are very rough and just for purposes of illustration.

30-year mortgage, $6\frac{1}{4}\%$*, monthly principal & interest = $1,231

15-year mortgage, $5\frac{3}{4}\%$*, monthly principal & interest = $1,660

Difference per month = $429

Increased Equity of $429 × 60 = $25,740

*You can get a rough approximation by adding or subtracting $15 for each $\frac{1}{8}$ percent rates go up or down.

In essence, making a bigger monthly mortgage payment goes a long way toward building equity and reducing the mortgage on your property. Question: Is it better to save/invest this way as opposed to contributing $429 to your 401(k) or IRA? Probably not. In fact, if all you did was to invest $429 per month in a 4 percent tax-free municipal bond, your principal would amount to approximately $29,000 by the end of five years.

Remember in Chapter 8 when we talked about how many people make the mistake of overwithholding their taxes when it would be better for them to withhold the minimum and invest the difference? Choosing a 15-year over a 30-year mortgage is a similar situation. The 15-year mortgage just forces you to save. It might be better to take the longer mortgage and its smaller mortgage payments and invest the $429 that you save each month into a tax-deferred investment. This way you get the tax break and the benefits of compound interest. Opt for additional retirement savings, and pay the mortgage off sooner that way.

> **Fiscal Facts**
>
> There is a capital gains tax exclusion on your home of $250,000 for an individual and $500,000 for a couple. But to qualify you must have lived in the house for at least two of the past five years. Are there any exceptions? Yes! For job (transfer) or health reasons. Simply divide the number of months you actually lived in the home by 24 months (minimum required). Now multiply that figure by either $250,000 (individual) or $500,000 (joint return) to get your exclusion. Want more info? Request IRS Publication 523.

The Relocation Package

If you are moving to take a new job or because you've been transferred by a new employer, look into whether your firm offers a "relocation package." Some aspects of a relocation package may be classified as compensation, meaning you'll have to pay income tax on it, but that's still better than paying all moving expenses out of pocket. The "job relo" may include any or all of the following:

♦ Prepaid moving services

♦ Special financing rates

♦ Purchase of your existing home (and/or the sub-leasing of an apartment for you in the new area until you sell your home)

♦ A "buyer's broker" paid for by your employer

If you don't have a job relo, go to a reputable real estate firm and ask for a licensed realtor with at least five years experience. Be specific about your housing needs, such as size, style, price range, transportation, and schools. If good schools are an important part of your decision, ask the realtor for the names of the best school systems and cross-check the list with your employer. And bore in on real estate taxes. Remember, it's not the current taxes on the home that matter, it's what your tax bill will be if you purchase the property.

Should you use a "buyer's broker"? Before answering that question, let's make sure you understand who pays and who receives residential real estate commissions. A typical real estate commission of, say, 6 percent is split 3 percent to the listing broker (and his/her firm) and 3 percent to the selling broker (and his/her firm). The home seller pays the 6 percent. The selling broker is a sub-agent who represents the seller, not you. You are free to go to as many brokers as you wish to be shown properties.

> **CAUTION**
>
> **Crash Alert**
>
> Choosing the 30-year over the 15-year mortgage is financially sound if you really, truly have the discipline to invest what you would have had to pay monthly on the 15-year mortgage in your retirement account. If you find you're just spending that extra few hundred dollars a month, then opt for the 15-year mortgage.

When you use a buyer's broker, on the other hand, you sign a written contract with a specific broker who will represent you, the buyer. You, in turn, agree to only work with that broker. That 3 percent selling commission still comes from the seller's proceeds, only it goes to your buyer's broker. We think tilting the odds a little away from the seller and toward the buyer makes sense, so we recommend that you use a buyer's broker.

Renting Out Your Home When You Move

Nobody wants to be temporarily owning two homes: the one you just purchased and the one that hasn't sold yet. But that situation arises more often than not. And if the prospective buyer knows your situation, you've lost some negotiating leverage.

What to do? Well, it depends primarily on market conditions and secondarily on your particular property. If the market is strong (or even stable), the economy is decent, and you have a tract home, one to two months of patience will probably pay off. Check with your broker to make sure your home is competitively priced; this is no time to be reaching for top dollar. Chances are, you know by the number of "showings" and offers (if any) whether or not you have a problem. If the market or the economy is weak, or if you have an atypical home (say, an offbeat architectural style or a less-than-accessible location), you may want to consider renting it out or renting it with an option to buy.

If you decide to rent your property, plan on offering a one- to two-year rental; shorter-term rental tenants are less likely to take care of your property. And remember, your end objective is still to sell your home. The complication is that you have to maintain your property while being geographically removed.

Unless you already have a willing tenant, you'll need to retain a broker to list your property as a rental. Typically, they will receive, up front, 10 percent of the yearly rent.

Real Estate Agents

We've all heard stories about how Jack and Mary sold their home themselves and saved $6,000, $12,000, or $18,000. What you don't hear about are the Bills and Nancys who overpriced their home, were excluded from multiple listing and relocation sources, and had no marketing plan. Their home sat on the market for months with few showings and no offers.

Not only do you waste time in this situation, you get a reputation for having an over-priced home. When you do get showings, it may simply be brokers using your home to show how attractive another property is on a price basis. We strongly urge you to get a broker; just be sure he/she is experienced. Ask for references and determine how much property the broker has sold during each of the previous three years. A good broker is worth more than the cost of the commission. Make sure your house is presentable, and don't restrict access to potential buyers.

If you are buying, by all means sign up with a buyer's broker. As we said, it's the only way to at least partially even the odds.

Closing the Deal

In a seller's market, you will get one or more offers at or very close to your asking price in a very short period of time. Lucky you! Make sure all parties agree to your closing terms, and let the process sort out the highest bidder.

In a buyer's market, you (and your broker) will have to "walk up" the bid. A low bid may be insulting, but don't let personal feelings get in the way of a business deal. Come down a little on your asking price and see what the prospective buyer does. Chances are the buyer was just trying to judge your level of desperation. After a few more rounds of this, your broker will offer this famous phrase: "Let's split the differ-ence." Now, your soul-searching begins. Yes … no … maybe? It's a fine line between keeping the negotiations going and killing the deal. Listen to your broker, and good luck!

The Least You Need to Know

- ◆ Don't borrow the money for your down payment; you might get turned down for a mortgage.

- ◆ Try to follow your local real estate market for several years before buying a home.

- ◆ Evaluate your mortgage-worthiness before a banker does.

- ◆ Continuing to rent is definitely preferable to buying the wrong home at the wrong price and time.

- ◆ Retire your mortgage before you retire yourself.

- ◆ If you must relocate because of your job, see if you can have your company pick up the expenses of moving.

Chapter 16

Educating the Little Rascals

In This Chapter

◆ Setting up educational funds

◆ Withdrawing from a Roth IRA to pay for college

◆ The Education IRA and EE savings bonds

◆ Evaluating qualified tuition programs

When it comes to educating your children (or grandchildren), there's both good and bad news. The bad news is that college expenses are continuing to grow by at least two times the overall inflation rate in this country and the average family income. The good news is that an increasing percentage of college enrollees are getting financial aid. In addition, several options, such as the Roth IRA and the Education IRA, make saving for college easier than ever.

Expenses for college vary dramatically, depending upon whether your child attends a state school or a private college or university. Gross expenses include tuition and fees, room and board, and books and supplies. Figure on spending roughly $12,000–$15,000 per year in gross expenses for a state school, if you reside in state. Add $3,000–$4,000 if you live out of state. Ivy League schools average around $34,000—$36,000. Over the last ten years tuition costs rose at about six percent per year so you can use that figure to estimate future tuition costs.

These are just ballpark figures, of course, but they give you an idea of the magnitude of the challenge faced by families trying to put several kids through college.

Put Your Financial Security First

Many parents go into debt to pay for their children's education. This is understandable, but financially questionable. Of course, you need to try your best to provide a good education for your children. But jeopardizing your retirement assets to bolster educational assets is not the answer. As we suggested in Chapter 3, of the 10 percent you should be saving out of your salary, commit 8 percent to your retirement and 2 percent to your children's education.

> **Super Strategy**
>
> Involve your child in the decision about where to go to college by getting him or her a copy of a great reference guide: *The College Handbook*, published by the College Entrance Examination Board. The handbook profiles 3,215 colleges and will definitely get you and your soon-to-be campus star excited and motivated.

Your child has many options at age 18: college first; work, then college; work-study program; no college; the military; etc. Your retirement only has two options; either you have the money to retire or you don't. And don't forget two other issues:

♦ Where your child goes to college is driven more by his or her academic and extracurricular accomplishments than by your checking account.

♦ Your child is capable of contributing to his or her college education via summer or part-time work, and probably will be a better person for doing so.

Setting Up Educational Funds

Set up educational funds for each of your children as soon as they are born—or you can start now! There are three questions that need to be answered when setting up funds for college education:

1. Which fund or funds are most appropriate? Your best choices include:

   ♦ Traditional IRA.

   ♦ Roth IRA.

◆ Coverdell Education Savings Accounts (ESAs). These used to be called Education IRAs.

◆ EE savings bonds (alone or as part of an IRA).

◆ 529 Plans or QSTPs (Qualified State Tuition Programs).

2. What scholarships, grants, and loans are available for student expenses or reimbursement? Presently, programs available include:

◆ Hope Scholarships

◆ Pell Grants

◆ Lifetime Learning Credits

◆ Student loans

◆ Qualified tuition programs (529s)

◆ Employer-paid educational assistance

3. Finally, should the securities or other assets you intend to save be in your name or the child's name?

Let's look at the fund options first.

Using a Traditional IRA to Save for College

Presently, each working or nonworking spouse can contribute up to $3,000 per year to a traditional IRA. The contributor must have an adjusted gross income (AGI, remember that?) of under $34,000 ($54,000 for a joint return). After $34,000, the contribution's deductibility is phased out incrementally, so that by $44,000, none of it is deductible. For married filing jointly the range is from $54,000 to $64,000.

The phase-out ranges move up over the next 5 years as follows:

Year	Status:	Single	Joint
2002		$34–44,000	$54–64,000
2003		$40–50,000	$60–70,000
2004		$45–55,000	$65–75,000
2005		$50–60,000	$70–80,000
2006		$50–60,000	$75–85,000
2007+		$50–60,000	$80–100,000

Most interesting for our purposes in this chapter, the 10 percent additional tax on withdrawals from a traditional IRA before age 59½ can be waived for qualified higher education expenses. "Qualified" expenses include tuition, room and board, books, fees, and supplies. These changes put a lot more muscle in the traditional IRA, particularly when applied to educational expenses.

Advantages of the Roth IRA

The Roth IRA was introduced during the 1998 tax year. It offers some great options for families saving for college.

♦ Funds can be withdrawn tax-free after five years under certain circumstances. Previously, investment earnings were taxable at the time of withdrawal. Funds can be withdrawn tax-free:

♦ On or after age 59½

♦ For a beneficiary after the death of the contributor

♦ For a "qualified special purpose"

This includes qualified higher education expenses, as discussed above, and up to $10,000 toward the purchase of the principal residence of a first-time homeowner.

♦ There is no mandatory distribution starting at age 70½, as with traditional IRA's.

♦ You can contribute to the Roth for as long as you wish. With the traditional IRA you have to stop contributing at age 70½.

Those are the positives. There are two negatives:

♦ The total amount that an individual can contribute to a Roth and other IRAs is currently $3,000 (excluding Education IRAs—more about those in the following sections).

♦ Contributions are limited by your adjustable gross income. Once your AGI hits $95,000, the amount you can contribute starts to decline, reaching zero at $110,000. (The limits kick in between $150,000—$160,000 for joint filers.)

Coverdell Education Savings Accounts (ESAs)

Like the Roth IRA, the Education IRA was introduced in 1998. They have since been renamed Coverdell Education Savings Accounts (ESAs). Contributions are tax-deferred, but not deductible and are limited to $2,000 per year, per beneficiary (little rascal). You can make contributions annually until your little rascal(s) becomes 18. Withdrawals for qualified educational purposes are tax-free. The income eligibility for married contributors was raised by the 2002 tax law changes to $190,000. As a couple's income increases from $190,000 to $220,000, which is double the range for unmarried persons—their contribution limit phases out.

Investor's Idiom

The **Education IR** was introduced in 1998. It has since been renamed Coverdell Education Savings Accounts (ESAs). The contribution limit was raised from $500 per year per child to $2,000. You can make contributions annually until your kids hit 18. Withdrawals for qualified educational purposes are tax-free.

Patriot Bonds (formerly EE Savings Bonds)

Following the events of September 11, 2001, EE Savings Bonds were renamed The Patriot Bonds. These savings bonds can be either plugged into Coverdell ESAs or Roth IRAs, or used on their own to save for college. There are some disadvantages to using savings bonds, however:

- The yield is fixed at 90 percent of a five-year Treasury note, with the yield recalculated every six months. If Treasury note rates fall, so does the rate on your bond. If the five-year Treasury note is yielding 3.25 percent, the Patriot Bond is yielding 2.925 percent. But if six months later, the Treasury note yield drops to $2\frac{3}{4}$ percent, your bond starts earning only 2.475 percent. Of course, the yields could go up, too!

- Although you can redeem (cash in) a Patriot bond after six months, you will pay a three-month interest penalty unless you wait five years to redeem it. To avoid the penalty, you have to really plan ahead when using savings bonds for college. You'll need to stop purchasing the bonds five years before the last college bills come due.

- You also have to deal with a limit of $15,000 purchase price per purchaser per year. If you remember from our discussion of savings bonds in Chapter 11, you buy the bonds at half price and wait for them to rise to full price at maturity. So a $15,000 Patriot Bond will eventually be worth $30,000.

Patriot savings bonds do have some great advantages:

- You can purchase them with as little as $25.

- They make great gifts from relatives.

◆ The interest income on an EE savings bond is free of state and local taxes. The federal taxes on interest income are due only when the EE savings bond is redeemed. And, in some instances, there is a tax exclusion if the proceeds are being used for postsecondary education.

Cool, but how does this work? First of all, the exclusion is limited to tuition and required fees. In this case, it may not be applied to room, board, or books. Second, the bonds must be registered in the name of the taxpayer, not the child, although the child can be named as beneficiary.

In addition, the qualified tuition and fees paid must be equal to or greater than the amount of money received when the bonds are cashed in. If you pay tuition and fees of $5,000 and the bond proceeds are no more than $5,000, you're qualified for the exclusion. If tuition and fees are $4,000 and the bond proceeds are $5,000, you can deduct only that ratio ($4,000 – $5,000 = 80 percent) of the interest income on the bonds (not the principal). Don't you love how confusing the IRS can make things?

Finally, to qualify for the tax exclusion, you have to earn less than the modified AGI limits. Currently, the range of modified adjusted gross income is $83,650–$113,650 for couples filing jointly and $55,750–$70,750 for single filers. In other words, you can get full exclusion if you earn under $83,650, and partial exclusion scaling down to zero once you earn over $113,650. Did you notice that we tucked in the word "modified"?

In this case, modified AGI is AGI plus the interest earned on the redeemed bonds. Ah, the tax code! But wait: there's another neat way to use EE savings bonds for a child's college expense. Buy the bonds in the child's name and file a tax return with the child's Social Security number. Then report the accrued (earned but not received) interest income on the bonds for that year. You won't need to file again and no tax is due unless or until the child's total income exceeds the threshold for taxes owed (e.g., $650). If tax is owed, it is at the parent's rate for children under age 14 and at the child's rate at age 14 or older.

It is unfortunate that the regulations on EE savings bonds are so complicated because they have a lot to offer parents saving for college. But that's the Feds for you.

Qualified Tuition Programs (Section 529s)

Public or private schools may now establish tax-exempt prepaid tuition programs, also referred to as Section 529 Plans. Section 529 plans are accounts that may be established by anyone—parents, other relatives, or friends of the family. The investment grows tax free and distributions are tax free when used to pay for tuition and other education expenses at any accredited college or university.

This is a smart idea for grandparents, who can contribute up to $11,000 per year ($22,000 for couples) without triggering the federal gift tax. You can even make a one-time contribution of as much as $55,000 ($110,000 from a couple) and spread the gift tax exclusion over the next five years. Not a bad way for grandparents to help out and avoid estate and gift taxes.

Interestingly, unlike ESA and custodial accounts, you don't give up control of the Section 529 plan when the child reaches 18. You still control when withdrawals are taken and for what purposes. A delight for the control freaks among us!

Prior to 1998, these programs had to be state-sponsored. Withdrawals from qualified programs may be made for tuition, fees, room and board, books and supplies. And, thanks to the Tax Relief Act of 2001, these specific withdrawals are tax free. You can't contribute to both qualified tuition programs and an ESA in the same year, however.

Here's how a typical plan, the UNIQUE College Investing Plan, sponsored by the State of New Hampshire and managed by Fidelity Investments, works.

The Unique Plan works like this:

- To fund your account, you can sign up for Fidelity Automatic Account Builder (FAAB), with automatic transfers from your checking account of as little as $50 per month. All contributions must be in cash (i.e., by check). Families who don't establish automatic contribution plans can start an account with as little as $1,000.

- Your funds are invested in a "lifestyle" portfolios consisting of Fidelity Mutual Funds. Remember lifestyle funds from Chapter 12? These are funds that automatically shift the allocation of your assets between equity and fixed income as you age.

  The Fidelity portfolio is similar, in that it shifts the assets in your Unique Plan account between equity, bond, and money market funds as the beneficiary (your child) ages. A newborn might be invested 88 percent equity/12 percent bonds, while at college age the ratios might shift to 20 percent equity/40 percent bonds/40 percent short-term bonds and money market—freeing up funds to pay for college. The stock/bond ratio for your child would be dependent upon his or her age upon entering the program. Alternatively, you can invest in fixed-asset allocations.

- Fidelity uses no-load mutual funds, so the account will be charged only the operating expenses for each mutual fund. In addition, there is a fee of 0.30 percent of your account assets per year and a $30 annual maintenance fee (waived for accounts over $25,000 or if you sign up for FAAB).

♦ You can increase your monthly contributions with FAAB at any time if you start earning more money or decide that you've underestimated potential education costs.

♦ Earnings grow tax-deferred until they are distributed. If the distributions are for qualified educational expenses, they are exempt from federal income tax. This is true of federal taxes; check with your state to determine state tax status.

♦ There is no adjusted gross income (AGI) to restrict or to pre-qualify you.

♦ Multiple accounts can be opened for your child by grandparents and other relatives. Joint accounts are not allowed, however. Currently (2002), the most you can invest in each account per beneficiary is $233,240.

♦ You can change the beneficiary to another child. If you distribute the assets to someone besides the designated beneficiary, however, or if the funds are not used to pay qualified education expenses, you will be socked with state and federal taxes, as well as a 10 percent penalty.

♦ Contributions are considered completed gifts, so the value of an account won't be included in the donor's estate when he or she dies. You can also give up to $55,000 ($110,000 if filing jointly) in one year without gift tax as long as you opt to apply the $11,000 annual exclusion over five years.

♦ You can invest in both a UNIQUE Plan and a Coverdell ESA in the same year. Your child can also benefit from Hope Scholarship and Lifetime Learning Credits, which are discussed below. If you claim these credits, however, you cannot make a tax-free withdrawal to pay for the same expenses. If you do, your 529 withdrawal may be taxable.

♦ You can use the assets to pay for qualified education expenses at any accredited institution of higher learning, not just New Hampshire schools.

♦ Qualified withdrawals may also be tax-free at the state level if you are a resident of that particular state.

♦ Qualified education expenses include tuition, fees, room and board, books and supplies.

This is just a summary of the Unique Plan. You will want to delve more deeply into the matter before proceeding, but it looks pretty nifty to us. Such 529 plans were limited and not widely recognized four years ago, but they have flourished since. At present some 36 plans are available, with total assets estimated at $10 billion. In an April 3, 2002 editorial on savingforcollege.com, editor Joe Hurley predicted that total assets in 529 programs would grow from $2.5 billion at the beginning of 2001 to $25 billion by the end of 2002!

Since word is still getting out, we expect 529 plans to be the most rapidly growing asset pool of this decade. Fidelity, Vanguard, TIAA-CREF, Merrill Lynch and Salomon Smith Barney are just some of the big names offering new 529 plans.

All the plans seem to use mutual funds exclusively and offer either age-based (meaning that a pre-set stock/bond ratio is used, depending on the tyke's age, e.g., heavy on stocks at age 2; heavy in bonds at 16, or fixed-asset allocations). Finally, each plan has different fees, so shop around. We suggest you start by contacting your State Treasurer's office. You can also mine the State Treasurers' website at www.collegesavings.org. Alternatively, check out www.savingforcollege.com.

Pros and Cons of 529 Plans

Just so we are on the same page, you understand that 529s are for college and university expenses, right? Good (just checking to make sure you're awake)! Now a quick summary of the pros and cons:

Pros

1. Contributions qualify for annual gift tax exclusion.

2. Assets enjoy tax-free growth.

3. You have the option of accelerating the annual gifting provision five fold (e.g., $11,000 \times 5 = $55,000$).

4. Distributions can cover tuition, fees, books, equipment, room, and board.

5. The donor (you) has the power to change the beneficiary.

6. Payment does not have to be made directly to the school; you can reimburse the beneficiary.

Cons

1. A penalty is assessed if the funds are used for any purpose other than education.

2. Contributions must be in cash.

3. Although you can change the beneficiary, there may be gift tax consequences.

4. Whatever you give for the 529 must be deducted from your annual max ($11,000) or the five-year max ($55,000).

5. Be careful if you mix 529s with the Hope or Lifetime Learning Credits we will discuss in the next section.

Tax Breaks for Education Expenses

As we said at the beginning of this chapter, there are all kinds of ways to defray expenses for college—and more are coming on line all the time. Here's a breakdown of the ... breaks!

The Hope Scholarship Credit

Started in 1998, the Hope Scholarship Credit allows parents to take a credit against federal income taxes for tuition and related expenses. The credit is limited to the first two years of undergraduate education and consists of 100 percent of the first $1,000 of qualified expenses, and 50 percent of the second $1,000. Thus, the maximum credit you can take in the first two years is $1,500 per year. Warning: The credit is phased out for married taxpayers filing jointly with a modified AGI between $80,000 and $100,000. The credit is reduced after $80,000 and hits zero at $100,000 or more. For taxpayers who aren't filing jointly, the phase-out range is $40,000 to $50,000 Beginning in 2002, however, these ranges will be adjusted for inflation.

Lifetime Learning Credits

Lifetime Learning Credits were also introduced in 1998. These are credits you can take for education expenses that are not eligible for the Hope credit. Included are expenses incurred to acquire or improve job skills. The credit is 20 percent of expenses up to $5,000 before 2003, and $10,000 thereafter. The Lifetime has income credit phase-outs on AGI identical to the Hope.

Mix and Match Carefully

Assume you are looking at a $3,000 tuition bill (obviously, your kid is going to a state school!), and you take the Hope credit, which reduces your income taxes. But you still have to come up with $3,000. Use the 529? Wrong! You can use the 529 for the first $1,000, but the other $2,000—equal to the Hope credit—must come from some-place else: your pocket, your checking account, Aunt Martha .... If not, you owe taxes and a 10 percent penalty on the amount involved.

The Education-Loan Interest Deduction

Qualified parents can now deduct interest paid on loans taken out expressly to pay college costs—whenever paid and regardless of the age of the loan. Prior to 2002, only interest paid for the first 60 months could be deducted, with the maximum being $2,500.

2002	$3,000
2003	$3,000
2004	$4,000
2005	$4,000

After 2004, the "sun goes down," meaning it's revoked!

As usual, the deduction comes with the dreaded AGI limits, but they have been raised from a previous phaseout range of $40,000–$55,000 ($60,000–$75,000 for joint returns) to $50,000–$65,000 (doubled for married couples filing jointly). Incidentally, the interest paid is deducted "above the line," meaning you do not have to itemize to claim the deduction. What's the best choice? Be guided strictly by your AGI. If you qualify, go for the Hope/Lifetime credits; otherwise, use the tax deductions.

There is a new tax deduction, starting in 2002. You'll be able to deduct up to $3,000 in tuition payments in 2002 and 2003, and up to $4,000 in 2004 and 2005. You qualify if you AGI is under $130,000 (couples) or $65,000 (singles). There is also a $2,000 deduction for those with higher AGIs in 2004 and 2005. However … here we go again! All these tax deductions vanish in 2006.

So which is your best bet, the credits (Hope, Lifetime) or the deductions? Be guided strictly by your AGI. If you qualify, go for the Hope/Lifetime credits; otherwise, take the deductions.

The 2002 tax law also added a new benefit. Taxpayers with incomes up to $65,000 (or $130,000 on a joint return) may deduct up to $3,000 for qualified higher education courses taken in 2002. You can't claim this deduction and a tax credit for education expenses for the same student in one year, however. Expenses paid by a tax-free distribution from a Coverdell ESA, a qualified tuition program or an education savings bond are not eligible either.

Other Options

We have no intention of exploring every conceivable option for financing your kids' education in this chapter. Our intention was to primarily explore investment options.

But do take a look at two other important prospects:

◆ Student loans or so-called Stafford loans. These are available from the government's "Sallie Mae" program (www.salliemae.com, 1-888-2-SALLIE). Stafford loans are for ten years and the interest rate is set annually on July 1, based on the last 91-day T-bill auction in May. Also, you can take one opportunity to consolidate any outstanding Stafford loans. With current rates at around 4 percent, this could be a timely decision.

◆ Scholarships. First, check with the college your child wants to attend to find out whether he or she is eligible to apply for any scholarships. Definitely call local organizations such as the Rotary Club or Kiwanis, which often sponsor scholarships for deserving students. Remember that grants or scholarships do not have to be repaid, loans do. Your college can also help you determine whether your child qualifies for financial assistance in the form of Pell grants or other government-sponsored grants. Financial aid is defined in terms of demonstrated need; total college expense less family contribution equals demonstrated need.

Sorting Out All the Options

Now, how do you sort out all these complicated alternatives? It seems that the best tax-incentive alternatives are available to low-income parents, who may also be most likely to obtain scholarship dollars for their child.

On the other hand, these parents face a level of complexity that would challenge an accountant. Parents over the AGI limits, meanwhile, can feel very frustrated. Let's list the alternatives we've discussed on a best-to-worst basis, both for those with a qualifying AGI and those above it.

If you earn at or below the AGI minimum:

◆ Coverdell Education Savings Account—Benefit specific (education) and ideal for larger families.

◆ Roth IRA—Not education specific, but same qualifications and benefits.

◆ EE savings bonds—Register in your name; also request gifts in child's name. Not all education expenses covered.

◆ Scholarships—Must pursue and apply shortly before matriculation.

◆ Hope/Lifetime Credits—If you have to borrow, use these tax deductions.

◆ Student Loans—Last resort.

If your earnings are over the AGI minimum:

 ◆ 529 Plans (Qualified tuition programs)—Choose the variable option over the fixed one; this gives you a better shot over time at making more money.

 ◆ Traditional IRA—Use the education expense option.

 ◆ EE savings bonds—Keep in child's name; ditto for gifts; don't bother with annual tax filing.

 ◆ Taxable portfolio—Invest in index equity funds or passive equities; mix with EE bonds.

 ◆ Hope/Lifetime Credits—See if you qualify.

 ◆ Student Loans—See Sallie as a last resort.

Finally, encourage your little rascal to study hard!

Sorting Out the AGI Level Morass

When you start looking into financing your kids' education, it seems every option has different rules about income limits. The chart below is a useful reference:

Program	Individual Tax Return		Joint Tax Return	
	Eligible below	Not eligible above	Eligible below	Not eligible above
Traditional IRA:	$34,000	$44,000	$54,000	$64,000 (for $3,000 deduction)
Traditional IRA: (nonworking spouse)	N/A	N/A	$150,000	$160,000
Roth IRA:	$95,000	$110,000	$190,000	$220,000 ($3,000 max allowed b/w Trad. and Roth)
Coverdell ESA:	$95,000	$110,000	$190,000–$220,000	($2,00 per child)
EE Savings Bonds:	$50,850	$65,850	$76,250	$106,250 (in your name, for interest deduction only)
Hope/Lifetime Credits:	$40,000	$50,000	$82,000	$102,000 (will be adjusted for inflation)

In Whose Name?

Parents ask us all the time whether they should keep education funds in their name or in the kid's name. This issue revolves around taxes vs. trust. If the assets are put in the child's name, the tax bite is going to be less. But if the assets are in the child's name, the child can choose to cash them in and move to Bali to study puppetry, rather than attend your alma mater. The very thought sends some parents into a spin. Then again, the young woman who designed the award-winning sets for Disney's Broadway production of *The Lion King* went to Bali to study puppetry, to the probable mortification of her parents—and she's doing awfully well! If the assets are in the child's name, it can reduce a child's financial aid eligibility.

We come down on the side of holding taxable education assets in the child's name, for the lower tax hit. If you are concerned that your child might abuse these assets, your problems are far greater than financing a college education.

The Least You Need to Know

- We've said it before, we'll say it again; don't jeopardize your retirement to pay for your kids' education.

- Put your education savings in traditional, Roth, and Coverdell ESAs and EE savings bonds.

- 529 College Savings Plans (QTPs) are tax-exempt, prepaid tuition programs; one of the most interesting is the Unique College Investing Plan.

- Several new income tax credits are now allowed by the IRS for education expenses.

- Hold taxable education dollars in your child's name for a smaller tax bite.

Chapter 17

Covering Your Assets

In This Chapter

- ◆ Determining your insurance needs
- ◆ Life insurance simplified
- ◆ Insuring your home and other assets

You might not think of insurance as related to investment, but a single unin-
sured catastrophe can wipe out years of gains in your portfolio. Making sure
you have adequate medical, home, auto, and life insurance is an important
piece of your life as a savvy investor. You don't want to ever have to sell off
great-performing stocks, or worse, dip into your retirement accounts to
cover a hospital bill or buy a new car because you didn't have your assets
covered. We've already discussed auto and health insurance in Chapters 6
and 13, respectively, so in this chapter we'll focus mostly on life insurance.

Don't Insure What You Can Afford to Replace

If you think of insurance as an offset to a catastrophe, you will save a lot in
insurance premiums. Take your car as an example (before we get to your
life). Most insurers offer you a deductible on collision insurance ranging
from $100 to $1,000. In other words, you pay out of your own pocket for
the first $100 or the first $1,000 of damage.

If your snazzy new auto is worth $30,000, what will your premiums be? Well, depending upon the insurer, the $100 deductible policy will cost you around $1,600, and the $1,000 deductible policy will cost you $660. You save roughly $1,000 per annum. In the first year, the extra cost of a collision (which is the difference in deductibles) is almost exactly offset by the lower premium! Admittedly, this data is from New Jersey, where auto insurance is very pricey. But the principle still stands.

You know we've got a rule of thumb for you, and here it is: Take the difference between the collision premiums for the minimum and the maximum deductible, and divide it by the difference in deductibles.

$$\frac{\text{Premium for max. deductible} - \text{premium for min. deductible}}{\text{maximum deductible} - \text{minimum deductible}}$$

If the resulting ratio is one-third or higher, opt for the maximum deductible.

Super Strategy

Once you realize that you should carry coverage for catastrophes but not for every conceivable expense, you can save or reinvest the premium dollars saved. "Ah," you say, "but what if I have a catastrophe? How do I deal with a thousand dollar out-of-pocket expense, smart guy?" Well, remember the emergency fund? That, in part, is what it's for. Emergencies.

Life Insurance Simplified

Life insurance has one purpose: to provide for your family in the event of your demise. Your beneficiary can use the proceeds of your life insurance policy to cover your funeral expenses, pay your estate taxes, and raise your children.

Determining Your Insurance Needs

Far too many people carry far too much life insurance, giving rise to the popular expression "insurance poor." There are two ways to estimate how much life insurance you really need.

- ◆ Make a list of expenses your family will need to cover if you die.

- ◆ Figure out how much of your salary your family would need to replace if you die.

Here's an example of an expenses list.

Funeral expenses: $20,000

Outstanding debts: $5,000

Remaining mortgage: $100,000

College costs for children: $60,000

Annual minimum: ($50,000 ÷ .06 or 6%) $833,000–$1,018,000

Less: Stocks, bonds, insurance, etc.: $300,000–$718,000

Less: Social Security and other retirement benefits (if operable): $50,000

Net new insurance needs: $668,000

The "annual minimum" of $833,000 is the sum that will generate $50,000 a year in income for the family to live on if it's invested at 6 percent. This family will need life insurance coverage for $668,000 should the breadwinner(s) die.

To determine how much life insurance you need to replace your salary, simply multiply your present salary times the number of years your family will need it. If your family will need your $75,000 a year salary for 15 more years, for example, you'll need $1,125,000 in life insurance. We don't necessarily endorse either method of estimating your life insurance needs. But at least they will get you thinking.

The Five Basic Types of Life Insurance

There are as many different types of life insurance policies as there are days in the year. And insurance agents sell them all, using every sales technique in the book. For the sake of simplicity (and your sanity), we are going to boil these down to five broad choices. It won't be easy going, but if you get through this next section, you'll be a lot more clued in than most people when you sit down with your insurance agent.

1. **Term Life.** The cheapest life insurance policies guarantee benefits only if you die before a specified term. They are called term life insurance policies. You pay X dollars in premiums and are insured for Y amount for Z years. If you die within the Z period, your beneficiaries get the Y amount. If you die after Z years, they get zip. The idea is to set Z years for a period after your kids are grown and able to take care of themselves.

   If this appeals to you, ask your insurance agent about declining term insurance. With this policy, the amount of protection decreases each year (just as your need does). Declining term insurance should be your cheapest option.

2. **Whole Life.** Whole life insurance is much more expensive than term insurance, but accumulates more value. A portion of your monthly premium goes to the insurer, who invests it on your behalf. Over time, compounding does its magic and the cash value of your policy grows exponentially. Upon your death, your family gets a death benefit plus the money that has accumulated in the policy.

3. **Joint Life and Survivorship.** Two popular variations used by two-worker families and business partnerships are joint life and survivorship. With joint life, two or more people are insured, and the face amount is paid upon the death of the first individual to the second individual. Survivorship policies are also called "second-to-die" insurance. With second-to-die, no payment from the insurance company is made until the second insured dies. Premiums are payable until the second death. As you'll learn in Chapter 18, the estate-planning chapter, if you die, your assets are sheltered by the marital deduction, but your surviving spouse's are not. The second-to-die policy can pay the taxes resulting from your spouse's death. This policy is also very popular with business partnerships.

4. **Universal Life.** This is a life insurance contract that, like whole life insurance, accumulates cash value. It is more flexible, however. The death benefit may be increased or decreased, and the premium changes to reflect that increase or decrease. A back-end load of around 7 percent is typically charged when you make any changes in your policy.

5. **Variable Life.** Variable life is a securities-based, whole life product. The insurance company sets up a separate account to hold the assets, which come from your premium payments, and invests them in common stocks, bonds, and/or money market securities. Because the value of the securities changes daily, so does your potential death benefit. The change is always on the upside, however. You are guaranteed the face amount of the policy. Premiums are fixed.

5A. **Variable Universal Life Policy.** This is like a Cadillac with all the options. It includes flexible premium payments, an adjustable death benefit, and two cash benefit options. The cash values are held in a separate account (as with a variable life policy), and the investment performance can affect the amount of the death benefit.

The policy holder may pay premiums in any amount and with whatever frequency (monthly, quarterly, etc.) he or she finds convenient. Loads are deducted from the premiums to cover sales and administrative expenses; and they can be either "front-end" or "back-end."

However—and it's a big "however"—there are monthly deductions from these separate accounts to pay for the insurance coverage provided by your policy. And if there is an insufficient sum in the accounts, the policy holder must deposit additional dollars to keep the policy in force.

What do all these options cost? That's not easy to answer, but here's as good a comparison as you will find, compliments of Gary Katz of Sagemark Consulting, a member of Lincoln Financial Group.

Rate Examples for $1,000,000 Policy

	Term	Universal Life	Whole Life	Universal 2nd To-Die	Whole Life 2nd To-Die
Age 45	2,325 for 10 years*	13,910 for 3 years. 9,193 thereafter	18,600	4,708	8,650
Age 65	13,575 for 10 years **	31,802	51,780	16,381	33,910

All Universal Life and Whole Life are full pay.

* 10-year level term. Client needs to requalify after 10 years. Premium increases substantially after 10 years, e.g., $13,765 in year 11; $21,295 in year 15, etc.

**10-year level term. Client needs to requalify after 10 years. Premium increases substantially after 10 years, e.g., $147,075 in year 11, $214,375 in year 15, etc.

Source: Gary Katz, Lincoln Financial Advisors

Are you totally confused? Maybe this will help:

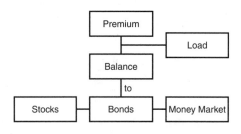

Comparison Data

| Features | Type of Policy | | | |
	Term	Permanent	Universal	Variable
Death Benefit	Fixed, level	Fixed, level	Adjustable, level or increase	Depends upon performance; guaranteed minimum
Premiums	Fixed schedule, increasing	Fixed schedule, fixed amount	Flexible schedule, flexible amount	Fixed schedule, fixed amount
Cash Values	None	Fixed and guaranteed	Current interest plus guaranteed minimum	Depends upon performance

Annuities

Insurance companies also sell annuities, which, you learned in Chapter 5, are regular payments for the length of the life of the person who owns the annuity contract. Like life insurance, an annuity is a contract between the insurance company and the purchaser (you). This person is called the "annuitant." Typically, you would designate yourself the annuitant and name a beneficiary, who will receive whatever value is left over in the annuity when you die.

Here's the interesting difference between life insurance and annuities. With life insurance, the insurer is hoping that you will live long enough to pay enough premiums to more than cover the death benefit. The longer you live, the better for the insurance company. With an annuity, on the other hand, the payments stop rather than start at death, so the shorter your life, the happier the insurance company. Kinda ghoulish, eh?

Importantly, for both fixed and variable annuities, your death benefit will at least equal the amount you paid for the contract. This is one of the features that insurers use to trumpet variable annuities over mutual funds. Your mutual funds, after all, could theoretically decline in value below what you put into them. A variable annuity, as we mentioned in Chapter 12, is basically a mutual fund with an insurance contract

Crash Alert

Life insurance is a commodity, so shop accordingly. You do want to be sure that the insurance carrier will be able to pay your death benefits, so always check into the financial capabilities of your insurer. A good way to start is to call your state insurance commissioner and see if any complaints or charges are outstanding.

wrapped around it. You get to invest in the possibilities of growth with the underlying mutual fund, plus you are assured a defined death benefit. However, we think you're better off buying mutual funds for your portfolio and separate term life insurance.

Your Kids Don't Need Life Insurance

Insurance agents will use three reasons to sell you on life insurance for your kids:

1. Premiums are low because of their young age.

2. It guarantees their insurability in the event of major health problems.

3. The cash value can be used for the child's education.

Okay, these are all valid reasons, but we just don't buy it. And we don't think you should. There are better ways to finance a child's education, as we discussed in Chapter 16. And if your child has major health problems, group health insurance, not life insurance, seems the more appropriate course.

Disability Insurance Is a Must

Disability insurance, on the other hand, is a must—for you, not your kids. Disability insurance replaces your income if you are disabled and can't work. Short-term (e.g., three months) disability is usually a part of your group health plan, but you'll need to buy long-term disability insurance (LTD) to cover you should a disability prevent you from working for a long time. Some employers offer this insurance to employees; if yours doesn't, contact your insurance agent.

Plan on paying about $50–$100 per month for disability insurance. It's a small price to pay for a lot of peace of mind. LTD will serve as a salary substitute if you are ever disabled.

Insuring Your Home and Other Assets

Finally, be sure to discuss homeowner's insurance with your agent. Your mortgage bank will require you to carry insurance at least equal to the outstanding mortgage. Your main concern should be coverage for fire, flood and wind damage.

Flood insurance, if you live in a flood plain, can be purchased most cheaply from the federal government. You may have seen articles about Topsail Island, one of the barrier islands off North Carolina. That's Hurricane Alley, and the people living there are in a continuing build/destroy/rebuild cycle. We can't imagine what they would do without flood insurance.

If you're not in a flood plain and the worse floods you face are one inch of water in the basement every 10 years, you don't need flood coverage. Fire will be your main concern. Be sure your coverage is for 100 percent of the current replacement value of your home.

If you own any important works of art or antiques, take out a fine arts policy. This insurance is not cheap, but it's the only protection available for such precious items.

> **Super Strategy**
>
> When you insure the contents of your home, be sure to go from room to room with a camera. Use up the roll to prove what you have and what it looks like, and store it in your safe deposit box, not in your home.

As a property owner, you should also seriously consider taking out liability insurance. This is insurance that will protect you from being wiped out by any lawsuits brought by someone who slips on your sidewalk or is otherwise injured on your premises. An "umbrella" policy providing a million dollars of coverage for various liability issues will cost around $200 a year. It's well worth it for the peace of mind, which, after all, is what covering your assets is all about.

The Least You Need to Know

- ◆ Don't insure what you can afford to replace.

- ◆ Life insurance has one purpose: to provide for your family in the event of your death.

- ◆ There are five basic types of life insurance: term, whole, joint, universal, and variable.

- ◆ Your kids don't need life insurance.

- ◆ Besides life and health insurance, you need disability and auto insurance. If you're a homeowner, you will need homeowner's and liability insurance.

Chapter 18

Keeping Uncle Sam's Greedy Mitts off Your Estate

In This Chapter

◆ Probate-proofing your will

◆ Saving on estate taxes

◆ Cons of passing everything onto your spouse

◆ Trusts and gifts

Most people react to estate planning the same way they do to pre-nuptial agreements: "That's just for the wealthy." But it's definitely not. Don't assume, for example, that if you were to die, your spouse would automatically inherit your assets. Without a will, that's not guaranteed. And, without careful estate planning, the government—not your heirs or spouse—is likely to end up with at least half of your hard-earned assets. There are two main definitions of the word *estate:*

◆ A sizable piece of land with a large house. This is what most people associate with the word "estate."

◆ All of one's possessions. This is what you should associate with the word "estate."

Do you care what happens to your estate—who gets what, and when? If you pay an accountant to make sure you pay the lowest possible income tax, does it not make sense to pay a tax/trust attorney to ensure that your estate will not take an unnecessary hit from estate taxes? Now, have we got your attention?

Why You Don't Want to Die Without a Will

Let's start with the most basic estate-planning strategy: the will. A *will* is a legal document, signed by you and witnessed, that gives explicit directions as to who or what is to get whatever specific assets of yours you choose to list. If you have children under the age of 18, you would specify in your will a guardian whom you want to take care of them upon your death.

Technically, you don't need a lawyer to draw up a will, but we strongly recommend that you use one. If you die without a will, it is referred to as dying "intestate." That means the state (and even potentially an ex-spouse), rather than you, decides how and to whom your assets will be distributed.

"The state," in this case, is that part of the judicial system known as probate court. Without a will, the state may give some of your assets to heirs who do not need them, while others who do need them get less or none. Even scarier, if you are a single surviving spouse with children and you die without a will, the court, not you, will appoint a guardian for your children. Finally, dying intestate delays the distribution of your assets and adds to the expense. None of these scenarios sound too hot, do they?

Investor's Idiom

A **will** keeps your assets out of probate court, or probate. With a will, you legally designate who will get your assets and your **executor** (i.e., a person you appoint to carry out the provisions and directions of your will) makes sure that happens after you die. If you die without a will, or if your will is contested, your estate can end up in your state's probate court, to be fought over by anyone who can demonstrate a claim to your assets.

We feel very strongly that everyone with assets needs to have a will. It should be reviewed every year to reflect any changes in your personal, legal, or financial situation. And you know when, don't you? That's right, on your birthday. Except, from now on, we are no longer referring to it as your birthday. After all, we all reach a point in our adult life when we don't want to acknowledge the date of our birth any more. So, henceforth, we will refer to your birthday as your *Review Day*. Okay? Reviewing your will each Review Day will literally take five minutes. And changing your will, for whatever reason, is a simple matter requiring a phone call to your attorney. It's also a good idea for both you and your spouse to make out your wills at the same time, so you can make sure you're not expressing conflicting wishes—regarding your children, for example, which could cause problems if you both die at or near the same time.

One final matter you should address with your will is the naming of an executor. Your *executor* will distribute your assets as you have set forth in the will. Although you can name anyone, we suggest appointing a professional, such as your attorney or someone from your bank trust department, and a close family member (spouse or sibling) as co-executors. Believe us, this is not an honorary position!

Probate: The Process of Administering Your Will

The next step in the estate planning process is coming up with ways to make sure your will doesn't end up in probate court. Probate is the process of administering your will (or divvying up your assets if you die intestate). Probating takes time, costs money and allows the public to view your personal assets (and you thought you had heard the last of your ex!). Fortunately, there are several ways to avoid probate court.

Living Trust

Perhaps the best-known way to avoid probate court is the *living trust*.

A living trust is a legal document that allows you to designate someone to manage your assets if you die or are incapacitated. The trust is typically managed by a trustee for you and for whomever else (your spouse, usually) you wish to include. This document is especially important if you have health concerns that could leave you incapacitated, but is important for most people to have these days because of medical advances that have resulted in more people "living" in incapacitated states.

Often you serve as trustee for yourself with provisions for someone else (a professional) to serve in the event of your death or incapacitation. You can also name a friend or relative

> **Investor's Idiom**
>
> One way to keep your estate out of probate court is to use a **living trust,** which names someone to actually manage your assets if you die or are incapacitated. The technical name for this trust is **inter vivos**—feel free to impress friends and neighbors with this phrase!

> **Crash Alert**
>
> If you create a living trust and choose to exclude specific assets for any reason, you can include or add them to the trust per the terms of your will. This is referred to as a "pour over" provision in your will. However, you will still need to have these specific assets probated since they were technically not in your living trust at your death.

as trustee/co-trustee. Because you created the living trust, you can change it whenever you wish, just as you can modify your will. A will and living trust are often created and modified at the same time, and drawn up by the same estate-planning attorney.

Joint Ownership

A simpler and less expensive way of avoiding probate is to keep some assets (home, securities, etc.) in joint ownership. Joint ownership does preclude several terrific estate-planning techniques that will reduce or eliminate state taxes. (We'll discuss those shortly.) Joint ownership is worth considering as an alternative to a living trust, however. Either joint ownership or the living trust is a good first step in the estate-planning process.

Before we leave probate, let's mention one class of assets that are automatically excluded: beneficiary-designated accounts. When you designate a beneficiary for your

- ◆ Retirement accounts (IRAs, pensions, 401[k]s, SEPs, etc.)
- ◆ Life insurance policies
- ◆ Qualified tuition programs (529s)

The assets in these accounts bypass probate and go directly to your designated beneficiary: spouse, child, etc. These sums are still included in your taxable estate, however.

Big Changes in Estate Taxes!

Now that we've taken care of the probate issue, let's proceed to ways to estate taxes. These taxes were among the most onerous in the U.S. tax system, starting at 37 percent and running up as high as 55 percent. It was a bummer to think that you might have a million dollars to leave to your kids, but the government could take half of it before the money even got to them.

Fortunately, what the government hath taken away, it hath slowly returneth. In 2002, it got a little easier to keep your hard-earned bucks in the family. A key section of the Tax Relief Act of 2001 creates a significant increase in the estate tax exemption, with a full repeal slated for 2010. Similarly, the highest estate (and gift) tax rates will gradually decline. Here are the details:

Year	Estate tax exemption	Highest estate/gift tax rates
2002	$1.0 million	50%
2003	"	49%
2004	1.5 million	48%
2005	"	47%
2006	2.0 million	46%
2007	"	45%
2008	"	45%
2009	3.5 million	45%
2010	—	—

On January 1, 2010, there will be a full repeal of all estate taxes. That's the good news. Now for the bad: The repeal will expire on December 31, 2010, and the law in effect prior to June 7, 2001 will be revived. That means the maximum estate tax exemption will return to $1.0 million, and the highest rate will jump back up to 55 percent. This so-called "sunset provision" (which we are betting the Feds will invoke, citing "budgetary safeguards" has given rise to a rather sick joke among legal eagles):

Fiscal Facts

The maximum rate for the estate tax and the gift tax is going down, down, down ....

Lawyer to aging client: "Try very hard to expire in 2010."

Only in America! Well, enjoy the respite while it lasts.

Year	Maximum Tax Rate
2002	50%
2003	49%
2004	48%
2005	47%
2006	46%
2007, 2008, 2009	45%

Unified Is Bifurcated

Until the Tax Relief Act of '01, there was a unified estate and gift tax system in the United States. Now there is a bifurcated system: a lifetime gift tax exemption ($1 million) and what's referred to as a deathtime exemption. The schedule for the deathtime is:

2002	million
2003	"
2004	$1.5 million
2005	"
2006	"
2007	1.5 million
2008	2.0 million
2009	"
2010	"
2011	3.5 million
2012	—

Do these years and numbers look familiar? You bet! The deathtime goes away in 2010 but, because it's "sunset" and because politicians are what they are, it would revert back to $1 million in 2011. How does the deathtime exemption work? If you give $20,000 this year, for example, versus the $11,000 maximum, the $9,000 difference goes to the deathtime side of the ledger, and the $11,000 goes to the gift tax side of the ledger. You can keep giving an extra $9,000 per year in this case until you reach the maximum exemption ($1 million in 2002 and 2003). Got that? Good, because we're not sure we do!

An estate tax return needs to be filed only if the gross estate exceeds this amount.

Year	Exclusion Amount
2002 and 2003	$1,000,000
2004 and 2005	1,500,000
2006, 2007, 2008	2,000,000
2009	3,500,000

Most drastically, estate tax rates have been cut. The top rate was reduced from 55 percent to 50 percent and is scheduled to keep dropping until it reaches 45 percent by 2009, and will be replaced altogether by the gift tax in 2010. Since the gift tax is capped at 35 percent, this is a dramatic reduction in estate tax. Or is it …?

The Estate Tax Repeal ... Not So Appealing?

Turns out it depends on what state you live in. Bear with us now, this is a bit confusing. In most states, for every dollar you pay in state estate taxes, you get a dollar in credit to apply to your federal death taxes. Under the 2002 Tax Relief Act, however, this credit will be phased out and replaced by a straight deduction which will be worth much less than the credit. About half the states plan to automatically reduce the tax as the credit is reduced, but in 23 states and Washington , D.C., the underlying tax will remain even as the credit disappears. The larger your estate, the more you could be hurt by the elimination of the credit. Estates in the millions could wind up paying more estate tax rather than less.

One more thing … although supposedly the estate tax will be repealed altogether in 2010, no one is convinced that will really happen. If the Democrats get control of Congress, if the government decides it can't do without the revenue from estate taxes … if, if, if! We wouldn't count on it. Our best advice: If you have a large estate, work with an expert in estate planning and prepare to be flexible.

They Can Tax *That?!*

Maybe you think you don't have to worry about estate planning because your estate isn't worth more than $1 million. But take a close look at what's included in the definition of *estate*. It adds up fast. Let's make a partial list:

- ◆ Taxable investments (stocks, bonds, mutual funds, CDs, money market accounts, etc.)

- ◆ Employer-sponsored retirement plan benefits

- ◆ All IRAs

- ◆ Personal residences less their mortgages

- ◆ Business/partnership interests

- ◆ Life insurance proceeds (at time of death)

Fiscal Facts

Federal Estate Tax Return Form 706 must generally be filed and taxes paid by the estate within nine months following the estate owner's death.

- ◆ Automobiles, boats (less loans)
- ◆ Jewelry and collectibles (antique furniture, paintings, coins, stamps, etc.)
- ◆ Other items of value (clothing, furniture, etc.)
- ◆ Taxable lifetime gifts

Does any of this look familiar? It should mimic what's on your personal balance sheet. (Have you gotten that together since Chapter 4? Nag, nag!)

Are there any deductions? Precious few. We've indicated some in our partial list (mortgages and car loans). Others include funeral expenses, transfers to charities of your choice, and the cost of administering your estate (trust bank fees and the like).

Super Strategy

As you get older, the value of your estate is going to continue to increase. You may not be a millionaire now, but you may be in 2006 or 2016 or 2026. Start protecting your estate now. First, carefully estimate the value of your estate. Have jewelry, collectibles and other property appraised. Think about what gifts you want to make to charities and to family members. In short, use this chapter as inspiration to get organized—then, see your attorney!

Cons of Passing Everything onto Your Spouse

There is one big deduction you can take on your estate: the unlimited marital deduction. The tax code says that you may deduct from your estate the value of all assets that are transferred from you to your spouse, either directly (via a will) or in a trust. In that case, there would be no tax on your estate: zero, zip, nada.

But yes, Virginia, there is a catch.

If you pass away, your assets (and your share of any joint assets) pass to your spouse and there is no estate tax on your estate. But what happens when your spouse dies? Your spouse's estate won't be able to use the unlimited marital deduction because you're dust.

What if your spouse dies first? Then you get the unlimited marital deduction benefit on his or her estate—and your own estate loses that benefit. Yes, as the surviving spouse you still get the unified credit exclusion ($1 million in 2002), but it has to apply to the total of both your and your deceased spouse's estate.

Are there any better options? Yes, and we will briefly outline a few of them for you in a minute, but first, let's bring up one more issue to make sure you are totally confused: The Generation Skipping Transfer Tax (GST).

Watch That Generation Gap

The GST tax was intended to prevent Rockefeller-rich families from preserving their wealth by giving to grandchildren instead of to children and thereby skipping an entire generation of tax.

It was an unbelievable 55 percent, tacked on top of other estate and gift taxes. If your total gifts (directly or via trust accounts) exceeds $1 million (or $2 million if the total is joint with your spouse), you're taxed at 50 percent on the excess. And you can't get around the GST tax by setting up a trust for your child that passes to your grandchild at the time of the child's death, although your child could set up the trust. The tax law changes reduce the GST amount and tax rate in lockstep with the estate tax exemptions and rates, with the tax repealed in 2010 but set to zoom back up to pre-Tax Relief Act levels as of January 1, 2011. All the new developments in tax law are another good reason to consult with an estate-planning attorney.

Tax-Saving Alternatives

Meanwhile, we can at least make you aware of some useful tax-saving strategies.

Gimme Shelter

A smarter way to use the unlimited marital deduction is to divide your assets in half and will only half to your spouse. Use the other half to set up a credit shelter trust (CST). Your spouse gets all the income generated by the trust's investments during his or her lifetime. The principal goes to your children when your spouse dies. Ideally, the assets used to set up the CST will be no more than the exclusion amount ($1 million in 2002)in the year of your death. At the time of your death, assets equal to the exclusion amount for that year go to create the CST, and the balance goes directly to your spouse via the unlimited marital deduction. At the time of your spouse's death, the CST is excluded from his or her estate. Voila! You've cut your and your spouse's estate tax bill in half.

QTIP: No, Not the Kind You Stick in Your Ear

In addition to the CST, you can also set up, via your will, a second trust that qualifies for the marital deduction. What kind of trust qualifies? The most popular choice is called the Qualified Terminable Interest Property Trust, or "QTIP" for short.

With a QTIP, your spouse receives the income during his/her lifetime. At the time of your spouse's death, the assets pass on to whomever you've named in your will. The assets are still included in your spouse's estate, but you retain control of the assets "from the grave." The QTIP is great for a second marriage, for example, because you can make sure some of your assets reach the children of your first marriage after your second spouse dies.

Charitable Trusts

There are two kinds of charitable trusts:

- Charitable Remainder Trusts (CRTs)
- Charitable Lead Trusts (CLTs)

With the CRT, you set up a trust for the charity of your choice, but you retain all rights to the income generated by the trust until you and/or your spouse dies. At that time, the assets go to the charity. You get a charitable gift deduction (Schedule A on IRS Form 1040) and the assets in the trust are excluded from your estate.

CRTs take one of two forms: either a Charitable Remainder Annuity Trust or a Charitable Remainder Unitrust. The former pays a fixed dollar sum to you each year; the latter pays you a fixed percentage of the assets.

Alternatively, the Charitable Lead Trust provides all income to the charity of your choice for a set period—20 years, for example. At the end of that period, the assets revert to whomever (son, granddaughters, etc.) you initially named as the remainder beneficiary.

You can establish a CRT or CLT:

- At the time of your death, via your will, protecting some of your estate from taxation.
- During your lifetime, improving both your income tax and estate tax situations.

Other Ways to Reduce Estate Taxes

There are several other ways to cut estate taxes and make sure more of your hard-earned money goes to the people you love, not to the IRS. Again, we recommend that you consult an attorney, but at least if you read this chapter, you'll walk into the law office reasonably well informed (always a plus, especially if you're paying by the hour). Consulting a licensed CPA wouldn't hurt, either.

Life (Saver!) Insurance

Life insurance can be used to pay any estate taxes, thereby nullifying the need for your heirs to sell estate assets to raise the cash for the tax bill. You can also create a life insurance trust to hold or purchase life insurance. At your death, the trustee would collect the proceeds and invest them for the benefit of whomever you named as beneficiaries. The proceeds won't be included in your estate as long as the policies are purchased at least three years before your death or transferred to the trust three years before death.

The Gift That Keeps on Giving

Gifting is another nifty way to lessen the burden of your pesky Uncle Sam. You can give $11,000 per person per year ($22,000 if you're making a joint gift with your spouse). This is an excellent way to reduce your estate, and thereby reduce your potential estate tax. Giving appreciated or potentially appreciating assets such as stock or real estate is a particularly good idea.

If you make medical or educational payments on behalf of your heirs, these payments are excluded from your estate—provided you make payments directly to the source. Education is limited to tuition, and you must pay the college directly. Medical payments must be paid directly to the hospital, doctor, or clinic, or to the insurance company, if you are paying for medical insurance. These exclusions only apply when you make payment on behalf of others, not for yourself.

Just a Little Token—Gifts to Minors' Trusts

You can also set up a trust for a child or grandchild and appoint a trustee (a parent, usually) to oversee the use of the funds in the trust. The trustee can pay out necessary sums for the minor's needs—college tuition, for example. At age 21 the child or grandchild has full access to the trust, however.

Super Strategy
If it makes you nervous that your child or grandchild can get into a trust at age 21, you can set up a Crummy Powers trust. A Crummy Powers trust gives the child or grandchild access to the trust for only a few days each year to make withdrawals. Technically, the child or grandchild has access to the principal, but for a very limited number of days each year. How much damage can they do?

Personal Residence Trust

You might also talk to your attorney about transferring your home to a trust, while retaining the right to use the home for a specified number of years.

For a personal residence trust, you make a member of your family the beneficiary. If you die before the specified number of years is up, the residence stays in your estate (and you have lost nothing). If you live beyond the specified time, you get an exclusion for one of the biggest assets in your estate. The downside to this arrangement, of course, is that ownership reverts to the named beneficiary. If you want to continue to live in the residence, you must pay this named beneficiary a "competitive" rent. Let's hope you are on good terms with him or her at that time!

This is but a short list of some of the more popular measures to save on estate taxes. We urge you to seek professional assistance if you wish to pursue any of these options; individual state laws differ, federal law is subject to annual change and interpretation, and we can't possibly cover all of the nuances for each of these alternatives. Above all, don't put off estate planning. As we've said throughout this book: It's your money!

What If You Inherit Money?

All this complicated talk about estate planning has probably got you wondering what to do should Uncle Fritz kick the bucket and leave you half of the $20,000 stuffed under his mattress.

When you inherit money, you will have two questions:

- How much do I get?
- How much do I owe?

What to Do When Your Ship Comes In

The first question, if it involves financial assets, is easy to answer, as nearly all securities have public market values.

The second question is a little more complex. In most cases, the cost of securities you inherit will be marked up to "date of death" (DOD). This is good news. It means that if you sell them shortly after receiving them, you will owe little or no capital gains taxes.

Although DOD minimizes your potential taxes, it maximizes the deceased's estate value. Depending on the final sum and the manner in which the assets were set up, therefore, you may owe estate tax after the estate is settled.

When an estate is being settled, the executor is concerned with determining the value of each asset as quickly as possible, and distributing these assets as soon as possible. Normally, marketable financial assets are sold, so the executor is distributing cash to the heirs. However, the heirs may jointly request that some or all of the securities be distributed "in kind." This means that if the estate holds 400 shares of General Electric and there are four heirs, each heir will receive 100 shares of General Electric.

Beyond Cash: Property, Businesses, and Valuables

Although most estates are valued on a date-of-death basis, the federal tax code also provides for an alternate valuation date: six months after the decedent's death. What's this alternate date for? Typically, the date is used if an estate is dominated by real estate or privately held businesses. The six-month leeway gives the executor time to hire an appraiser to estimate the "fair and sound value" of the estate. If the executor is able to "distribute, sell, exchange, or otherwise dispose" of the property within six months, it will be valued as of "date-of-death," not six months hence.

Household and personal items, such as watches, rings, antiques, paintings, etc., are considered what you probably consider them already: valuables. Their worth is estimated by the IRS's "willing buyer/willing seller" rule, which reads: "The price at which the property would change hands between a willing buyer and a willing seller, neither being under any compulsion to buy or to sell and both having reasonable knowledge of relevant facts."

If you didn't catch that, it just means the price is whatever the market will bear for the item(s) at the time, regardless of the circumstances under which they're being sold (i.e., the death of your great Aunt Tilly). The executor will most likely hire an appraiser to do an item-by-item, room-by-room appraisal. The appraisal will help you determine which items, if any, hold more than sentimental value. For those items, ask your insurance agent for a "fine arts" insurance policy.

What to Do with the Dough

After the first two questions have been answered, you will have a third: "What should I do with the dough?" In order of priority, until the money runs out, do the following:

- Pay off "bad" debt: credit cards, auto loans, etc.

- Pay off student loans, if you have any.

- Replenish emergency funds.

- Bring retirement plan assets up to the level you've determined (using our handy guide, of course) they need to be to reach your retirement savings target.

- Put the balance in educational funds, if you have children.

- Pay down your mortgage with any remaining proceeds.

Please, do not do the following:

- Buy a bigger house.

- Buy that new luxury car.

- Buy a boat, snowmobile, or any other large, expensive piece of recreational equipment for the heck of it.

If you want a treat, take a nice vacation. It's a lot less expensive and won't stick around to haunt you.

The Least You Need to Know

- A will is a legal document, signed by you and witnessed, that gives explicit directions as to who or what is to get your assets.

- A living trust is a document that allows you to choose someone to manage your assets should you die or become incapacitated.

- Estate taxes are among the most onerous in the U.S. tax system; use a good attorney to help you protect your estate.

- You can reduce your estate (and therefore your estate taxes) by giving $11,000 per person per year while you're still living.

- When you inherit money, use it to strengthen your finances by paying off "bad" debt and replenishing emergency funds.

Part 5

Investing Online

Computers rule when it comes to investing. They make it incredibly easy and convenient. (Perhaps *tooooo* easy and convenient, which is why you have to be so careful.) In this part of the book, we sort out the basics for you. If you're not online and don't even know quite what it means, that's fine. We start from the ground up, baby. What kind of computer to buy, where to get software, the best online services to subscribe to for investing. We'll get you up and running.

Once you are, you need never bother with trying to reach a broker on the phone ever again. We'll show you how to bank online and how to research investments and manage your portfolio online. We'll direct you to the best discount brokerages and top investment-related web sites. You'll also learn how to spot fraudulent schemes. Welcome to the future. It's fun!

Chapter 19

Getting Started with Online Investing

In This Chapter

- How the Internet developed and what it can do for you
- What you need to invest online
- Choosing an Internet service provider
- Banking online
- Selecting an Internet broker

In the next two chapters, we will show you how to bank, research investments, track your portfolio, and trade online. There is no substitute for poking around on your own, however, and we encourage you to do so.

A word of caution: Because websites are proliferating so rapidly and the information on each site is subject to change daily, we can't guarantee what we show and tell will be necessarily your experience when you go on the 'Net. With that caveat, let's buckle up and take a ride.

Once Upon a Time There Was a Big Fat Computer ...

If we asked you how long the *Internet* has been around, you'd probably say that it came into being in the last 10 years or so. Well, believe it or not, the Internet has been around for more than 30 years. (And you thought you were such a hotshot getting a modem in the '80s!) The Internet is a computer network that was developed in 1969 as a way for government scientists and military departments to communicate with each other via computer and have access to information stored on computers around the world. The first version of the Internet was the Department of Defense Advanced Research and Projects Agency (ARPA), which was a Cold War network designed to be less penetrable by "the enemy" (okay, the Russians) than the computer networks available at the time.

By the 1980s, university professors were hooked up, too, as were the Department of Energy and the National Institutes of Health. But the Internet was still primarily a geekfest until e-mail was developed in 1990, and both regular folks and commercial businesses got wise to the fun and the financial potential inherent on the 'Net. Fax machines were already transmitting data over phone lines, so hooking up computers to do the same was not a stretch for most businesses.

The World Wide Web

The next step was the development of a computer language, *HTML*, that allowed graphics and sound to be combined in a document. These HTML documents were a lot more fun to look at than the complicated, code-strewn documents previously available online. When you look at a page on the World Wide Web, you are looking at HTML documents. The web is a subset of the Internet and is coordinated by an organization called the World Wide Web Consortium.

Investor's Idiom

Chatting on the web **in real time** simply means that you and whomever you are speaking with are having a discussion in the present time. The keyed messages you receive on-screen in a chat room occur in the same amount of time that it takes for you to type them.

The Internet is not controlled by any one government or organization, but there is an Internet Society, the ISOC, that helps develop programming standards so computers can continue talking to each other. For your purposes, you will spend most, if not all, of your time online within the web. Documents on the web begin with "home pages" and are accessed by their Uniform Resource Locators (URLs), or addresses. The URL for the World Wide Web Consortium, for example, is www.w3.org. You will probably also explore newsgroups, which are special-interest groups whose members "meet" online to exchange information and discuss topics by leaving each other messages. You can also meet new friends and business associates in chat rooms, which are online sites where people meet to talk *in real time.* In a chat room, your message appears as you type it and anyone signed into the chat room can see it and type a response that you'll be able to see on your screen.

Then, of course, there's *e-mail,* or electronic mail. Once you're online you can send and receive mail from over 150 million users in the United States alone. That's a whole lot of mail.

Take a Test Drive

The Internet has been likened to the old, early days of the Wild West: It's big, boisterous, growing, exciting, and loaded with open-ended opportunities, but it is also unregulated and unpoliced. So caveat emptor (or for those of you who missed that Latin lesson, "let the buyer beware"). Anyone can leave a message or create a website on the 'Net, and some get pretty weird. Also, on some websites you will be annoyed by pop-up ads or probed by a cookie, a program that gathers marketing information from you without your being aware of it when you explore a given website. Next thing you know, you are getting tons of unwanted junk e-mail. If computers give you the Orwellian heebie-jeebies, remember: You don't have to use the Internet. Probably 90 percent of what you want or need can be found in traditional forms: periodicals (newspapers, magazines), on-site visits (libraries, malls), and telephone contact.

Investor's Idiom

The **Internet** is basically a worldwide network of computers talking to each other over phone lines via modems. Modems translate the data coming from the computer to a form that can be sent over the phone. **E-mail,** or electronic mail, is one type of document that can be sent via modem over the Internet; HTML documents are another. **HTML,** or hypertext markup language, is a computer language that allows sound and graphics to be included in a document and viewed on the Internet. HTML documents make up the colorful subset of the 'Net called the World Wide Web.

Consider taking a test drive on the 'Net before signing up. Many metropolitan areas have Internet cafes where you surf the 'Net for the price of a cup of cappuccino. If you're in the Big Apple, for instance, try Cyberfelds Internet Café at 20 East 13th Street. A test drive is a much cheaper first step than bulking up with a new PC system just to get on the 'Net. Your public library may also offer free Internet access. There are thousands and thousands of sites on the Internet, and it is very easy to become overwhelmed and confused. We can help a little, but you'll have to do a lot of experimenting and eliminating on your own. And, remember, new sites emerge every day, and existing sites are constantly updated and revised.

Super Strategy

Worried that you won't be able to keep track of all those sites on the web that you want to revisit? Never fear. When you get onto your Internet browser page, you'll notice on the menu at the top there will be an option called "Favorites." If you click on this, you will see an option called "Add to Favorites." Anytime you go to a web page that you like and know you'll want to go back to, simply click on "Favorites" and then "Add to Favorites," and you will have saved the address of the page. To get back to that page, click "Favorites," then select the page from the pop-up list on your screen.

Hey, How Do I Turn This Thing On?

Thus far, we've assumed you have a PC (personal computer). But maybe you're part of what we'll call the electronically challenged segment of the population. Don't worry, we're going to tell you exactly what you'll need to get up and running (or surfing, as the case may be) in no time.

Your first choice is used versus new. If you don't have to have the newest and latest, think used. We checked several sources and confirmed that you could access the Internet for around $400. This buys a CPU (or central processing unit), a keyboard, and a monitor. If the CPU doesn't include a modem, you will need to buy a separate modem to attach to the computer. To further investigate buying a used machine, look in the Yellow Pages under "Computers—Dealers" or "Computers—Service and Repair." Or shop online using a friend's computer. Some of the best websites that let you compare prices and options are the ones run by the top computer magazines, including:

- *PC World*, www.pcworld.com—Use the Product Finder to help you narrow down your choices.

- *Macworld*, www.macworld.com—If you are more interested in getting a Macintosh computer, check out the pricing search engine on this site.

Prices have really come down since our last edition of this book! And you can get a lot for your money, including internal DVD players, scads of memory … the works.

Next, you will need an Internet service provider (ISP).

Compare the telephone to a computer. If you have a telephone and a friend you are trying to reach also has a telephone, you two cannot communicate until your phones are "hooked up" via a telephone wire connection. Similarly, your computer can't talk to another computer hooked up to the Internet without that "wire."

The company that provides that wire is going to charge you a monthly fee (just like the telephone company). In fact, many phone companies, such as AT&T, Sprint, and MCI WorldCom, have gotten into the ISP business. If you want the comfort of dealing with them, go for it, but you may get better deals elsewhere. Be sure that your particular modem works with the ISP you select; if it doesn't, replace it.

Dial-Up, DSL, or Cable?

A few years ago most of us had only one choice for our Internet connection—a dial-up connection. Using this connection required a phone line, so you could either get a second phone line for your Internet connection or resign yourself to not being able to use your phone while you were online. In addition, connections available for your average home computer user were not terribly fast—up to 54K tops. Internet speed is measured by the number of bits of data that can be sent or received per second.

"Bits" is short for binary digits. Computers use binary numbers, which are composed only of two digits: 0 and 1. A 54k speed modem, therefore, is moving 54 kilobits of data per second. At this speed, it takes several minutes just to receive a photograph over your modem. Yawn!

Luckily, the newer DSL and cable modems provide connection speeds many times faster than a 56k modem, maxing out at about 10 megabits per second, but this is still not fast enough to provide streaming video. In other words, to view a movie you would first have to download it and save it onto your hard drive, which is irritatingly time-consuming. A new DSL is on the horizon, however, called VDSL, for very high bit-rate DSL, that will run at about 52 megabits per second. This could turn your computer into a full-on home entertainment center.

Super Strategy

Our grandchildren will no doubt roll their eyes in boredom and disbelief as we regale them with stories of how "back when I was your age, we could only access the Internet at 128k!" For that matter, they might even ask, "What's the Internet, grandpaw?" The mega-geeks at the Defense Advanced Research Project Agency (DARPA), the same agency that funded the Internet, are already cranking away on SuperNet, the next generation's Internet. DARPA plans to increase the speed at which the average user can access the Internet by a factor of 1,000 within the next 5 to 10 years.

Today DSL, which stands for digital subscriber line, is widely available. This is super-high-speed access to the Internet via your existing phone line. You can talk on the phone and surf at the same time ... yippee! DSL comes at a price, though—about $50 a month, which includes Internet access, compared to the average price for dial-up of about $20. Still, when you factor how much you save by not having to install a second phone line, you might find that's not so bad. And the price is coming down steadily. Other advantages of DSL include:

- You can keep your connection open all night long, should you feel the need, since it doesn't block your phone line and since you are typically not charged by the amount of time you use it. No need, as with dial-up, to go through the tedious connection process every time you want to zip around online.

- DSL offers speeds of 1.5 MBps, as opposed to 54K. Take our word for it, it's fast. And it doesn't slow to a crawl when there are lots of users on, the way dial-up networks can.

- Most DSL companies will offer you the modem for free.

If you have cable, chances are you've been annoyed by phone and mail solicitations for your Internet business. The cable companies quickly realized that the *Bonanza* reruns they are pumping into your home only take up 6 megaherz on the cable. But the coaxial cable can carry hundreds of megahertz. Hmm ... can you say piggyback ride? If you have cable TV, you can get a high-speed Internet connection along with your programs.

Price-wise, cable is competitive with DSL, but with one drawback that may or may not bug you: If your cable company is in charge of your Internet access, it can route you to what it wants you to see. New Disney movie coming out and your cable company is in Disney's pocket? Chances are you'll see ads for the latest animated feature when you log on.

Cable companies are also motivated to discourage the kind of free-for-all trading of digital movies and music that is flourishing on the web. They are seeking to establish tiered pricing that would force consumers to pay for the bandwidth they use when they download big files like pirated movies or MP3s.

If none of this bothers you, check out cable, but don't be naive about what you're getting—Internet access monitored by a company with a vested interest in where you go and what you do when you surf the web.

Choosing an ISP

So once you decide between dial-up, DSL, and cable, which provider do you choose? Do you go with a national service like America Online or Earthlink, or regional, or even local (for the lowest cost)? Check out three issues: cost, reliability, and service.

◆ **Cost.** If you are a "light" user of the Internet—i.e., under 10 hours a month—look for an ISP that offers a low-use fee (say $7–$9 per month). If you are a heavy user (e.g., three hours per day), get a plan with unlimited usage. Most plans charge $20 to $22 per month for unlimited usage, but you can save with a one-year subscription. Also, ask about any start-up fees.

◆ **Reliability.** We think this is the most important factor to consider. If you get a lot of busy signals when you try to use the service, chances are there is a reliability problem. Inverse Network Technologies is an independent research firm that audits and rates ISPs. Most ISPs that are reliable will freely give their Inverse Network Technologies rating for an honest evaluation of its network availability and connection speed. We feel very strongly that you should check this out before making a final decision.

CAUTION **Crash Alert**

Make sure the ISP of your choice has a local access number; otherwise, you could be paying phone charges of up to 10¢ per minute of dial-up online usage. You want your access to your ISP to be a local (read, free!) phone call. If you are in doubt, check the ISP access number with your local telephone company to make sure it's a free call for you.

◆ **Service.** If you are having a problem, you don't want to be on hold for what seems like hours—you want to talk to a human being, and pronto. Check out the ISP's customer service and help lines before you sign up.

SmartMoney magazine always offers the latest up-to-date choices among ISPs on its website, www.smartmoney.com. Just go to the Best Buys area and look for the newest article on Internet service providers.

You Need a Surfboard ... We Mean, a Browser

Okay, you've got your PC, your modem, and your ISP. Now, you need a browser. This is software that enables your computer to surf (browse) the web and read all those groovy HTML documents. Most computers come equipped with Microsoft Internet Explorer (IE), or you can download Netscape Navigator for free at a website like www.downloadalot.com. Here's a bonus factoid: Free software available on the web is called "shareware."

Secret Agent Man

If you want to trade and bank online, you will need a browser that meets bank and broker security standards. Specifically, you will need a qualified browser that supports 128-bit encryption. Both IE and Netscape do.

> **Investor's Idiom**
>
> *En*-what? **Encryption** is the scrambling of information as it is transmitted over the Internet to ensure your privacy and confidentiality. In other words, it's like sending messages in code.

The strongest form of *encryption* available for commercial use over the Internet today is 128-bit encryption. There are billions of possible keys to de-encrypt information ("crack the code") that is passed over the Internet. Only one key can be used to allow access to your account information. And every time you initiate a new session by logging onto a site for trading or banking, a new key is randomly selected.

Banking and Shopping Online

Now you're ready to bank and shop online. *Time* magazine reported a study by World Research that compared shopping online with more traditional methods and found no significant savings when consumers bought books, airline tickets, and other items online.

Of equal interest were the reasons people were not buying online:

Fear of hackers: 21 percent

Lack of products: 16 percent

Can't see the products: 15 percent

Must reveal personal information: 13 percent

(Source: World Research)

We think that there are savings, be they real or implied, because the Internet rips out an entire layer of costs: the salesperson. Security trading on the Internet is surging for this reason, and we expect the same to hold true for clothing. But as mail-order consumers will tell you, shopping from the J. Crew catalog is very convenient, but not necessarily cheaper than buying at one of their retail stores.

Last, but not least, not everything is free on the Internet. You can get some basic research on a company free, but if you want more in-depth investment info, it'll cost you money. You can download a company's prospectus for free, for example, but not an in-depth research report from a Wall Street analyst.

Fiscal Facts

After the terrorist attacks on the United States on September 11, 2001, online shopping dropped 25 percent, according to ComScore Networks, a company that tracks online activity. Travel spending was especially hard hit, dropping 54 percent the week of the attacks. On the other hand, use of the web to get information increased after the attacks. The most common words entered into search engines were "Taliban," "anthrax," and "bin Laden."

Banking Online

This is a fairly simple financial task that is really a delight to do from home. It's a good warm-up to more advanced activities like trading stock online.

To illustrate Internet banking, we are going to describe the requirements, options, and services of Fleet Bank.

Sign Me Up!

The first thing you need to do in order to bank online is register. Using America Online as the ISP in this example, you can access Fleet HomeLink online banking as follows:

- Launch AOL and connect to the service.

- Minimize AOL after connecting (click on the little box in the far upper-right-hand corner with the "–" sign in it).

- Launch your qualified Microsoft or Netscape browser.

- Go to www.fleet.com and select "Personal Financial Services."

You can follow a similar procedure with any other ISP. Fleet charges $4.50 per month for unlimited bill payments (free for the first three months). Enrollment is by mail. Within 10 business days of applying at the website, you will receive your log-on ID in the mail. Your password will be received under separate mailing.

No More Waiting in Line When You're Online

Once you are registered, you can bank! Here's how you do it with Fleet.

- ◆ Navigate to the Fleet home page at www.fleet.com and click on "Fleet Web Banking Logon."

- ◆ Type in your log-on ID and password.

- ◆ You will see five choices:

  - ◆ Account Information

  - ◆ Transfers

  - ◆ Bill Payments

  - ◆ Investment Services

  - ◆ Other Services

  Click on "Account Information" and you will see your account information illustrated as follows:

Account Name/Number	Account Type	As Of	Balance
Checking/12345678	Checking	09/25/02	$2,456.19
Savings/32145768	Savings	09/25/02	$7,000.00
Credit Card/87654321	Credit Card	09/25/02	$934.78
Money Market/35791357	Money Market	09/25/02	$5,000.00

Once you're in your account, you can do pretty much everything you would if you were at a bank or at an ATM machine. You can:

- ◆ Click on "Transfer" to transfer funds between accounts.

- ◆ Click on "Payments" to pay down on one or more accounts or to pay bills to any business or individual in the United States.

- ◆ Click on "Other Services" to send e-mail within the bank and log-out to end your session.

It's really that simple.

> **Super Strategy**
>
> Banking online makes it easy to find the best rates for your deposits. BanxCorp, Inc., provides current rates for various savings instruments, such as money markets and CDs. At BanxCorp's website (www.banx.com), you can browse by term or location.
>
> Valuable info is also available via the Gomez Advisors, Inc., website at www.gomez.com, which profiles the top 20 Internet banks as ranked by users.

The Best Financial Software

Once you get into banking online, it becomes a breeze to manage your finances the same way—but you'll need some specialized financial management software. Among the most popular are the following:

- Quicken (new versions coming out in 2003, including Quicken 2003 Deluxe for personal finance management)

- Microsoft Money

- Managing Your Money

These each retail for around $90 to $100, but if you're buying a new PC, your dealer may be willing to include your choice of the above for free (hey, it doesn't hurt to ask!).

Now Can I Trade? Selecting an Internet Broker

Well, you're not quite ready to run with the bulls and bears just yet. You have to select an Internet broker! And that's not easy. Gomez Advisors, Inc., offers a list (and an evaluation) of all 71 brokers with transactional Internet sites. Gomez evaluated the Internet brokers on five criteria:

- Ease of use

- Customer confidence

- Onsite resources

- Relationship services

- Overall cost

The scores in each category were then totaled for an overall score. The top five discount online brokers, according to Gomez, are the following:

- Charles Schwab

- Fidelity Investments

- E*TRADE

- Harrisdirect

- Ameritrade

For a list of other websites that provide online broker evaluations, check out www.consumersearch.com/www/personal_finance/online_brokers/index.html. Finally, the October 2001 issue of *Kiplinger's Personal Finance* magazine had a very good evaluation of online brokers. If you can't find the magazine, try www.kiplinger.com or call 1-800-544-0155. *Kiplinger* ranked Fidelity Brokerage number one, even though its commission rate is fairly high. Muriel Siebert & Co. was a close second, with Charles Schwab coming in third. In terms of market share, Charles Schwab is currently the world's number one online broker, with 27.5 percent of the U.S. market as of August 2002. E*TRADE is running a close second, and is first in some other countries, such as the United Kingdom.

For cheap trades, however, Kiplinger ranked Scottrade as number one, followed by National Discount Brokers, TD Waterhouse, and Brown & Co. (E*TRADE declined to participate in Kiplinger's evaluation process.)

Now, just to make things even that much easier for you, here is a list of the brokers we have mentioned thus far with their URLs and phone numbers. We also included a couple of our favorites:

Broker	Website	Telephone
Ameritrade	www.ameritrade.com	1-800-454-9272
Datek Online	www.datek.com	1-888-463-2835
E*TRADE	www.etrade.com	1-800-387-2331
Fidelity	www.fidelity.com	1-800-544-5555
Harrisdirect	www.harrisdirect.com	1-800-825-5723
TD Waterhouse	www.waterhouse.com	1-800-934-4410
WebStreet	www.webstreet.com	1-800-932-8723
Muriel Siebert & Co.	www.siebertnet.com	1-800-872-0444
National Discount Brokers	www.ndb.com	1-800-888-3999

Broker	Website	Telephone
Brown	www.brownco.com	1-800-822-2021
Fidelity	www.fidelity.com	1-800-544-7272
Schwab	www.schwab.com	1-800-435-4000
Scottrade	www.scottrade.com	1-800-619-SAVE
Quick & Reilly	www.quick-reilly.com	1-800-837-7220

We believe Gomez and Kiplinger are the best resources for evaluating online brokers. We strongly urge you to visit their websites and use all the evaluation pages to help you select an Internet broker. Hey, it's free advice! What's better than that?

Evaluating Your Online Trading Needs

No matter what Gomez et al. recommend, however, the final decision regarding an Internet broker must be yours, and this means critically evaluating your online trading needs. For example: Do you really need to trade online? If you are an infrequent trader and a long-term investor happy with your present broker, why bother?

If you're definitely going to the 'Net, then carefully consider the following:

♦ The type of accounts you want to open online: Will you open just an IRA account, just a taxable account, or one or more of each? If an IRA account is involved, you will want to flag those brokers that

  ♦ Charge either no or minimal fees for opening, closing, transferring, and so on.

  ♦ Provide good legal updates, reminders, and follow-ups.

  ♦ Have "stone walls" that prevent you from accidentally adding to your IRA account or taking a withdrawal prematurely. Simple mistakes here can cost you taxes and/or penalties, which a "warning flag" can avert.

♦ For a taxable account, check the web pages for the manner in which the broker records gains and losses. Also, does the broker allow you to designate specific lots of a given security for realizing gains and losses?

♦ If you bought shares of the same stock at different times and three different prices, you have three different "lots," e.g.,:

100 shares purchased at $20 on 4/11/92
100 shares purchased at $40 on 5/13/95
100 shares purchased at $60 on 7/7/97

Total: 300 shares   Average price: $40

Your statement may just show "300 shares at 40"—but what if you want to sell the first lot you purchased to realize the gain now that the price of the stock has moved up to $60? You need a statement that allows you to designate specific lots so you can make buying and selling decisions and have them properly reflected in your records.

◆ Types of assets in which you plan to invest:

Do you plan to invest in equities, treasuries, other fixed income, or mutual funds? Some brokers won't trade fixed-income securities or only Treasuries, and discourage such transactions with high fees or charges.

If you want to invest in mutual funds online, find out if the broker offers funds you presently own or like. Check the fees and compare to your offline broker. If you use mutual funds in an IRA, dividend and capital gains reinvestment is important; will your prospective broker accommodate?

If you are interested in purchasing stocks on margin or playing the options and futures markets (see Chapters 21 and 22), the rates the broker offers on margin loans are a very significant factor for you to consider.

◆ Activity: How frequently do you intend to trade online? The greater the number of trades, the more important the following should be to you:

  ◆ Cost of trading

  ◆ Real-time quotations

  ◆ Quick and consistent entry to website

  ◆ Good, prompt execution

The Online Commission Picture

All 'Net brokers advertise low commission rates of around $5 to $25 per trade. But some also charge 1¢ to 3¢ per share for trades over 5,000 shares. This is still much cheaper than full-service brokerage and discount brokerage, but the differential is narrowed. Let's say a broker charges $14.95 per trade plus 1¢ per share for trades over 5,000 shares:

4,999 shares = $14.95

5,000 shares = $14.95 + $50 = $64.95

Wow, that 1¢ per share adds up!

Not all 'Net brokers charge for larger orders like this, but some do. So ask before you enroll!

If You Are a Frequent Trader ...

If you are an infrequent trader with a long-term perspective, whether you are looking at a current quotation or one with a 20-minute lag may be immaterial. But if you are a frequent trader, and certainly if you are a day trader, you are looking to ring up many small gains. These three things are essential to your success:

 ◆ You must have current quotations, especially during periods of high market volatility.

 ◆ You must be able to reach and log on to your broker's website quickly.

 ◆ Your broker must provide a Touch-Tone telephone order system as a backup. You don't want to miss making a critical trade because your broker's website was down.

Finally, good and prompt execution is critical for frequent/day traders. How long does it take to execute your order once it's placed? Note your order time and check the time of order execution (if the time is not shown, request it). Remember, most orders are not going directly to the Exchange, they are being executed via a market maker, so time is of the essence. Ask friends and associates for recommendations on brokers who can handle frequent trades efficiently. And stick to market orders, which usually confirm the price of the trade before you go offline. (This might be a good time to revisit our discussion of market and limit orders from Chapter 10.)

None of these issues regarding activity is critical if you are an infrequent trader. However, you should still follow our recommendations regarding market versus limit orders.

Investment Research

Is research critical to your investment decision-making process? Then focus on those 'Net brokers that offer the widest array of research. You're looking for Securities & Exchange Commission filings, consensus earnings estimates, Standard & Poor's reports, and so on.

There are some amazing research sites on the web that you can access yourself, such as:

♦ **www.briefing.com** (analysts' upgrades and downgrades)

♦ **www.hoovers.com** (company profiles and financial data)

♦ **www.marketguide.com** (earnings estimates from First Call, insider trading from Vickers, and stock screening from Stock Quest)

♦ **www.sec.gov** (essentially all Securities & Exchange Commission filings by companies)

♦ **www.zacks.com** (consensus earnings estimates, broker recommendations, and insider trading)

We especially like www.marketguide.com. Be careful of leaning on a given broker's in-house research. Just like a baseball team, a broker's research team includes a mix of superior, average, and inferior analysts.

There tends to be at least an indirect correlation between low commission rates and minimal additional services (including research). So if research is important to you, plan on paying higher commissions for quantity and quality.

The Comfort Factor

Some people are uncomfortable turning their money over to a "stranger," i.e., a broker they've never heard of, no matter how strongly recommended the broker may be. If you are that type of person, you may wish to simply tap into the online equivalent of your present brokerage. Many brokerages now have an online presence.

> **Crash Alert**
>
> Beware of "teaser" research: bare-bones research offered at no charge to entice you to purchase "in-depth" research at an additional charge. The in-depth reports may be worth the money, but just be conscious of when a carrot is being dangled in front of you.

Similarly, you may be most comfortable dealing with bank-related brokerage firms, especially if the bank is one you presently use. Examples include Fleet Bank, which has Quick & Reilly; Citibank; Mellon (Dreyfus); Fifth Third Bank; and Wachovia. You may even find that your existing bank relationship enables you to receive "freebies" on the Internet brokerage site not offered to nonbanking customers. Check it out.

Ancillary Services

Is there something else you want from your online broker? Free checking, for example, or perhaps free credit/debit cards? One appealing feature is the ability to transfer funds back and forth electronically between a bank checking account and a brokerage account—at no or minimal cost, ideally. Make out your wish list, then see which broker comes closest to matching it.

Now you're ready to trade!

Super Strategy

Choose an online broker by …

- ◆ Drawing up your wish list.
- ◆ Prioritizing it.
- ◆ Checking out the references we recommended (Gomez, Kiplinger's).
- ◆ Talking to friends/business associates about their own experiences, good and bad.

One service that should not be compromised in any way is a same-day "sweep" of any of your uninvested cash into a money market fund with a competitive interest rate. And make sure you are given a choice between taxable money market funds (where you can stash IRA cash) and tax-free money markets (for protecting uninvested cash from taxable accounts).

The Least You Need to Know

- ◆ The Internet is basically a worldwide network of computers talking to each other over phone lines. The World Wide Web is a subset of the Internet made up of websites that can include text, graphics, and sound.

- ◆ Make sure you choose an Internet service provider (ISP) that you can access with a local (free!) call.

- ◆ If you want to trade and bank online, you will need a browser that meets bank and broker security standards; specifically, you will need a qualified browser that supports 128-bit encryption.

- ◆ If you intend to trade frequently online, carefully research your choice of an online broker—look into fees and execution lags, and make sure your broker offers a telephone backup trading system.

Chapter 20

What's New in Online Trading and Tracking

In This Chapter

- Avoiding online fraud
- How to use an online broker
- The best search engines for investors and how to use them
- Lots of great financial websites

In this chapter we will explore the basics of how to trade and manage your portfolio online. This chapter is also loaded with the URLs for some of our favorite financially friendly websites. So plug in and hang on!

Speed and System Backups

Okay, you've narrowed your choice of Internet brokers to just a few, based on our criteria. Before you make that final choice, please, we beg of you, run your top choices past a few experienced friends. The surveys we've recommended in the previous chapter are terrific starting points but do tend to over-look one important factor: speed. Speed of order entry and reporting, that is. Many brokers' sites are so heavily secured that the basic order entry process moves at a crawl. If speed matters to you, ask fellow investors if a particular broker is quick or slow.

Another issue is system failure backups; what happens if the site crashes or is unavail-able? Can your order be phoned in? Many online brokers have had system failures without any backup systems in place for their customers to use to continue trading. This situation can cost you plenty and wipe out any savings from trading online.

Finally, try to get a feel for your broker's telephone responsiveness before you sign up. Some brokers will keep you on hold for a half hour—not fun when you're trying to execute a trade or get some help.

Crash Alert _____

Online investing is ripe with fraud. Here are some tips for avoiding fraudulent brokers:

- ◆ Stick with brokerages that appear in national magazine surveys.
- ◆ All legitimate brokers are SIPC insured. If you're thinking about using a lesser-known broker, ask for proof of SIPC insurance. "SIPC" stands for Securities Investor Protection Corporation. It currently insures securities and cash in a brokerage account for up to $500,000, no more than $100,000 of which may be in cash.
- ◆ Avoid penny stockbrokers, online or otherwise.
- ◆ Chat room and newsgroup advice should be treated with great caution. Many participants are there to promote their interests, couching their sales pitches as hot tips. Remember, free advice is unregulated by the SEC!

How to Use an Online Broker

Once you have selected your online broker, you need to complete the "paperwork." Nearly all brokers offer a form that you can fill out from your PC keyboard, print out, sign, and mail in. You can e-mail the form, but the broker still needs your signa-ture on file, so you will have to use the good old U.S. Postal Service (affectionately known as "snailmail"). By return mail, you should receive a log-on ID and password.

When you receive your ID and password, you may be able to "save" them to avoid having to reenter (and remember!) them each time you trade. Most online brokers offer this feature.

The Typical Broker's Home Page

Once logged on, you will find yourself at the broker's home page, which is like a book's table of contents. Typically, the home page is subdivided into three sections:

♦ **About the broker.** This is for prospective customers and typically includes the firm's history, information on how to open an account, and sample screens and portfolios. Look over this section for every broker you are considering before making your final decision.

♦ **Your account information.** Included here will be trading-related pages, including a verification page you can use to look over a trade order you've placed. In other words, this is your last chance to "chicken out" of a trade! Next, you'll see a series of pages relating to the status of your account, including the individual assets in your portfolio, the current market value of your portfolio, gains and losses year-to-date, and a trading-history page showing all transactions going back three months to a year (depending on the broker). You should also expect to receive monthly statements and daily confirmations of your trades, via mail or your PC.

♦ **Investor-related information.** Just as Section 2 was customer specific (you), Section 3 tends to provide information for all the broker's customers. Examples would include individual stock quotes, current stock and bond market statistics and information, general news items, and links to other websites. Many of these websites are merely online versions of printed material (e.g., *Wall Street Journal*, *Fortune*, *USA Today*). At this point, most brokers will remind you to use a browser (Netscape or Microsoft) to expedite your visit to other websites. Check out each site initially to see which, if any, you will want to return to on a more or less daily basis, and keep a list of these handy. As we mentioned in the last chapter, your browser probably includes a feature that allows you to keep a "hot list" of the websites you'd like to note and return to under the item on your toolbar titled "Favorites."

How an Online Broker Works

Let's look at how a typical online discount broker works.

E*TRADE requires a $1,000 minimum to open an account. E*TRADE commission rates are $14.99 for "listed" (New York Stock and American Stock Exchange) securities and $19.99 for NASDAQ securities, up to 5,000 shares, for the first 29 trades. Add 1¢ per share once you go over 5,000 shares—and that's for all the shares, not just those over 5,000. This policy discourages investors from purchasing large blocks of "penny" stocks. (Remember those from Chapter 10? Penny stocks sell for a few dollars or less) E*TRADE rewards frequent traders with commission discounts. After 29 trades, the commissions drop to $9.99 for listed stocks and $14.99 for NASDAQ stocks. After 75 trades, all commissions drop to $9.99.

At E*TRADE, you can talk to a "live" broker, if necessary, for a $15 fee. E*TRADE doesn't charge set-up fees for IRAs but it does charge $25 to set up other retirement plans like money purchase plans or profit-sharing plans.

When opening an account with any web dealer, you first print out an account form from the website, fill it out, sign it, and mail it to the brokerage. Once you've been informed that your account has been opened and you're given a password, you can log on.

When you log onto E*TRADE, you will see a page with the following subheadings:

Home

Portfolio & Markets

Stocks & Options

Funds

Trading

My Accounts

Community Marketplace

Click on "Portfolio & Markets" and you will see the day's price charts on the Dow Jones Industrial Average as well as the NASDAQ composite. Down below you will see your portfolio holdings prices plus market headlines. E*TRADE offers price quotes in real time; if any quotes are delayed, they are noted as such on the screen.

Click on "My Accounts" and you will see the value of the account as of the current date, broken down between cash (held in money market funds) and equities. Again, you will notice a number of account records options in the left-hand margin. You've just looked at "Account Balances," so click on "Account Positions." This will show you each of your equity holdings by symbol, name, number of shares, and current price.

If you click on "Account Activity" in the left margin, you will see listed all the transactions in your account for the last three months. This includes principal transactions (B for buys, S for sells) as well as income transactions (interest and dividends received).

Again in the left margin, you can click on "Unrealized Gains & Losses" to see individual holdings broken down between cost and current market value, with the net gain (or loss) in the far-right margin. You can also click on "Tax Records" in the left margin to see realized gains or losses year-to-date.

If you wanted to make a trade, you would click on "Trading" in the top margin. A stock-order page would appear, allowing you to enter an order, with options in the left-hand margin. You would indicate the type of transaction (buy, sell, and so on), number of shares, stock symbol, and type of order (market, limit, and so on). Next you can click either "Place Order" to execute or "Cancel Order."

If you wanted to check out the broker's mutual funds offerings or look at your mutual fund holdings, you would click on "Funds." E*TRADE provides ratings and performance data for each fund showing the fund's performance (up to 10 years if available), fees, and composition. If you wished to purchase the fund, you would click on "Trading" in the upper margin, then "Funds," and then "Enter Order" from the left margin.

An online broker like E*TRADE will also supply business and company news, as well as its analysts' stock reports.

Super Strategy

Develop an alternative plan for those frustrating moments (and they will occur) when you can't get online or can't get your online broker account to work. Backups might include telephone contact, a full-service or discount broker, or patience (what's your hurry, anyway; aren't you a long-term investor?). E*TRADE, for example, allows you to talk to a broker directly (1-800-STOCKS-5), or you can use their automated telephone system (Telemaster).

Researching Investments Online

There's a lot of hype about how the web is "empowering" individual investors. But it may sometimes seem as if the web is overwhelming infoseekers rather than providing them with useful tools to manage and make more money.

Avoiding Investment Research Overload

To avoid investment research overload, try to prune. Most of the better stuff is still disseminated the old-fashioned way: books, newspapers, and magazines. The quality of some of the magazines, such as *SmartMoney*, *Fortune*, *Worth*, and *Forbes*, is constantly improving. Many offer online versions—we list some URLs at the end of this chapter.

But don't go nuts and sign up for pricey subscriptions for a bunch of online magazines. You can receive most online subscriptions on a trial basis. Go that route first and see whether a subscription adds true value to your investment life. If you have a subscription to *The Wall Street Journal*, however, you may want to subscribe to its interactive edition for a small additional fee. The *WSJ* is still the paper of record for financial news.

Many online brokers are offering research at their websites for their customers. This research is generally from highly regarded outside parties such as Standard and Poor's, Zacks, or Reuters. If you have some extra cash to burn and find yourself deeply into investing after reading this book, you may wish to sign up for a Bloomberg terminal for about $1,200 a month. Bloomberg is the Tiffany's of investment information systems, providing up-to-the-second price quotes and tons of exclusive info.

Search Engine Fun

Okay, you can snap out of your Bloomberg fantasy now! The average investor will do just fine without a Bloomberg terminal, especially if he or she becomes familiar with search engines. *Search engines* are businesses that collect and index web pages. Search engines (or portals, as they are sometimes called) are like electronic libraries. And, obviously, the largest libraries with the most "books," or web pages, are the most convenient. Your browser or online service will include a link called "Net Search" or "Search Engines" that will hook you up with an array of search engines.

By far, the number one search engine is Yahoo!, which logs about 111 million web-page views per month. It is definitely the largest electronic library and is usually rated number one by investors for the following reasons:

♦ Yahoo! provides both comprehensive and dynamic financial information, 24 hours a day.

♦ Yahoo! provides rudimentary data that most investors can use.

> **Fiscal Facts**
>
> The great majority of search engines are free, because the site developer sells advertising space. Eventually, you will either adapt to the advertising or develop an acute case of nausea and swear off the portals. When you think about it, though, the ads are no different from what you face in your local newspaper, so please don't get too annoyed.

- It's easy to use.

- The investment information on Yahoo! tends to be quite timely. We particularly like Yahoo! Finance at finance.yahoo.com.

Other excellent search engines include Excite, Lycos, and Infoseek. Excite is probably Yahoo!'s closest competitor. Excite may be more appropriate for the beginner investor, because it provides broader information (on home mortgage rates, for example).

Using a Search Engine

When you visit a search engine's website, you will see a flashing cursor inside a small box. You type in that box a word or phrase that best describes what kind of information you are looking for, then you click "Search" and within minutes the search engine will provide you with a bunch of URLs for sites with information on your topic. The search engine will also provide tips to help you narrow your search.

Use a search engine the same way you would look up an author's books in the library or a service in the Yellow Pages. If you want to research Patriot bonds for example, type in "Patriot bonds" using quotation marks so the search engine knows to provide only sites about Patriot bonds and not every bond site out there! Some search engines recommend that you type +Patriot+bonds to communicate that you want only sites that include both "Patriot" and "bonds."

Finally, use that ancient implement known as the telephone to call a company you are researching. Where do you find the telephone number? On the company's website. Or use Yahoo!'s phone directory.

Investor's Idiom

A **search engine** is a business that collects and indexes the zillions of proliferating websites (so you don't have to!). Think of it as a big electronic library with a super-fast librarian who can find you any book in the world in a matter of minutes. Search engines are also referred to as "portals."

Portals Just for Investors

The portals listed below are those we find particularly useful for investors. Be careful, though, as some research, such as company profiles, is provided for free, while more in-depth research may be pricey.

- **Yahoo! Finance,** finance.yahoo.com.

- **Bloomberg,** www.bloomberg.com. A very good source for general business news and both broad-market and security-specific information. Anyone who has ever used a Bloomberg machine appreciates its many attributes. Really a must. (The site, not that expensive terminal!)

♦ **CEOExpress,** www.ceoexpress.com. A portal that bills itself as "for the busy CEO," it provides a very broad variety of business-related website links, alphabetically listed.

♦ **Kiplinger Online,** www.kiplinger.com. Kiplinger Online provides stock quotes; lists of great Internet sites for investors; lists of top mutual funds, business news, and forecasts; and even online calculators to help you track your portfolio.

Tracking Your Portfolio

Most brokers keep a log of your portfolio that will show its value on a daily basis. You will also receive a confirmation for each trade, either in the mail or via your PC. Monthly statements are mailed if the account was active; these statements include dividends, margin activity, and trading.

Brokers also provide year-end summaries that will help you file Schedule D on your tax returns. These summaries include dividends, margin interest, and a 'Net proceeds summary that is also furnished to the IRS. The latter is referred to as a 1099. Active traders ought to consider buying a commercial software program such as Quicken to tabulate their "buys and sells." This will come in especially handy when it's time to fill out that Schedule D.

Portfolio-Management Programs

Your online broker automatically updates your portfolio, but what if you have several different accounts with different brokers? How do you keep track of it all?

Programs are available online that can help you keep excellent records of every security you own. These programs will automatically apply daily price changes to your holdings, calculate your portfolio's value, and compare your current return to your financial goals. Most portfolio-management programs will also help you with asset allocation and even alert you when securities hit prices at which you may want to buy or sell.

There are two kinds of portfolio-management programs available online:

♦ Web-based portfolio-management programs. These are programs you can access by registering at websites that offer them:

- ◆ **Thomson MarketEdge Portfolio Tracker,** www.thomsoninvest.net

- ◆ **Stockpoint Portfolio Management,** www.investor.stockpoint.com

- ◆ *The Wall Street Journal's* **portfolio tracker,** www.wsj.com

- ◆ PC-based portfolio-management programs. These are software programs you download from the Internet to your computer. These programs can offer more functions than web-based programs, but, on the other hand, they don't provide the daily stock quote and other financial information that the web-based programs can. Some popular PC-based portfolio management programs include the following:

  - ◆ **PointCast,** www.pointcast.com

  - ◆ **Inside Track Lite,** www.quote.com/info/microquest/liteinst.html

  - ◆ **StockTracker Lite,** www.stockcenter.com

Three Isn't Necessarily a Crowd

Finally, we'd like to briefly discuss a technical matter generally overlooked by most articles and books about investing online, yet which should be understood by all: third-market execution.

How can an online broker offer to trade thousands of shares for average commissions of only about $15? The answer is that your broker may well be selling your order to a third-market dealer or broker that pays your broker a fee for that order. In Wall Street jargon, this arrangement is known as "payment for order flow." It is perfectly legal and has the blessing of the regulators. Your purchase of a New York Stock Exchange stock through an online broker is not actually executed on the NYSE but through a third-market dealer.

Do you receive an inferior trade execution as a result? We don't think so. In fact, you are benefiting from tapping into the world of specialized traders who move huge amounts of capital in the blink of an eye. It is our view that if you can get NYSE executions at cheap Internet rates, go for it!

Now, to send you merrily surfing across the 'Net, here's our final offering—a list of our favorite financial websites! One last piece of advice: Don't believe any "hot tips" or "insider information" you come across on the web. Odds are it's been planted to get you to do something stupid (and potentially profitable for the planter).

Financial Markets

biz.yahoo.com/reports/stocks.html (U.S. markets news)

www.amex.com (American Stock Exchange)

beta.nasdaq.com (Nasdaq)

www.nyse.com (NYSE)

dir.yahoo.com/Business_and_Economy/Finance_and_Investment/Bonds (Bonds)

dir.yahoo.com/Business_and_Economy/Finance_and_Investment/Futures_and_
Options (Futures and Options)

Quotes

quote.yahoo.com

www.bigcharts.com (BigCharts)

www.dbc.com (DBC Online)

biz.yahoo.com/zacks/extreme.html (earnings surprises)

www.justquotes.com (Just Quotes)

finance.lycos.com/home/stocks/quotes.asp?symbols=

www.thomsonrtq.com/index.sht (real-time quotes)

www.stockmaster.com (Stockmaster)

www.stocksite.com (StockSite)

www.iclub.com/investorama.html (stock screening sites)

Financial News

djnewswires.com (Dow Jones News)

dailynews.yahoo.com/headlines/business (Yahoo's financial news)

biz.yahoo.com/industry (financial news and info by industry)

biz.yahoo.com/reports/world.html (international business news)

biz.yahoo.com/bw (BizWire)

headlines.yahoo.com/Full_Coverage/Business (Financial News)

dir.yahoo.com/Business_and_Economy/Finance_and_Investment/News_and_Media
(Financial News)

dir.yahoo.com/News_and_Media/Business (Business News)

dir.yahoo.com/Business_and_Economy/Finance_and_Investment/News_and_Media/
Quotes/International_Markets (Quotes and News)

Investment Research

djindexes.com (Dow Jones averages and other indexes)

biz.yahoo.com/research/earncal/today.html (company research)

biz.yahoo.com/reports/ipo.html (reports on initial public offerings)

www.hoovers.com (IPO Central)

tfc-charts.w2d.com/ (TFC Commodity Charts)

www.bbb.org (Better Business Bureau)

www.annualreportservice.com (Annual Report Service)

www.corporateinformation.com (CorporateInformation.com)

www.thomsonib.com/ (Thomson Financial market analysis)

www.investware.com/aaii.stm (American Association of Individual Investors)

www.investools.com (Investools Research)

Investment Message Boards and Chat Rooms

messages.yahoo.com/yahoo/Business___Finance/Investments/index.html (Yahoo!'s list
of finance message boards)

chat.yahoo.com/?room=investments@news (stock chat; note, you have to register to
participate in chats)

mb15.mb.scd.yahoo.com/yahoo/Business_and_Finance/Stocks/index.html (stock message board)

boards.fool.com (The Motley Fool discussion boards)
features.yahoo.com/finance/survey (marketplace poll)

www.thestreet.com/tsc/boards.html (members-only message board for The Street)

ragingbull.lycos.com/cgi-bin/static.cgi/a=index.txt&d=community (Raging Bull message boards)

www.siliconinvestor.com/stocktalk/ (Silicon Investor StockTalk)

groups.yahoo.com/group/gloomanddoomclub/ (Yahoo! Doom and Gloom Club for
bearish investors)

Investment Clubs and Community-Based Sites

clubs.yahoo.com/Business_Finance

www.blackstocks.com (African American network)

www.gfn.com (the Gay Financial Network)

socialfunds.com (socially responsible investing)

www.wfn.com (Women's Financial Network)

www.msmoney.com (investing for women)

www.latinstocks.com (investing for Latinos)

Mutual Funds

www.morningstar.net (Morningstar)

www.fool.com (Motley Fool)

www.brill.com (Mutual Funds Interactive)

www.thestreet.com (The Street)

Financial Magazines

www.businessweek.com (*BusinessWeek*)

www.cfonet.com (*CFO Magazine*)

www.economist.com (*The Economist*)

www.feer.com (*Far East Economic Review*)

www.fastcompany.com/home.html (*Fast Company*)

www.ft.com (*Financial Times*)

www.forbes.com (*Forbes*)

www.fortune.com (*Fortune*)

www.hbsp.harvard.edu (*Harvard Business School Publishing*)

www.industryweek.com (*IndustryWeek*)

www.investors.com (*Investor's Business Daily*)

www.joc.com (*Journal of Commerce*)

www.kiplinger.com (*Kiplinger*)

business-times.asia1.com.sg (*Singapore Business Times*)

www.smartmoney.com (*SmartMoney*)

www.strategy-business.com (*Strategy & Business*)

www.worth.com (*Worth*)

Technology Magazines

www.byte.com (*BYTE*)

www.computerworld.com (*Computerworld*)

www.eb-mag.com (*Electronic Business*)

www.electronicmarkets.org (*Electronic Markets*)

www.techweb.com (*TechWeb*)

www.webfinance.net (*Web Finance*)

www.hotwired.com/frontdoor (*Wired*)

www.pcworld.com (*PC World*)

www.macworld.com (*Macworld*)

Insurance Sites

insurance.yahoo.com/auto.html (auto insurance)

insurance.yahoo.com/life.html (life and health insurance)

insurance.yahoo.com/home.html (home and renters insurance)

Government Agencies

www.federalreserve.gov (Federal Reserve)

www.business.gov (U.S. Business Advisor)

www.sec.gov/news/newsindx.htm (SEC News Digest)

www.sec.gov/edaux/searches.htm (SEC database)

Investor Services

www.ameritrade.com (Ameritrade)

www.datek.com (Datek)

www.etrade.com (E*TRADE)

www.fid-inv.com (Fidelity Investments)

www.schwab.com (Schwab Online)

www.waterhouse.com (TD Waterhouse)

www.jpmorgan.com (JP Morgan)

www.lehman.com (Lehman Brothers)

www.ml.com (Merrill Lynch)

www.ms.com (Morgan Stanley)

www.smithbarney.com (Salomon Smith Barney)

www.vfinance.com (Venture Capital Resources)

www.wellsfargo.com (Wells Fargo)

Media and Other Resources Available Online

Here's a list of media and other resources available online, just to get you poking around. It's not remotely conclusive, but you can use it to find your bearings in the vast world of Internet information. Just enter the name of the resource into a search engine (surround the name in quotation marks if it's longer than one word), and you're off to the races. Have fun!

Online Television News: ABC | BBC | CBS | CNN | CNNfn | Fox | MSNBC | PBS

Business Magazines: *BusinessWeek* | *CFO* | *The Economist* | *Electronic Business* | *Far East Economic Review* | *Fast Company* | *Forbes DigitalTool* | *Fortune* | *Harvard B. School Publishing* | *Inc.* | *Industry Week* | *IW-Growing Co.* | *Money* | *Newsweek* | *Red Herring* | *MIT Sloan Management Review* | *Smart Money* | *The Standard* | *Strategy & Business* | *Time* | *Upside Online* | *U.S. News & World Report* | *Web Finance* | *Worth*

Technology Magazines: *BYTE* | *CIO* | *c|net* | *CNET Radio* | *Computerworld* | *Electronic Markets* | *Emmerce* | *First Monday* | *Intranet Journal* | *MIT TechReview* | *TechWeb* | *Wired* | *ZDNet*

Custom News: CNN | Excite | Infobeat | Inquisit | My Yahoo! | Netscape Business

Newspage Newsfeeds: AP Wire | Bloomberg | Bloomberg Audio | Broadcast.com | Business Wire | Canada Newswire | Drudge Report | Industry.net | NewsLink | NewsReal | PR Newswire | Reuters

Internet Search Engines: Alta Vista | Deja News | Dogpile | Domain Name Search | Excite | Google | HotBot | Infoseek | LibrarySpot | Magellan | Metacrawler | Northern Light | Snap | Wall Street Search | WebCrawler | Yahoo! | Search Tips

Financial Markets: AMEX | Averages & Composites | NASDAQ | Nikkei Net | NYSE | Commodities Charts (T-bills, etc.) | Futures/Options Markets | Other Stock Exchanges

Analysis: Deutsche Bank | Dismal Scientist SEC: Edgar Online People | FreeEdgar | SEC Digest | SEC Database | SIC Codes

Government Agencies: Federal Reserve System | Federal Web Locator | Foreign Government Resources | Government Printing Office | International Trade Administration | IRS | OSHA | U.S. Business Advisor | U.S. Patents & Trademarks | Statistics: Bureau of Labor Stats | Cyber Atlas | Fedstats | Population Lookup | Economic Research Data | U.S. Statistical Abstract | Statistics USA | U-Michigan Documents Center | U.S. Census Datamaps

Legislature: C-SPAN | Congressional VoteWatch | Federal Register | Legislator Search Engine | State Legislatures | Thomas Legislative Search | U.S. House (e-mail) | U.S. Senate (e-mail)

Business Links: CorpFinet | Financial Data Finder | FinWeb | Invest-o-rama | IOMA Business Directory | Research Links

Real Estate: HomeAdvisor | HomeScout | IRED | Move Central | National Real Estate Investor | Net Properties | Real Estate News | Shopping Center Database

Quotes and Market News: BigCharts | DBC Online | Earnings Surprises | Just Quotes | Quicken on fn | Quote | Real Time Quotes (free) | Stockmaster | StockSite | Stock Screening Sites | Upgrades & Downgrades | Yahoo! Finance

Online Investor Services: Ameritrade | Datek | E*TRADE | Fidelity Investments | Harris Direct | Schwab Online | Waterhouse Securities

Banking & Finance: Bank Rate Monitor | Cowen & Co | Finance Student's Web World | Hambrecht & Quist | Internet Banking Index | JP Morgan | Lehman Research | Merrill Lynch | Morgan Stanley | Salomon Smith Barney M&A: Venture Capital Resources

Small/Family Business: Better Business Bureau | Business Forms | Business Toolkit | Chambers of Commerce | Government Resources | Idea Cafe | Institute for Family Business | MoneyHunter | Sample Business Plans | SCORE | SBA | SmallbizNet | Small Business State Profiles | Smartbiz | Taxes | Yahoo! Small Business

Investing & IPO Research: 2001 Fortune Investor's Guide | Alert IPO | American Association of Individual Investors | CDA Insider Watch | Final Bell | First Call | Investools Research | IPO Central | Microsoft Investor | MoneyNet | Money Talks | Morningstar | Motley Fool | Mutual Funds Interactive | The Street | Syndicate | Tech Investor | Zacks

Bankruptcy: American Bankruptcy Institute | Bankruptcy Stats | Internet Bankruptcy Library

References: Dictionary | Encyclopedia.com | Hypertext Dictionary | Internet Public Library | Learn2 | Library of Congress | Virtual Reference Desk | National Archives | NetLingo | One Look Dictionary | Technical Support Search | Thesaurus | World Holiday Calendar | Beginner's Central

Directories: AnyWho (AT&T) | Area Code Finder | Four11 | Switchboard | 800 Directory | Yellow Pages | Zip Code Finder

Computers/Software: Buy Direct | CDW | Cyberian Outpost | Egghead | Insight | NECX | Shopper.com

The Least You Need to Know

◆ If speed matters to you, ask fellow investors if a particular online broker is quick or slow.

◆ Treat chat room and newsgroup advice with great caution. Many participants are there to promote their interests, couching their sales pitches as hot tips.

◆ Have an alternative trading method for those frustrating moments when you can't get online or can't get your online broker account to work.

◆ Search engines are businesses that collect and index web pages.

◆ Portfolio management programs are available online that can help you keep excellent records of every security you own.

Part 6

Advanced Investment Plays

By now you've developed your own investment I.Q. And it's pretty darn high. You're now capable of understanding some fairly complex investments and can decide whether or not to include them in your portfolio.

Most of us will never trade pork bellies or gold, but we can use the same tools that commodities traders use—such as options and futures contracts—to strengthen our own portfolios and protect them from volatile market swings. This section builds on everything you've learned so far and shows you how to apply advanced plays to your investments.

Take a look at the offerings in this part. It'll feel good to have a clue when you hear about hedge funds, or real estate investment trusts, or private equity funds at a party or on the news. You may even find that not only do you understand these investments, but they may also help you meet your goals.

Chapter 21

Hedging Your Options

In This Chapter

- All about options
- Protecting your portfolio with puts and calls
- Selling short vs. trading options
- Protecting stock positions
- Advanced hedging strategies

Well, we promised that at the end of this book we would get into some advanced investment plays, and here we are—about to tackle options. Can you believe you even know enough to get into this topic? But if you've been with us so far, you definitely do! Options are contracts that give you the option, but not the obligation, to buy or sell a specified quantity of stocks or bonds. Options have two purposes:

- To protect you against a sickening drop in stock prices
- To enable you to profit from an exciting rise in stock prices

Both options and futures contracts, which we'll discuss in the next chapter, are called *hedges*. You've no doubt heard the phrase, "He's hedging his bets." Options and futures contracts can be used to hedge your bets on the stock market. A caveat: The strategies we'll be discussing in this and the next few chapters are quite sophisticated and should not be undertaken without careful research and the support of a trusted pro.

Our goal is simply to give you enough background so you can ask that trusted pro intelligent questions. Toward that end, we've gone a bit deep on some topics; if you can get through it, great, but if you can't, don't sweat it now. Just keep us around as your personal reference. Should you find yourself considering any of these investments in the near future, we'll still be here. Right on your shelf.

> **Investor's Idiom**
>
> An **option** is a contract that is listed on an exchange just like a stock. The contract states what is to be delivered for what price and what time period. At the end of the designated time period, the option loses all its value. The option is a right, but not an obligation, to exercise the rights stated in the contract.

> **Investor's Idiom**
>
> The **strike price**, also called the **exercise price**, is the price at which the holder of an option contract can buy ("call") or sell ("put") the underlying security. For example, a Computer-Nerd, Inc., 50-call option means you can buy 100 shares of ComputerNerd, Inc. at $50 per share. A ComputerNerd, Inc., 50-put option means you can sell 100 shares of ComputerNerd, Inc., at $50 per share.

Puts and Calls

There are two kinds of option contracts: *puts* and *calls*. When you buy a call option, you are buying the right to purchase a stock at a set price, called the *strike price*, for a specified period of time—usually a few months.

Here's a very simple example of how a call option contract works. Let's say you're thinking about buying 100 shares of ComputerNerd, Inc., stock, which is currently selling for $40 a share. You've heard that the company's coming out with an awesome new spreadsheet software and the stock price could rise sharply as a result. Hmmm … what to do?

You could lay out the $4,000 now for the 100 shares and hold them, praying nightly that you were right about that software and looking forward to selling your stock for $6,000 when the share price rises to $60 for a tidy $2,000 profit. But what if there's a glitch in the software and ComputerNerd doesn't release it on schedule and the stock price sinks to $20? Oy! This could make for some very restless nights.

Hedge Your Bet with a Call

This is where an option comes in very handy. Instead of laying out $4,000 for 100 shares of ComputerNerd, Inc., contact your broker and buy a three-month call option on 100 shares of Computer Nerd stock at a strike price of $40. The option will only cost you, say, $400. Now, if the stock does rise to $60 before your three months are up, you have a contract entitling you to buy the stock for only $40. You'd pay only $4,000 for $6,000 worth of stock. You could turn around and sell the stock right away for a $2,000 profit. Pretty nifty!

If the stock price falls below $40, simply don't exercise the call option. Sure, you're out the $400 you spent on the option contract, but that's a lot easier to swallow than having spent $4,000 on the stock and watching its value shrink to $3,000 or $2,000 or less. With the call option, you've hedged your bet.

A put option is the opposite of a call option. A put is a contract that gives you the option to sell a security at a specified price until the contract's expiration date. With a call, you are hoping for the price of the security to rise, but with a put, you are praying for the price to fall.

Prevent Portfolio Wipeout with a Put

Let's say you're bearish on ComputerNerd, Inc. You're convinced the company's spreadsheet software, which everyone else thinks is going to turn the industry on its ear, is a stinker. Unfortunately, your spouse thinks differently and insisted on buying 100 shares of ComputerNerd at $40 a share. How do you protect yourself from disaster?

Call your broker and buy a three-month put option with a strike price of $36. This contract guarantees that for three months you can dump those 100 shares of ComputerNerd for at least $36 per share. If the stock tanks within the next three months, you can get out at $36, even if the share price drops to, say, $18. Instead of watching helplessly as your $4,000 stake in ComputerNerd drops to $1,800, you can exercise your option when the stock price hits $36 and get out with $3,600 intact. Because you've hedged your spouse's bet, you lose only $400, plus whatever you spent on the put option contract.

Investor's Idiom

An option **expires**—becomes worthless—on its expiration date. Options expire on the Saturday following the third Friday of the month in which they can be exercised. For example, ComputerNerd, Inc., December 50 options expire on December 19, 2002. Nine months is typically the maximum expiration date on an option.

How Did This Get Started?

Options trading has been around about as long as securities trading, but until the 1970s, options traded in an informal, unregulated manner. Brokerage houses specializing in "puts and calls" would advertise their specials of the day in publications like *The Wall Street Journal*. There was no regulated market.

Fiscal Facts

Options trade in "round lot equivalents" of 100 shares. Each option contract covers 100 shares of the underlying security. Options are quoted in dollar terms, with the 100 shares underneath each option implied; a $2 option, for example, really costs $200—$2 for each share.

After the 1973–1974 bear market for stocks took prices of popular indices like the Dow Jones and the S&P 500 down some 40 percent, it became clear that options could play an important role in stabilizing the market and protecting investors from severe drops. The government got involved in standardizing options trading. This led to the creation of the Chicago Board Options Exchange (CBOE). With the creation of the CBOE and its sister institution, the Options Clearing Corporation (OCC), trading in options grew phenomenally.

Risk-Loving Speculator Seeks Cautious Hedgehog

Options can be viewed in two ways: as rank speculation ("I bet you $200 that ComputerNerd, Inc., stock will go up 20 points in 90 days") or as a hedge ("I can protect myself against my ComputerNerd stock going down by buying put options with a $40 strike price for three months"). When you think about it, it takes both a speculator and a hedger to complete a contract.

An option's price is called a *premium*. The premium is the price the options buyer pays and the options writer receives for the option. The premium is like a commission, except that the premium diminishes in value steadily until the contract expires. A three-month contract offered June 1, 2002, to buy a ComputerNerd, Inc., 50-call option might sell for $3, for example, when it's first offered. The price will decline, however, over the course of the three months. Why? Because as time passes, the option is protecting the buyer for less and less time.

Investor's Idiom

An **options writer** (or "seller" or "issuer") creates the options contract, and must stand ready to honor the terms of the contract. If you write an option on 100 shares of ComputerNerd, Inc., common stock and the buyer of your options contract exercises his or her option, you must be prepared to deliver the requisite shares of ComputerNerd, Inc., to the buyer. The **options buyer** (or "holder") pays the options writer a premium for the right to buy the shares of ComputerNerd, Inc., in a call option or sell the shares of ComputerNerd, Inc., in a put option.

The option's price, or premium, is the maximum loss that the buyer of the contract can experience. An option for 200 shares at $3 costs $600. That's the premium. If the price of the stock doesn't go your way and you never exercise the option, you lose the $600. But that's all.

In the Money

Options are referred to as either:

♦ "In the money"

♦ "Out of the money"

♦ "At the money"

This swinging lingo simply defines the difference between the option strike price and the current price of the underlying stock.

If the strike price is less than the current market price, for example, a call option would be described as "in the money." You are already ahead by the difference (or spread) between the strike price and market price.

This same situation would be described as "out of the money" for a put option, however. Why? Because, you are behind by the same amount for the put. You are betting the stock will go down, but, darn, it's going the other way.

"At the money" means the stock price and strike price are equal.

Reading an Option Table

Let's take a look at several examples from Section B of the August 8, 2002, *The Wall Street Journal*, using AOLTW (AOL Time Warner).

Option/Strike		**Call** Exp.	Vol.	Last	**Put** Vol.	Last
AOLTW	7.50	Jan	26	4.20	3819	1.10
10.80	10	Aug	1428	1.15	1308	0.40
10.80	10	Sep	843	1.80	668	1.05
10.80	10	Jan	49	2.90	4003	1.85
10.80	12.50	Aug	1151	0.10	36	1.75
10.80	12.50	Sep	1362	0.65	101	2.45

Let's look at the first contract, on the first line. This is the AOL January 7.50-call option. The buyer of the contract has the right to purchase 100 shares of AOL at $7.50 per share, which is $3.30 less than where the stock closed on August 7, 2002. This is an example of a call option that is "in the money," because the buyer has the right to purchase the stock for a lower price than it is selling for on the open market.

The contract runs out on January 18, 2003. How do we know? Because *Jan* stands for January, and all contracts expire on the Saturday following the third Friday in the month. The volume on August 7 was 26, or 26 contracts. Since each contract equals 100 shares, the AOL Jan 7.50-call options traded an equivalent of 2,600 common shares.

The last (or closing premium) of 4.20 means that it would cost you $4.20 times 100 (everything being expressed in 100 share terms), or $420, to purchase this call option contract. And notice that your break-even point (strike price + premium – closing price) is 7.50 + 4.20 - 10.80, or 0.90. If the stock price goes up more than 0.90 the next trading day, you are ahead of the game. Of course, each day, the stock price and the premium are subject to change (but that's the exciting part, right?).

Now, check out the put. Notice that there is a put option for the same contract. Here, the purchaser is wagering that the share price will decline. Since the strike price is less than the closing price, the put option contract is presently "out of the market." The stock would have to decline by more than the difference, or more than 3.30 to be "in the market." Notice that the break-even point is different: first, you have to get back to "at the money," which is the 3.30 strike price; then, you have to recover your premium, or 1.10, for a total stock price decline of 4.40.

Options Galore

The second contract listed on the table, with the strike price of $10 has an August 2002 expiration. Each stock has options with four different months: the two closest months (in this case August and September, plus two other months). However, newspapers can't justify showing data on all the months. See how the August 10 premium is less than the September 10 premium? The closer an option is to expiring, the smaller its premium.

Most Active Contracts

Finally, let's take a look at the "most active contracts" list in the *Journal* for August 8, 2002. Under the most active contract list for that day, you would have found the following information for Cisco:

Option/Strike	Vol.	Exch	Last	Net Chg	Close
CISCO Aug 12.50 P	20,350	XC	0.35	-0.80	12.99

The P stands for Put; since August 7 was an "up" day in the market, the contracts with the biggest losses were put contracts. XC stands for the Exchange Composite. The net change of -0.80 means that the premium declined 0.80 from the August 6 close 1.15! In other words, had you purchased the put option (CISCO Aug 12.50) at the close on August 6 and sold it at the close on August 7, you would have lost 69.6 percent for the day (-0.80 / 1.15 = -69.60 percent)! In dollar terms, if you spent $115, you received $35, for a loss of $80.

Selling Short vs. Trading Options

Before the options market developed, speculators who wanted to bet that a stock's price was going to fall had only one play—to "short" the stock. When you short a stock, you don't actually buy the shares—you borrow them from a broker. You take the stock you've borrowed and sell it. Then you pray (a lot!) that the price of the stock will fall before you have to give the shares back to the broker.

Because what are you going to use to buy the shares to give back to the broker? That's right, the money you made selling the borrowed stock. What if you don't make any money selling the borrowed stock? You're in big trouble.

Let's say you borrowed 100 shares of ComputerNerd, Inc., agreeing to return them the next day. You go out and sell the 100 shares for $40/share and make $4,000. If the stock price falls to $32, you'll only need to use $3,200 to buy the 100 shares to return to the broker. You can pocket $800 profit. Pretty swift.

But what if the stock price shoots up to $50/share. Uh oh, you're gonna need $5,000 to purchase those 100 shares. Well, you've got $4,000 from selling short. That other $1,000 is going to have to come out of your pocket. Big bummer.

Since August 7 was a strong up day in the stock market, very few put instruments were profitable on the day. But let's look at one that did work: The Verizon October 25 put contract. The contract closed August 7 at $1.50, v. $1.40 on August 6. So you made, for one day. $.10/$1.40, or 7.1 percent. If you had simply "shorted" the stock at the close of August 6, at $29.87, and sold it at the close on August 7 at $29.47, you would have made a piddling 1.4 percent.

Now you understand why the vast majority of option contracts are not exercised: the buyer of the put or call option is interested in trading the contract, not the underlying stock. The potential for profit is so much greater with option contracts.

Risky Business

Throughout this book, we've harped on the relationship between risk and return—and options are no exception. The very fact that you can reap such high returns with options should tip you off that they are very risky.

The day someone lost 69.6percent on Cisco August 12.50-put contracts, for example, someone else could have made a bundle on Cisco October 15-call contracts. The contract closed at 0/65, up 0.10 for a day gain of 18.2 percent (+0.10/0.55)! The underlying common stock of Cisco gained only 7.6 percent that day. The option gave a much bigger bounce.

> **Crash Alert**
>
> If you are a buyer of an option contract (put or call), you stand to make *or* lose a lot in percentage terms. And don't forget that any gains are going to be short-term, which means they are subject to income tax, at rates up to 38.6 percent (2002).

Sellers of option contracts take on even more risk. As we said before, the buyer's maximum loss per contract is the amount of the premium. If you sold a call option on the AOL January 10, for example, you would receive the $290 premium. But if the stock rose to $12 in November, you would have to spend $1,200 to be in a position to deliver if, by some chance, your contract was exercised. So worst-case scenario, you could suffer an out-of-pocket cost of $910 ($1200 - $290). Oh, the pain.

Option Strategies That Protect Your Stock Positions

In the previous example, we assumed that you, as the option writer, did not actually own the stock and would have to go buy it if the option you sold was exercised.

> **Super Strategy**
>
> A variation of the covered call strategy is called a "buy-write" program, where you simultaneously buy, let's say, 100 shares of AT&T and write a call option on them. This can be an especially effective tool in tax-deferred accounts, such as IRAs, and defined benefit accounts, but using it is not a part-time job. Some professional firms hire individuals specifically for their buy-write expertise to add value to the retirement accounts under their management.

But suppose you did own the stock. You could write (sell) an option contract on the stock. This is called "covered call writing." When you own the underlying stock, writing a call is a conservative course of action. When you do so, you earn additional income minus the premium the option buyer pays you—which can help offset any minor price weakness in your stock. If the stock moves up in price and, for some reason the option is exercised, you already own the stock, so you won't take a hit on the price. Pretty much a win-win deal.

Using Puts for Downside Protection

An even more conservative step is to purchase a put option for a stock you already own. This gives you unlimited downside protection for simply the cost of the put. And, of course, you would fully benefit if the price of the stock went up.

You get unlimited upside, as well as protection on the downside, because the value of the put increases as the price of the stock decreases. This works especially well if the strike price is at or close to the market price, and you purchase the longest put contract, which has the lowest premium and provides more time for the strategy to pay off. This strategy works best if you are concerned about a significant correction in the stock market or your particular stock.

Again, remember that all these strategies involving put and call options trigger income tax events for taxable accounts. Repeat after us: "I will visit my trusted professional should I become intrigued with these strategies."

Stock Index Options

Unlike individual stock options, stock index options give you a chance to hedge your entire equity portfolio—assuming it is diversified as we have advised.

Stock index options dominate the options scene now due to the broad acceptance of the product by money managers. *The Wall Street Journal* lists 37 different indices upon which options can be written/purchased. These include well-known broad indices, such as the Dow Jones Industrials, S&P 500, S&P 100, NASDAQ 100, Russell 2000, sector or industry indices, and indices for foreign stock markets.

S&P Index Options

The contracts are listed under Index Options Trading in *The Wall Street Journal*. Let's take a look at the options contracts for two indices: the S&P 100 and the S&P 500 in the August 8, 2002, issue.

If we look under S&P 100 Index (OEX) and scan down to Aug 440c and Aug 440p (c standing for call and p for put), we can see the volume, last price, and net change for each:

Strike	Vol.	Last	Net Change
Aug 440c	1,881	10	+1.10
Aug 440p	724	10.50	−7.10

We selected these two contracts because they are closest to the current price ($441.46). How do we know that? Because there is a table set into the Index Options Trading page called Ranges for Underlying Indexes. And the fourth index down is the S&P 100. The value of the contract, the total exercise price, and the premium are each derived by multiplying each by 100:

$100 \times \$441.66 = \$44,166 =$ contract value

$100 \times 440c = \$44,000 =$ total exercise price

$100 \times 10 = \$1,000 =$ cost to purchase option

You can exercise the contract on any day, just like with individual stock options; however, the contract is settled with cash, not with the security.

The S&P 500 follows the same format and procedure as the S&P 100, with one important difference: the S&P 500 option can be exercised only on the expiration date. This is referred to as a European-style option. American-style options can be exercised on any given day.

Hedge Strategies for Index Options

Hedge strategies for index options are similar to those for individual stock options. Suppose you wanted to hedge your diversified stock portfolio by purchasing the correct number of put contracts. By "correct number" we mean that you would buy put contracts with values that approximate the decline in your equity portfolio that you are worried about experiencing.

Similar to purchasing insurance—which, in effect, this is—your premium is your maximum cost. Let's assume your equity portfolio is presently worth $1 million and is invested similarly to the S&P 100. Multiply $100 times the current value of the S&P 100 ($441.46) and you'll get $44,146. Divide this into $1 million and you'll get $22.64 (round up to 23). To hedge your portfolio, you'll need to buy 23 put contracts.

Pick the put contract closest to the current index price, or 440p, for the month you want. The premium for 23 October 440-put options is 32. What's the maximum cost to you? 32 times $100 is the cost per contract, and you need 23 contracts. Your cost is

$73,600, or 7.4 percent of your equity portfolio. As you can see, this is not cheap insurance. Equity index hedging is not for your everyday amateur.

The Braveheart of Wall Street

Still with us? Good! If you're hankering for more, we've got two more aggressive strategies for you:

- **Straddles.** These are the simultaneous purchase of a put and call for the same stock or index at the same strike price and expiration date. The straddle buyer makes money if the price of the stock moves significantly up or down. The straddle writer makes money even if there is little or no stock price movement by capturing two premiums. This is a very hot strategy among professionals.

- **The spread.** This is the purchase and sale of options on the same stock, only the options have either a different strike price with same expiration date or the same strike price and different expiration dates.

  - A bull spread involves purchasing an option with a lower strike price (i.e., "in the money") and the sale of an option at a higher strike price (i.e., "out of the money").

  - With a bear spread, you sell the option at a lower strike price and purchase the option at a higher strike price.

These strategies can get quite esoteric and should not be tried in the comfort of your own home. And remember, again, that any success translates into short-term gains, which means you'll be paying income tax on them. So don't even consider using these strategies for any portfolio except your tax-sheltered IRA account.

LEAPS

Finally, we have LEAPs, which stands for Long-Term Equity Anticipation Security. These are long-term option contracts that are very popular with individual investors. There are two main differences between LEAPs and regular options:

- LEAPS can be written for up to a three-year expiration date vs. a maximum of nine months for traditional options. If you are really convinced that the market is going to move strongly in a certain direction, a LEAP gives you more time than a traditional option to wait for that move to happen. All LEAPs expire in December on the Saturday following the third Friday.

◆ The price of a LEAP is one-tenth the price and size of a traditional option. This is much more manageable for individual investors than having to buy 100 round lots every time you want to buy a regular option.

The combination of a longer-term and lower contract size (one-tenth the size of standard contracts) make LEAPs attractive to individual investors. Just be sure you look before you leap—all the strategies in this chapter are from a very volatile and sophisticated game best left to experts.

The Least You Need to Know

◆ Options are contracts that give you the option, but not the obligation, to buy or sell a specified quantity of stocks or bonds.

◆ Options and futures contracts are called "hedges."

◆ A "put" is an option to sell; a "call" is an option to buy.

◆ You can conservatively use options to protect your portfolio from stock market moves.

◆ Enlist the aid of an experienced broker if you want to get involved with options.

Chapter 22

Fancy Futures

In This Chapter

- ◆ How a future differs from an option
- ◆ Butter to zinc—the seven main types of commodities
- ◆ Buying on margin
- ◆ Using futures to offset uncertainty

Looking for a bright future? Well then, you've come to the right chapter. A futures contract is a legal agreement between two parties. One agrees to purchase from the other a specified asset at a specified price at a specified time in the future. Futures contracts are made on everything from commodities, like pork bellies or sugar, to stocks and indexes.

There are also options on futures. Now, don't let this confuse you. Just remember that the purpose of these "advanced play" chapters is simply to give you some background in these complicated investments.

Both options and futures are called *derivatives* because they "derive" their value from the underlying security, index, or commodity they represent. Derivatives tend to be short-term "plays" dominated by large institutions. You participate at your own peril. If you do decide to participate, be sure you work with a very experienced full-service broker specializing in options/ futures.

What Is a Commodity?

A *commodity* is a basic food or raw material. If you turn once again to our old friend, *The Wall Street Journal*, you will see toward the back of Section C a subheading entitled Cash Prices. Listed here are cash prices for seven broad commodity categories, plus the London Metal Exchange Prices. The seven categories are:

1. Grains and Feeds (barley, bran, corn, cottonseed meal, hominy, bonemeal, oats, sorghum, soybean meal, and wheat)

2. Foods (beef carcass, broilers, butter, cheddar cheese, cocoa, coffee, eggs, flour, hams, hogs, pork bellies and loins, steers, and sugar)

3. Fats and Oils (coconut oil, corn oil, grease, lard, palm oil, soybean oil, and tallow)

4. Fibers and Textiles (burlap, cotton, and wool)

5. Metals (aluminum, antimony, copper, lead, steel scrap, tin, and zinc)

6. Miscellaneous (rubber and steer hides)

7. Precious Metals (gold, platinum, and silver)

Investor's Idiom

A **commodity** is a basic food or raw material, such as cotton, gold, or pork bellies. There are seven main categories of commodities that trade on specialized exchanges.

Fiscal Facts

Futures trading is regulated by a federal agency: the Commodity Futures Trading Commission (CFTC). The CFTC, in turn, oversees the National Futures Association (NFA), which is the industry's self-regulating body.

For each of these items, the *Journal* reports the previous day's closing price. On August 8, 2002, the *Journal* reported that Top Quality Minneapolis Barley was priced at $2.70 per bushel (note: "Minneapolis" here refers to the exchange on which the barley is traded, not a type of barley). The London Metal Exchange reports prices per metric ton for aluminum, tin, copper, lead, nickel, and zinc.

It All Began with Farmers

The first commodity exchange in the United States, and currently the largest futures exchange, is the Chicago Board of Trade (CBOT). The CBOT was formed some 150 years ago to serve as a medium of exchange for farmers' cash crops—wheat and corn. Futures trading began shortly after the end of the Civil War. Today, futures contracts are made not only for commodities but also for:

- Interest rates on all kinds of notes and bonds, including Treasury bills, notes, and bonds

- Indices like the Dow Jones Industrials, the S&P 500, and the NASDAQ 100

- Currency, from the Japanese yen to the Euro

How a Future Differs from an Option

An *option* is a right, but not an obligation, to buy or sell something at a specified price within a specified time. A *futures contract*, in contrast, is an obligation accepted by both the buyer and seller to make a specific trade at a specified time and price. Where an option buyer pays a premium, both parties in a futures contract put down a deposit, which is called *margin*.

The buyer of a future is "long" or has a "long position." A seller is "short" or has a "short position." Futures orders are entered with a broker just like stock orders.

Buying or selling futures is like trading stocks. "Long" means you own "it" (a stock, a bushel of wheat, whatever) and are betting that "it" will rise in price. "Short" means you do not intend to buy it and are betting that it will decline in price (and if it declines enough, you'll buy it then).

- "Market" means at the market price

- "Limit" means at or below the limit price to buy, at or above the limit price to sell

- "Stop loss" means execute the order if the contract declines (or rises) to a predetermined price, at which point the order is executed on a "best price" basis

In the old days, a futures contract could literally result in 5,000 bushels of wheat being dumped on your front lawn! Today, few contracts go to the delivery date, and when they do, delivery is acknowledged by warehouse receipts. The reason delivery rarely takes place is because the buyer doesn't really want the commodity; he or she simply wants to make money by trading it! So, at some point before delivery date, the buyer will sell, and the seller will buy, canceling the contract.

Investor's Idiom

A **future**, or **futures contract**, is an agreement between a buyer and seller to make a specific trade at a specified future date and price. Both parties put down a deposit, called a **margin**.

It's like a stock trade: If you buy 100 shares of General Electric at 10 a.m. and sell those 100 GE shares at noon, you no longer have a position in the stock. You probably bought the stock because you thought the price was going to go up and you could sell it for more than you paid for it. Once you've sold the stock you have what we in the biz call "no position."

How Margins Work

When you buy a futures asset, you need to put down that deposit, called a margin. Before you can buy a future, your broker needs to be sure that you have sufficient money in your account to cover the margin.

Margin takes two forms:

♦ Initial or original—what you have to have in your account to initiate the purchase of the futures contract

♦ Maintenance—what you have to have in your account to maintain (keep) the futures contract

The initial margin is set by the exchange that trades the futures contract you are interested in purchasing. This amount will vary, depending on market conditions, but is usually around 10 percent. Your brokerage firm, however, may require a higher margin. Its decision is binding (unless you choose to take your business elsewhere).

Crash Alert

If your maintenance margin falls below the level required by your brokerage, you will receive a "margin call" warning you to put up sufficient cash to return your balance to the original margin level. If you fail to respond, your broker will liquidate your position by selling securities in your account. Maybe even the ones Grandma gave you. Yes, it's a cold, cruel world.

The maintenance margin is also determined by the exchange. Typically, the maintenance margin is 75 percent of the initial margin.

Here's an example: Let's say you buy a $10,000 futures contract with an initial margin of $1,000. If the contract value declines to $9,750, your margin will drop, as a result, to the maintenance level, which is $750 (75 percent of $1,000).

Why? Well, your initial margin was $1,000, but the contract's value has since declined by $250 ($10,000– $9,750 = $250). That decline comes out of your margin, reducing it from $1,000 to $750 ($1,000 – $250 = $750). At this point, you're still okay, because your margin hasn't fallen below the maintenance level. If the contract drops further, though—to $9,500, for example—your margin is cut to $500. You will be informed that you must deposit an additional $500 to bring your account back up to the initial margin of $1,000.

This simple example shows just how risky futures contracts can be. A small move in the price of the underlying commodity translates to a large dollar gain or loss for the contract holder.

Using Futures to Offset Uncertainty

Why do people mess with these risky investments? Because, just as with options, there are hedgers and there are speculators. Speculators are in the market to "make a killing" (or get killed). Hedgers are trying to offset a future unknown. Let's look at a couple of examples of how ordinary people use futures contracts as hedges against risk and uncertainty.

Suppose you're a cotton farmer. The current price of 40¢ per pound would provide you with a decent profit, but your crop won't be ready to go on the market for another six months. What if the price of cotton declines to 30¢ per pound by then? You could be wiped out. So, you sell (go short) March '03 cotton futures. If cotton does drop to 30¢, you make money on your short—the premium for which you sold it. This money offsets the loss on your "cash" crop. If cotton stays at 40¢, you can cover your short position by purchasing a contract at 40¢. Now you have a loss, but you can offset it with the profitable sale of your cash crop.

Here's another example: Suppose you are a home builder about to open up a new development. You accept contracts for completion of new homes six to nine months from now. You've agreed to sell each house at a fixed price—but what if lumber prices go through the roof in the next six months and eat up all your profit?

Well, you could buy lumber futures at $288.70 per 1,000 board feet. If the price of lumber goes up, you have two choices:

♦ You could pay the higher price for the lumber and offset it by selling your lumber futures contract for a profit. Remember, if the price of lumber has gone up past $288.70 per 1,000 board feet, somebody out there will be happy to buy your contract.

♦ You could accept delivery of the lumber from your futures contract.

What if the price of lumber goes down? Well, the loss on the contract is offset with the lower price you actually pay for your lumber. Either way, you've hedged very nicely. This is a form of insurance, and that's what a hedger is looking for.

Financial Futures

Financial futures currently dominate the futures market. How would an investor use financial futures to hedge? Suppose you are the proud owner of a $1 million equity portfolio (taxable). You have a feeling that stock prices are going to start falling, but you're not absolutely sure, and if you sell some or all of your stocks and prices rise, you've lost an opportunity. And incurred taxable capital gains. You look in *The Wall Street Journal* on August 8, 2002, and under the Future Prices heading you see the following:

DJ Industrial Average (CBOT) – $10 Times Average

	Open	High	Low	Settle	Chg	High[(L)]	Low[(L)]	Open Interest
Sept	8,329	8,460	8,205	8,440	155	10,705	7,450	33,633
Dec	8,390	8,445	8,190	8,422	152	10,740	7,425	559

(L)=lifetime

These are futures contracts on the Dow Jones Industrial Average. *Open, high, low,* and *settle* are the prices for the previous day, August 7, 2002. *Chg* is the change in price for that day's trading. Here, it's —155 points. High and low are the lifetime high and low prices for the contracts, and open interest is the number of outstanding contracts.

If your portfolio is fairly similar to the Dow Jones Industrials, you could use these futures contracts to neutralize the negative effect a market decline would have on the value of your portfolio.

The December contract, for example, is valued at 8422 × $10 = $84,220. Your $1 million equity portfolio divided by $84,220 per contract would require 11.9 contracts ($1,000,000 ÷ $84,220) to neutralize a market decline. You could buy 12 contracts and plan to sell them for December 2002 delivery. If the market declines, your profit on the sale of the contract offsets your "paper" (unrealized loss) on your equity portfolio. If the market goes up, your equity portfolio appreciation offsets the loss on your contract.

Note, however, that if the market declines, and you close out your contracts at a profit, that profit will be taxed at ordinary income tax rates (you have to hold an investment for at least a year to get the better capital gains tax rate). Hence, this hedging works much better for tax-deferred accounts. The taxable investor fearing a market decline has three options:

◆ Use futures contracts, accepting the margin costs and tax consequences

◆ Sell stocks, incurring capital gains and commission dollar consequences

◆ Do nothing and ride out the potential storm

As we've noted throughout this book, over time the stock market has consistently recovered from even the most wrenching declines. Individual investors do best when they choose option 3, and just ride it out. But we thought you should know a little about financial futures anyway, if only to impress somebody.

Options on Futures—Oy!

Options on futures contracts are about as risky as you can get. Like regular options, options on futures are a right, not an obligation, to buy or sell. As with regular options, you can either buy calls or sell puts. Interest rate options on futures, especially on Treasury bonds, are extra hot right now.

In *The Wall Street Journal*, under "Futures Options Prices," you will find "Interest Rate," and under that subheading the following:

T-Bonds (CBT)

$100,000; points and 64ths of 100%

If you wanted to purchase September 2002 call options with a strike price of 106, your premium would be 1-61. Since the option is quoted in 64ths, 1-61 means $1\frac{61}{64}$, or 1.953125. Each premium point amounts to $1,000, so the premium would cost you 1.953125 times $1,000, or $1,953.13. You can also buy puts/calls on stock index futures.

The contracts are for specific months and can extend out to two years.

Spread Strategies for Speculators

Speculators toy with all these different futures contracts. Spreads are one of the more famous commodity futures strategies used by speculators. Typically, the speculator is looking for the price differential to widen or narrow between two different crops, like wheat and oats. He buys a futures contract on the commodity he expects to go up more in price, and sells a contract on the other. What happens to the spread in price between the two commodities is critical, not whether one or both go up or down in price.

If you expect oats to increase in price versus wheat, for example, you would buy an oats contract and sell a wheat contract. If you're right, you can make a lot of money. If you're wrong, you can lose a bundle. That's why it's called speculation.

Program Trading

"Program trading" is an expression you've probably heard on the news to describe why the stock market went up or down sharply in the last hour or so of a trading day. Program traders work for large institutions and set up automated hedges that are triggered when the market hits certain key prices. In effect, they establish a spread—between the S&P 500 Index and a future contract on the index, for example.

When the spread widens because the future price rises, program traders automatically sell futures and buy the index. If the spread narrows via a lower futures price, they sell the index and buy the futures contract. Because the process tends to be highly automated, several institutions buying or selling large sums at any given time can have a dramatic impact on the stock market.

Gold Nuggets

Earlier in this chapter, just for fun, we showed you where to find prices for all kinds of commodities in *The Wall Street Journal*. Unless you're a farmer or building bridges, these markets should not concern you, with one possible exception: precious metals.

> **Fiscal Facts**
>
> Whether gold will ever regain even a vestige of its former allure is open to question. "Gold bugs" argue vociferously that the only long-term financial discipline for individual nations in a global economy is direct linkage of local currencies to gold. Fortunately or unfortunately (depending on your views), national leaders don't want to have their economic policies limited by a fixed amount of currency in circulation.

For centuries, the civilized (and sometimes not-so-civilized) world measured wealth in gold. Paper currencies were backed by it, dreams were spun from it, and wars were fought for it. It was, without exception, the one insurance policy against the ravages of inflation. In this country, some 25 years ago, President Richard Nixon severed the last direct tie between our currency and gold, freeing the dollar to seek its ultimate value. With the quadrupling of oil prices and double-digit inflation during Nixon's term, gold had soared from around $30 per ounce to over $800 per ounce. It currently trades for a little more than $300 per ounce.

As a result of the severance of gold's link with the dollar, investors no longer view gold as a monetary asset, but rather as a commodity. If this view is correct, gold will trade in the same wide cyclical ranges as other commodities, and will attract more speculators than investors. Will gold wrench back its rightful role of inflation hedge from the current holder: the U.S. dollar? We think it's possible, hav-ing seen the dollar's value fluctuate over the years and the varying degree of respect shown to it by other nations. Right now the dollar is king, but we don't subscribe to those who think its reign will last forever.

The question for you, the investor, is whether you should own some or no gold. The answer depends entirely on how you feel about infla-tion and the dollar. If you decide to own some gold, we suggest that it compose no more than 5–10 percent of your total portfolio.

> **Super Strategy**
>
> How to hold gold (and other pre-cious metals): You can buy and store gold bars or coins, but these provide no income return, and storage—even in a safe deposit box—costs money. A bet-ter strategy is to hold shares of precious metals companies or precious metals mutual funds.

Precious Metal Companies and Funds

Because we're your pals, here's a list in alphabetical order of 6 precious metal compa-nies, along with phone numbers and exchange list/ticker symbols:

- Barrick Gold Corp. NYSE ABX 416-861-9911
- Coeur D'Alene Mines Corp. NYSE CDE 208-667-3511
- Echo Bay Mines Ltd. ASE ECO 303-714-8600
- Hecla Mining Co. NYSE HL 208-769-4100
- Newmont Mining Corp. NYSE NEM 303-863-7414
- Placer Dome Inc. NYSE PDG 604-682-7082

If you prefer the diversification of mutual funds (and, as you well know by now, we do), the five largest no-load precious metal funds, listed alphabetically, are:

- American Century Global Gold 1-800-345-2021
- Invesco Gold and Precious Metals 1-800-525-8085
- Midas Funds 1-800-400-6432
- Scudder Gold and Precious Metals Fund 1-800-225-2470
- Vanguard Special Gold and Precious Metals 1-800-662-7447

The Least You Need to Know

- A futures contract is a binding agreement between two parties. One agrees to purchase from the other a specified asset at a specified price at a specified time in the future.

- A commodity is a basic food or raw material.

- When you buy a futures asset, you need to put down a 10 percent deposit, called a margin.

- Futures are used to hedge against anticipated changes in prices.

- If you want some precious metal in your portfolio, consider shares in mining companies or in precious metal mutual funds.

Chapter 23

Realizing Real Estate Dreams

In This Chapter

- ◆ Bad reasons to invest in real estate
- ◆ REITs—great "hands-off" real estate investments
- ◆ How rental income hits your tax return
- ◆ What to look for in a location

Everybody needs a place to live, and in Chapter 15 we talked about how to put a roof over your head and finance it, too. In this chapter we take a look at real estate as investment, not just shelter.

Why Own Real Estate?

Investors are attracted to real estate for many of the same reasons they own common stocks and bonds. Most of the reasons investors cite for wanting to include real estate in their portfolios, however, are not all that strong. Let's take a look:

- ◆ **Income.** Real estate can generate income (rent!). With real estate, the income you earn from the investment is the difference between the rental income you receive and your operating expenses. Bonds and most stocks also generate income, however, and it's typically more reliable and secure than the income coming from a rental property. This is especially true of U.S. Government securities and high quality, above-average-growth common stocks.

◆ **Appreciation.** Real estate's value can increase over time. But, again, so can stocks and, to a limited degree, bonds.

Investor's Idiom

To buy something on **leverage** means to finance its purchase with debt. When you take a mortgage on a real estate property, you are borrowing money from a bank to buy the property. Leverage is measured by the debt-to-equity ratio:

Debt ÷ Equity = debt-to-equity ratio

As you pay off the mortgage, your debt-to-equity ratio changes because the debt gets smaller and equity (ownership) gets bigger.

◆ **Leverage.** Real estate can be bought on leverage. You might, for example, put $20,000 down to buy a $100,000 property. If the property's value increases 10 percent in two years, or $10,000, you've made a 50 percent return on your $20,000 investment. Of course, if the property's value declines 10 percent, you lose 50 percent! If the leverage game appeals to you (it doesn't to us), you can satisfy it with less hassle using options or futures.

The REIT Stuff

We hate to break it to you if you had visions of becoming the next Donald Trump, but there's another reason real estate may not be a great investment for taxable accounts—gains on real estate are taxed as ordinary income! You don't get that nice capital gains tax break you get when you hold stocks or bonds for over one year.

There is one way you can rake in some of the benefits of investing in real estate while avoiding the potential tax hit. Real Estate Investment Trusts (REITs), which were created in 1960, are exempt from taxes as long as they distribute at least 95 percent of their operating income to the shareholders and as long as they invest primarily in real estate. All the larger REITs are listed on either the New York or American stock exchanges.

CAUTION

Crash Alert _____

For years, there was one excellent reason to own real estate: Any losses on your real estate could be used to offset income and reduce your taxes. This was a great way to build up equity (because you gain ownership as you pay off your mortgage) and also cut your taxes.

Unfortunately, the 1986 Tax Reform Act took away what was perhaps the greatest appeal of a real estate investment for a taxable portfolio. The Act rules that real estate loss may be used only to offset other real estate income—not your income from salary or other investments. The Feds strike again.

Because operating income typically exceeds net or reported income, a portion of the income received by the shareholder and reported on Form 1099 is considered a tax-deferred return of capital. This means, among other things, that that portion may be converted to capital gains income and taxed at capital gains rates.

Types of REITs

There are three categories of REITs:

♦ Equity REITs invest primarily in real estate properties.

♦ Mortgage REITs invest primarily in real estate mortgages.

♦ Hybrid REITs invest in a combination of properties and mortgages.

Super Strategy
We recommend that you exclude mortgage REITs and concentrate on equity and hybrid REITs. Mortgage REITs fill basically the same purpose in your portfolio as fixed-income securities, and, as we've discussed throughout this book, Treasuries are your best bet there. If you insist on a mortgage-based product, focus on three U.S. government-created agencies discussed previously: Federal National Mortgage Association, Federal Home Loan Mortgage Corporation, and the Government National Mortgage Association. Their short names are: Fannie Mae, Freddie Mac, and Ginnie Mae, respectively.

REITs respond to two different investment stimuli: the bond market and the real estate market. They are considered conservative investments and tend to mimic the bond market. On the other hand, they are sensitive to trends in their particular real estate market (apartments, commercial or shopping centers, and industrial structures/parks). They are especially sensitive to trends in property values and rental rates. As a result, prices of REITs often run counter to the general stock market.

Emphasize Quality and Safety

If you want to pursue REITs for five-to-ten percent of your equity portfolio, we strongly suggest that you emphasize quality and safety. To get you started, we have taken the REITs followed by Value Line and isolated those with at least a 2 safety rank (1 being highest), and a B++ financial strength rating. And the winners are ...

Name	Symbol	Type of Investments
1. Archstone-Smith	ASN	Multi Family Properties
2. BRE Properties	BRE	Apartments
3. Federal Realty	FRT	Shopping Centers
4. Kimco Realty	KIM	Shopping Centers
5. New Plan Excel	NXL	Shopping Malls
6. Washington REIT	WRE	Mixed

Please note that these ratings are as of July 31, 2002; you should check current ratings before buying any of these REITs. Source: Value Line Investment Survey (1-800-833-0046).

Types of Real Estate Ownership

A REIT is as far removed from the day-to-day management as you can get and still retain the basic benefits of real estate investing. More hands-on types of investment in real estate include:

◆ Single ownership: you and you alone.

◆ Partnership: a way to finance the purchase of larger, more expensive buildings. Partnerships don't always go smoothly, so be sure you have the right or option to buy a controlling interest.

◆ Corporation: not a good move for the individual investor because you will end up paying taxes at both corporate and individual levels. Also, you lose the tax shelter benefit of deducting any depreciation on your property from your personal income.

◆ Limited Partnership: We delve into this type of ownership in greater detail in Chapter 24. But, basically, a limited partnership comprises a general partner and a number of limited partners (including you). This form was popular in the 1980s but has dropped in popularity because investors have realized how hard it can be to sell your share in the partnership and get your money back. Liquidity and marketability are drawbacks of limited partnerships. Limited partnerships are also used for energy (oil and gas) investments.

So, You Want to Own Real Estate

If we haven't talked you out of investing in real estate yet, here are the eight basic forms of real estate you can explore:

- **Duplex.** Typically, you live in one half and rent out the other half.

- **Apartment building.** Here again, you could live "on site," or retain a resident manager to live on site and perform necessary odd jobs. Depending on the size and age of the building, you might need a property manager. The property manager would be responsible for collecting rents, paying bills, maintaining the grounds, contracting for repairs, etc. This could run you up to 10 percent of your gross rental income from the building.

- **Hotels/motels.** Years ago, "Ma and Pa" motels were fairly common, but the chains have turned this into a tough business. The "bed and breakfast" business, though a charming fantasy for many beleaguered urban couples, is even tougher. Sure, that cozy inn in Vermont looked good on Bob Newhart's show, but bear in mind that to run a bed and breakfast you've got to be on call 24 hours a day as chef, handyman, and concierge.

- **Office buildings.** Unlike singles, duplexes, and apartment buildings, office buildings rent on a per-square-foot basis. Leases are usually longer for offices—five years with additional option years, for example, compared to one/two year rentals for residential property.

- **Shopping centers.** Mini-malls, medium-size malls (with one major or anchor tenant plus local tenants), larger malls (two anchors, one on each end plus local stores in between), and super regional malls, like the Mall of America—this country loves malls. But unless you're very wealthy, you probably wouldn't be invited to invest in the partnerships and corporations that own most malls. If you invest in REITs, though, you'll end up with a piece of the action, as most REITs eventually own the best shopping centers.

- **Warehouses and industrial buildings.**

- **Mobile home parks.**

- **Land.**

Land is the most speculative real estate investment because there is no depreciation to help cut your taxes and no rental income. You could sell cutting rights to a logger or grazing/planting rights to ranchers/farmers, but that's about it. You could get lucky and sell out for big bucks to a developer. But while you're waiting, you'll be paying taxes and loan payments (if you borrowed to purchase the land). We maintain that the only really good reason to buy land is if you intend to build a home for yourself on it. Then again, there is only a fixed amount of land. In the spirit of Will Rogers: "Buy land, they ain't makin' any more of it."

Purchase and Rental of Homes and Apartment Buildings

In Chapter 15, we discussed the purchase vs. rental decision, pointing out that owning a home at the first opportune moment is not necessarily the best move. Let's review these thoughts, as they also apply to buying real estate as an investment.

Financially Prepared and Market-Wise

First and foremost, be financially prepared and market-wise. "Financially prepared" means, ideally, to have your down payment set aside. Having to hustle up the down payment by selling assets for cash or borrowing (mortgaging your future) is not smart. Also, you should already have spoken to a mortgage banker to ensure that you will qualify for the mortgage. In fact, if you can be pre-approved, it adds to your attraction as a prospective buyer. Check with a realtor or mortgage banker about what you need to do to be pre-approved.

"Market-wise" means you know what's available in the area where you would like to own and have researched the prices of the types of properties you want to own. Market-wise also means you've regularly taken the market's pulse for at least a year. You can tell when it's rising sharply, flat, or declining—and you can spot a buying opportunity.

Many newspapers include information on recent home/condo sales to assist you. Brokers will also give you data on recent sales and trends. The Sunday *New York Times*, for example, listed a home in New Jersey on June 20, 2002, that sold for several thousand dollars more than the asking price, in less than a week. What does that indicate about that market? Several other homes in the area also sold within one/two weeks of listing, very close to the asking price. This is a sign of a hot—if not overheated— residential real estate market.

How Rental Income Hits Your Tax Return

Let's say you're about to make your first foray into real estate investment by renting out a home that you own. How does the rental income hit your income tax statement? See the following page for an example of what Schedule E (Supplemental Income and Loss) of Form 1040 would look like, assuming that the rental contract begins July 1.

Because it's a July 1 rental, you are going to record 5/12 of your annual income and expenses. And in this case, the tenant is paying (or reimbursing) you for telephone, heat, and electricity, but not cable TV (which is the $137 next to Line 18). Now, let's go over this form blow by blow:

♦ Under Line 1 you would put "residential property" and the specific address.

♦ Line 2 is primarily for people who rent out a second or vacation home. You are entitled to up to 14 days for your personal use. If you use the home for more than 14 days, your tax situation gets more complicated, and you should work with an accountant.

♦ Line 3 is actual rents received. $10,000 is equivalent to a monthly rent of $2,000 (times 5 months).

♦ Line 8 is the broker's commission of 10 percent.

♦ Line 9 is homeowner's insurance, again apportioned.

♦ Line 12 is mortgage interest (but not any portion allocable to principal pay-down).

♦ Line 16 is real estate taxes.

♦ Line 18 is the aforementioned cable bills.

♦ Line 19 is the subtotal of expenses.

♦ Line 20 is depreciation.

♦ Line 21 is total expenses after depreciation.

♦ Line 22 is a loss, but one that we cannot use unless we have a gain in other "passive" (e.g., real estate) income.

Note that even though we can't use the tax loss, we still have a "profit" of $1,422 (Line 3 less Line 19) on which we have no tax due. Pretty snazzy.

SCHEDULE E (Form 1040) Department of the Treasury Internal Revenue Service (99)	**Supplemental Income and Loss** (From rental real estate, royalties, partnerships, S corporations, estates, trusts, REMICs, etc.) ▶ **Attach to Form 1040 or Form 1041.** ▶ **See Instructions for Schedule E (Form 1040).**	OMB No. 1545-0074 20**02** Attachment Sequence No. **13**

Name(s) shown on return | Your social security number

Part I   **Income or Loss From Rental Real Estate and Royalties**   **Note:** *Report income and expenses from your business of renting personal property on **Schedule C** or **C-EZ** (see page E-1). Report farm rental income or loss from **Form 4835** on page 2, line 39.*

1 Show the kind and location of each **rental real estate property:**		2 For each rental real estate property listed on line 1, did you or your family use it during the tax year for personal purposes for more than the greater of: • 14 days, **or** • 10% of the total days rented at fair rental value? (See page E-1.)	Yes	No
A	**Residential Property**	A		XX
B		B		
C		C		

Income:			Properties			Totals (Add columns A, B, and C.)	
			A	**B**	**C**		
3	Rents received	3	10,000			3	10,000
4	Royalties received	4				4	
Expenses:							
5	Advertising	5					
6	Auto and travel (see page E-2) .	6					
7	Cleaning and maintenance . . .	7					
8	Commissions	8	1,000				
9	Insurance	9	195				
10	Legal and other professional fees	10					
11	Management fees	11					
12	Mortgage interest paid to banks, etc. (see page E-2)	12	5,546			12	5,546
13	Other interest	13					
14	Repairs	14					
15	Supplies	15					
16	Taxes	16	1,700				
17	Utilities	17					
18	Other (list) ▶	18	137				
19	Add lines 5 through 18	19	8,578			19	8,576
20	Depreciation expense or depletion (see page E-2)	20	5,388			20	5,388
21	Total expenses. Add lines 19 and 20	21	13,966				
22	Income or (loss) from rental real estate or royalty properties. Subtract line 21 from line 3 (rents) or line 4 (royalties). If the result is a (loss), see page E-3 to find out if you must file **Form 6198**. . .	22	3,966				
23	Deductible rental real estate loss. **Caution:** *Your rental real estate loss on line 22 may be limited. See page E-3 to find out if you must file **Form 8582**. Real estate professionals must complete line 42 on page 2*	23	(0)(	)(	)		
24	**Income.** Add positive amounts shown on line 22. **Do not** include any losses					24	
25	**Losses.** Add royalty losses from line 22 and rental real estate losses from line 23. Enter total losses here					25	( )
26	Total rental real estate and royalty income or (loss). Combine lines 24 and 25. Enter the result here. If Parts II, III, IV, and line 39 on page 2 do not apply to you, also enter this amount on Form 1040, line 17. Otherwise, include this amount in the total on line 40 on page 2					26	

For Paperwork Reduction Act Notice, see Form 1040 instructions.   Cat. No. 11344L   **Schedule E (Form 1040) 2002**

Investor's Idiom _____

In real estate, **depreciation** is defined in terms of the minimum useful life of the property. For residential property, the useful life is defined as 27.5 years (or 3.64 percent per year); for all other real estate, the useful life is 39 years (2.56 percent per year). How do we get these numbers? One hundred percent divided by 27.5 = 3.64 percent. And remember, you cannot depreciate the land on which your residence resides.

Location, Location, Location

Location, location, location: the three rules of real estate investing! But what's "location?" Let's define it this way (you want as many of the following as possible):

◆ **Good schools.** Good schools act like a magnet (who doesn't want their kids to go to a good school?). They are the first thing many potential buyers or renters look for when planning a move into the area.

◆ **Low taxes.** You can avoid high property taxes, in part, by avoiding smaller municipalities where the school, police, and fire costs are spread over a smaller taxable populace. But high taxes are only one issue; the other is the rate of increase in taxes. Rapidly growing townships often mean rapidly increasing costs and, for you, higher tax bills. So, look for areas that are already largely built up.

◆ **Convenience.** Buy property with easy access to main roads or arteries as well as convenient public transportation to shops, entertainment, and places of worship.

Fiscal Facts _____

How do we deal with the depreciation of the land portion of your real estate investment? Your tax bill should be broken down into an appraised value of the land and an appraised value for "improvements" (or your "structure" or "building"). Take the land dollar sum and divide it into total appraised value to get a percent (e.g., $20,000 ÷ $100,000 = .20, or 20 percent). Multiply your current professionally appraised market value by this percent and deduct it. This is your depreciable value (e.g., $150,000 × .20 = $30,000; less from 150,000 = $120,000 depreciable base).

These are the three issues that will be important to whoever rents or buys your property.

Financing Real Estate Investments

A mortgage is a generic product, and there is no advantage to shopping around with local banks, except that they may be familiar with the property you want to buy. Remember, the mortgage amount is driven by the appraised value of the property, and banks tend to use the same limited list of appraisers.

You want a mortgage at the lowest rate (excluding points that you do not want to pay) per term (15 years, 20 years, 30 years, or adjustable). The term depends on your ability to pay—a 15-year will cost you about 30 percent more per month than a 30-year, but will enable you to reduce the mortgage principal much more rapidly. An adjustable rate is initially quite low but can rise beyond a 30-year mortgage's rate quickly, especially when interest rates are rising.

The first thing you should do when seeking a mortgage on a property is check the yield curve. The *yield curve* is the difference in yield between one interest rate and another, as it would appear on a graph. If the line between the two yield points is steep, there's obviously a big difference between the yields. If it's flat, there's very little difference.

Fiscal Facts

Want to use the Internet for online quotes? Here are three websites:

♦ E-loan at **www.eloan. com**

♦ Quicken Home and Mortgage at **www.quicken. com/mortgage**

♦ HomeShark at **www. homeshark.com**

If the yield curve is flat, there is no incentive to opt for an adjustable-rate mortgage (ARM), and the "spread" (yield difference) between 15-year and 30-year mortgages may not lead you to a 15-year mortgage. Check with your broker, check all the local mortgage companies locally yourself, and check further on the Internet.

Best of luck making your real estate dreams come true!

The Least You Need to Know

♦ Most of the goals investors cite for wanting to include real estate in their portfolios would be better met by investments in stocks and bonds.

♦ The 1986 Tax Reform Act rules that real estate losses can be used only to offset real estate income, thus ending one of the best reasons for individual investors to own real estate—the tax break.

♦ Gains on real estate are taxed at income tax rates, not at capital gains rates.

♦ Real Estate Investment Trusts (REITs) are an opportunity to rake in some of the benefits of investing in real estate while avoiding the potential tax hit.

♦ Don't buy mortgage REITs; concentrate on equity and hybrid REITs.

24

Alternative Investments

In This Chapter

- ◆ Investments once available only to the rich
- ◆ Exploring hedge, venture capital, and LBO funds
- ◆ Investing in business dealings via private equity funds and limited partnerships
- ◆ Pros and cons of UITs and SPDRs

"We're so glad we've had this time together …." Sorry, got caught up in a Carol Burnett moment. But seriously, we hope you've enjoyed this book. If you've read all (okay, most) of the chapters, you now have a solid grounding in investment basics that will help you sail through your financial life. You've also explored some fun stuff, like options, futures, and precious metals. In this, our final chapter, we'll zip through a few of the "alternative investments" that used to be discussed only in exclusive country clubs among millionaires but have, in the last decade, become available to the average investor (that's you!).

How Regular Folk Discovered Alternative Investments

"Alternative investments" are equity products like hedge funds or venture capital funds that used to strictly be the province of very wealthy investors, large public and private retirement plans, or universities with huge endowments like Harvard or Yale. These funds used to require $10–$20 million minimum investments, so they were only reasonable investments for people or institutions who had at least 10 times that much in their portfolios—because you wouldn't want to invest more than 5–10 percent of your portfolio in these investments.

A few years back, however, two events occurred that introduced alternative investments to the rest of us. One was a made-for-TV movie on HBO called "Barbarians at the Gate," which depicted, in an entertaining way, the efforts of firms like Kohlberg Kravis Roberts (KKR) to take over R.J. Reynolds via a "leveraged buyout."

In a *leveraged buyout* (LBO), one firm will offer to buy up any and all stock of another company at a price significantly higher than the current trading price of the stock. The idea is that the stockholders will be so excited by this higher price that they will sell all their stock to the takeover company. Once KKR owns all of R.J. Reynolds stock, for example, it owns R.J. Reynolds and can do with it what it will. And what it will do is send in a team to pare down debt and cut costs (meaning fire lots of people), making the revamped R.J. Reynolds lean and mean and very attractive to new potential stockholders. Then it will take the firm public again, selling its stock and making a fortune on the sale.

> **Investor's Idiom**
>
> A **hedge fund** is an unregistered investment fund whose managers can pretty much do whatever they want—invest in currencies or commodities, go short or long, use options and futures, etc. Some funds are very conservative. Others are quite aggressive and make all kinds of risky currency and interest rate plays.

The second event was the media spotlight turned on investors like George Soros, whose hedge funds were blamed by several national leaders for adversely affecting and artificially manipulating currency values around the world.

Hedge Funds

Hedge funds historically had limited the number of investors to fewer than 100 participants, which meant that they didn't have to register under the Investment Company Act of 1940 ("The '40 Act"). Because they are unregistered, hedge funds can invest in currencies, commodities, public stocks and bonds, or whatever they like, and can do so by going long (buying), going short (selling borrowed shares), or using options and futures, etc.

Venture Capital and LBO Funds

While hedge funds move in and out of markets quickly, basically speculating with options and futures and the like, other funds invest for the long haul in new or recently created businesses. These "private equity" funds are more like partnerships than traditional mutual funds. With a straightforward mutual fund, you own shares in whatever publicly traded stocks the mutual fund managers buy. Private equity funds invest in privately owned businesses that do not have stock trading in a public market.

Venture capital funds, for instance, provide the capital for start-up businesses. Investors in a venture capital fund are limited partners. The manager of the fund is the general partner.

Leveraged buyout funds are also proliferating. LBOs use primarily, if not entirely, borrowed money to purchase the outstanding stock of a publicly traded company by offering to purchase it from stockholders at a premium. This turns that company from a public to a private company, owned by the LBO's investors. Then the LBO team rigorously reduces the company's costs, pays down its debt, and takes it public once again—kind of like taking a race car with a blown engine off the track, rebuilding the engine, and putting it back on the track.

The rewards? Industry data is hard to come by since there are no reporting requirements for these funds, but they seek to do at least 150 percent better than the Standard & Poor's 500 Index.

Fiscal Facts

Unlike publicly traded funds, which are corporate entities owned by shareholders, private equity funds are partnerships. More specifically, there is a general partner, who creates the fund, and limited partners who provide the capital. Typically, the general partner (GP) receives a 1–2 percent annual fee for managing the fund, and 20 percent of the profits realized. The limited partners (LP) receive the remaining 80 percent of the profits (after the return of their capital).

The Private Equity Fund of Funds

Historically, as we said, investment in hedge funds and private equity funds was limited to large institutional investors and wealthy individuals. In effect, Wall Street was servicing Park Avenue. In part, because of the voracious appetite for new capital, Wall Street, along with some major trust banks, have introduced a new concept: the private equity fund of funds. This doesn't mean Wall Street is serving Main Street USA, but it is a step in that direction.

A private equity fund of funds also has a general partner (GP) and investors who are limited partners (LPs). The GP receives typically a 1–2 percent annual fee, and a 5 percent share of the profits. What does the GP do? The GP selects other private equity funds (typically 10–15) in which to invest.

If you are a limited partner in a private equity fund of funds, you become, essentially, a limited partner in whatever funds your GP chooses to buy.

> ### Investor's Idiom
>
> A **venture capital fund** invests in new businesses by providing start-up capital. The investors in a venture capital fund are limited partners in the businesses in which the fund invests and are entitled to a share of its profits. A leveraged buyout fund, on the other hand, borrows money to buy a company, revamp it, and take it public. Investors profit from what the LBO fund makes when it resells the company's stock.

What You Need to Qualify for a Fund of Funds

How do you get to be an LP in a private equity fund of funds? Let's start with financial requirements. A limited partnership interest typically requires a minimum commitment of $500,000. This doesn't mean you write out a check for $500,000 and sit back to wait for the profits to roll in. (For one, who has an extra $500,000 just lying around?) It means that over the next three to six years you will receive "calls" to kick in as much as $500,000, typically in 5 percent pieces ($25,000), with the first 5 percent due when you sign the partnership papers. Obviously, this is a much easier check to write out!

Because the partnership interests are not registered as securities under the Securities Act of 1933, you also have to qualify as an "accredited investor." This is defined as someone with more than $1 million of net worth or more than $200,000 ($300,000 if filed/filing a joint return) of adjusted gross income (remember what that is?) for the previous two years and expected for the current year.

On top of that, you are required to affirm that you are acquiring your LP interest as an investment and not for resale or distribution, and that you will not assign or transfer your interest without the consent of the GP. Got that? Now you can dazzle your cocktail crowd!

But wait, there's more! Congress also stated in a follow-up bill passed in 1940 that to participate in a limited partnership you must also be a "qualified purchaser." Today that's typically defined as meaning that you must have more than $5 million in investments (stocks, bonds, real estate held for investment purposes, commodities, and cash all qualify). How did Congress know back in 1933 and 1940 what current dollar worth would qualify someone as an "accredited investor" and a "qualified purchaser"? They didn't. What they did do was entrust the Securities and Exchange Commission (SEC) to establish and revise, from time to time, the definitions of an "accredited investor" and a "qualified purchaser." The General Partner (GP) of a limited partnership knows that if any of his limited partners is not qualified, the GP could lose his or her exclusion from the 1933 Act and 1940 Act. Therefore, the GP takes on the responsibility and ultimate authority to approve your application to be a limited partner.

How Limited Partnership Works

Assuming you are approved to invest as a limited partner in a fund of funds, what is the sequence of events?

1. You will honor the first capital call, which is 5 percent of your total commitment at the closing. So if you have agreed to a total commitment of $500,000, you will write out a check for $25,000 at the closing.

2. You will receive additional capital calls of, say, 5 percent over the first 6 years or so.

3. You may begin to receive distributions (moolah!) from the fund as early as the third year.

4. As a limited partner, you are entitled to a return of your "invested" capital, plus a pre-determined return (called the "preferred return").

5. After the LPs receive back their invested capital and the preferred return, the GP is entitled to a "carried interest amount" equal to 5 percent of the "carried interest account." The carried interest account is the difference between the aggregate portfolio distributions and the invested capital—in other words, 5 percent of the gain. This is called a "catch-up distribution."

Crash Alert

If you fail to honor a capital call from a limited partnership within 20 days you could, at the least, face interest charges, and at the worst, run the risk of having your interest sold for as little as 50 percent of book value. You definitely don't want to miss a call!

6. After #4 and #5 have been honored, subsequent distributions are split (e.g., 5 percent GP, 95 percent LPs).

7. The fund will last for the number of years in the contract or until all assets are distributed, whichever occurs last.

Pros and Cons of LP Investments

There are several points to consider before getting involved with a fund of funds:

♦ You will receive an IRS Form K-1 to use to report partnership income each year. These are not usually available to meet the April 15 tax deadline, however. You can choose to either file an amended return or pay 110 percent of the previous year's taxes. We recommend that you choose the latter option.

♦ Because your fund has multiple fund holdings and multiple investment holdings in each fund, you will probably face state tax returns in at least several states other than your own.

So if you are able to invest and decide that investing in an LP is for you, keep in mind the following advantages:

♦ Potentially (and historically) superior returns to the public equity market

♦ A diversified portfolio of private equity investments

♦ An opportunity to participate in an equity class traditionally reserved for very wealthy individuals

… and disadvantages:

♦ These are risky and illiquid investments.

♦ You have to make a very long-term commitment to the fund.

♦ The tax filing requirements are a pain in the neck.

Unit Investment Trusts

Another alternative investment product that might be dangled in front of you at some point is Unit Investment Trusts, or UITs. This is a hybrid product within the mutual fund category. UITs have two distinguishing characteristics: front-end loads (remember them?) and a fixed maturity or termination. Originally, UITs were fixed-income products that provided investors with a predetermined sum at a fixed rate.

More recently, equity UITs have been developed, the most notable being the "Dogs of the Dow." The concept is simple: the UIT invests in the 10 highest-yielding or the 10 worst-performing stocks in the Dow Jones Industrial Average. The trust matures after one year, and you "rollover" (if you wish to continue the game) into another new UIT, repeating the process every year. The original "load" may be $2^3/_4$–3 percent, and the rollover load may run $1^3/_4$–2 percent.

Although the management fees are low (approaching those of index funds), we think the loads make the product, which is sold by brokers, pricey compared to mutual funds or individually investing. There is one possible exception: SPDRs.

Along Came a SPDR

Standard & Poor's Depository Receipts (SPDRs) are American Stock Exchange–traded securities that represent ownership in the SPDR Trust. The Trust, in turn, is a UIT that holds securities intended to track the performance of the Standard & Poor's 500 Stock Index. SPDRs are perhaps the best-known example of Exchange-Traded Funds (ETF), which we discussed in Chapter 12. To refresh your memory, these are index funds that trade on an exchange. SPDRs are index funds that trade on the American Stock Exchange.

ETFs use brand names, created by their sponsoring financial companies to help market the funds. Brand names include SPDRs (sponsored by State Street Global Advisors), HOLDRs (Merrill Lynch), iShares (Barclays Global Investors), and VIPERs (Vanguard). This information could come in handy at your next bar trivia game.

Specifically, the shares attempt to represent one-tenth of the value of the S&P 500. So, if the S&P 500 closes on any given day at 1,000, the SPDRs would close at an approximate price of $100. They are listed on the American Stock Exchange with the symbol SPX, and if you purchase them, you pay only a commission, not a

> **Super Strategy**
>
> SPDRs are very marketable, and, almost without exception, they are the most actively traded stock on the American Stock Exchange each trading day. And, as with any listed stock, you can sell short as well as go long.

> **Investor's Idiom**
>
> Standard & Poor's Depository Receipts (SPDRs) are a subset of Unit Investment Trusts, or UITs. Both are mutual fund hybrids that trade for a fixed period of time.

load. Like other stocks, SPDRs trade in round lots of 100, and can also be purchased in odd-lot numbers. Total expenses are 18.45/100 of one percent (0.1845 percent), which is competitive with most, if not all, S&P 500 Index mutual funds. More recently, MidCap SPDRs (symbol MDX) have been introduced. These trade on the American Stock Exchange and track the S&P MidCap 400 Index.

The SPDR Trust has an interesting termination date: January 22, 2118, or (according to the Standard & Poor's Depository Receipts SPDR Trust, Series 1 Prospectus) "the date 20 years after the death of the last survivor of 11 people named in the trust agreement, the oldest of whom was born in 1990 and the youngest of whom was born in 1993," whichever occurs first!

It's an interesting product! And no doubt the investment world will continue developing new products for you, the savvy individual investor. Be smart, and have fun!

The Least You Need to Know

- ◆ "Alternative investments" are equity products like hedge funds or venture capital funds that used to be strictly the province of very wealthy investors.

- ◆ A hedge fund is an unregistered investment fund whose managers can pretty much do whatever they want—invest in currencies or commodities, go short or long, use options and futures, etc.

- ◆ Private equity funds invest in privately owned businesses that do not have stock trading on the stock market.

- ◆ Venture capital funds provide the capital for start-up businesses.

Appendix A

Useful Investing Info

Government and Regulatory Contacts

Federal Reserve Board's World Wide website: www.federalreserve.gov

Federal Trade Commission, Consumer Response Center:
For information on credit reporting agencies, call 202-326-2222. The FTC website is: www.ftc.gov.

Internal Revenue Service:
www.irs.gov

Call 1-800-829-1040 for free help with filing the 1040 income tax return. Order all tax forms from the IRS by calling 1-800-829-3676.

Securities and Exchange Commission (SEC):
www.sec.gov

The Office of Consumer Affairs
Securities and Exchange Commission
450 5th Street N.W.
Washington, D.C. 20549

Social Security Administration:
Call 1-800-772-1213 or visit www.ssa.gov. If you want information on Medicare, call Social Security at 1-800-772-1213 and request Publication No. 05-10043 (Medicare), which explains Medicare hospital and medical insurance.

U.S. Treasury:
You may purchase T-bills directly from the U.S. Government via the Treasury Direct Program or via banks or brokers, usually for a service fee. If you buy

direct from the Treasury, you can do so in person, by mail, by phone (1-800-722-2678), or via the Internet at www.publicdebt.treas.gov. To utilize the latter two alternatives, you will need to provide a signature to open your account.

Financial Exchanges

Most exchanges will let you come in and check out their pits full of screaming traders. It's a sight (and sound) worth experiencing at least once in your life!

New York Stock Exchange (NYSE)
11 Wall Street
New York, NY 10005
212-656-3000
www.nyse.com

American Stock Exchange (AMEX)
86 Trinity Place
New York, NY 10006
212-306-1000
www.amex.com

Other exchanges include the Chicago Mercantile Exchange, Boston Stock Exchange, Montreal Stock Exchange, and the Philadelphia Stock Exchange.

Credit Reporting Agencies

For personal credit histories, contact:

Trans Union National
760 W. Sproul Road
Springfield, PA 19064-0390
1-800-888-4213
www.tuc.com

Experian (formerly TRW)
National Consumer Assistance Center
P.O. Box 2002
Allen, TX 75013
1-888-EXPERIAN (1-888-397-3742)
www.experian.com

Equifax
P.O. Box 740241
Atlanta, GA 30374-0241
1-800-685-1111
www.equifax.com

If you own a business, you'll want to run a credit check on it periodically, too. The three top credit-reporting agencies in this field are the following:

Dun & Bradstreet
One Diamond Hill Road
Murray Hill, N.J. 07974-1218
1-800-234-3867
www.dnb.com

NCR Corp.
1700 S. Patterson Blvd.
Dayton, Ohio 45479
1-800-CALL NCR
www.ncr.com

Experian (formerly TRW) Business Credit Services
National Consumer Assistance Center
P.O. Box 2002
Allen, TX 75013
1-888-EXPERIAN (1-888-397-3742)
www.experian.com

Consumer Info

Consumer Reports:
1-800-205-2445 or visit the website at www.ConsumerReports.org.

Edmund's Automobile Buyer's Guide:
www.edmund.com

Kelley Blue Book (indispensable when selling or trading cars):
www.kbb.com

Investment Research

Value Line:
1-800-833-0046. A one-year subscription costs $598.

Standard & Poor's Stock Guides:
1-800-852-1641 or visit the website at www.stockinfo.standardpoor.com.

The Wall Street Journal:
To order a subscription to the *Journal*, call 1-800-521-2170, ext. 247. The Internet address is wsj.com.

Amazing Online Research Sites

There are some amazing research sites on the web that you can access yourself, such as the following:

- www.briefing.com (analysts' upgrades and downgrades)

- www.hoovers.com (company profiles and financial data)

- www.marketguide.com (earnings estimates from First Call, insider trading from Vickers, and stock screening from Stock Quest)

- www.personalwealth.com (Standard & Poor's info, including Wall Street analysts' recommendations and consensus earnings estimates)

- www.sec.gov (essentially all Securities & Exchange Commission filings by companies)

- www.zacks.com (consensus earnings estimates, broker recommendations, and insider trading)

Mutual Funds

Large-Cap Growth: Asset size => $2.0 billion, expense ratio <= 1.0%

American Century Ultra	1-800-345-2021
Fidelity Blue Chip Growth	1-800-544-8888
Fidelity Independence	(same as above)
Harbor Capital Appreciation	1-800-422-1050
Janus Growth & Income	1-800-525-8983
T. Rowe Price Blue Chip Growth	1-800-638-5660
Vanguard Index Growth	1-800-662-7447

Large Value: Asset size $2.0 billion, expense ratio max. 0.75%

Dodge & Cox Stock	1-800-621-3979
Fidelity Equity-Income	1-800-544-8888
Vanguard Equity-Income	1-800-662-7447
Vanguard Windsor II	(same as above)

Large Blend: Asset size $2.0 billion +, expense ratio max. 0.75%

Elfun Trusts	1-800-242-0134
Fidelity Asset Manager: Growth	1-800-544-8888
Fidelity Growth & Income	(same as above)
Schwab 1000	1-800-435-4000
State Farm Growth	1-800-447-0740
Vanguard 500 Index	1-800-662-7447

Mid-Cap Growth: Asset size $1.0 billion +, expense ratio max. 1.25%

Hartford Midcap HLS	1-888-843-7824
T. Rowe Price Mid-Cap Growth	1-800-638-5660
Brandywine	1-800-656-3017

Mid-Cap Value: Asset size $1.0 billion+, expense ratio mx. 1.25%

American Century Equity Income	1-800-345-2021
Longleaf Partners	1-800-445-9469
Oakmark Select 1	1-800-625-6275

Mid-Cap Blend: Asset size $1.0 billion +, expense ratio max. 1.25%

Meridian Value	1-800-446-6662

Small Growth: Asset size $0.5 billion +, expense ratio max. 1.25%

Liberty Acorn Z	1-800-426-3750
Vanguard Explorer	1-800-662-7447

Small Value: Asset size $0.5 billion +, expense ratio max . 1.25%

Ariel	1-800-292-7435

Small Blend (Value and Growth): Asset size $0.5 billion +, expense ratio max. 1.25%

Royce Premier	1-800-221-4268

Foreign Stock: Asset size $1.0 billion +, expense ratio max. 1.25%

American Advantage Int'l Equity	1-800-967-9009
Artisan Intranational	1-800-344-1770
Bernstein Tax-Managed Int'l Value	212-756-4097
Harbor International	1-800-422-3750
Liberty Acorn International	1-800-466-3750

Long Government: Asset size $1.5 billion +, expense ratio max. 0.50%

Vanguard Long-Term U.S. Treasury	1-800-662-7447

Intermediate Government: Asset size $2.0 billion +, expense ratio max. 0.50%

Vanguard GNMA	1-800-662-7447
Vanguard Interm. US Treasury	(same as above)

Long-Term Bond: Asset size $2.0 billion +, expense ratio max. 0.50%

Vanguard Long-Term Corporate Bond	1-800-662-7447

Intermediate-Term Bonds: Asset size $2.0 billion +, 0.50%

Fidelity Investment Grade Bond	1-800-544-8888
Fidelity Spartan	(same as above)
PIMCO Total Return	1-800-927-4648
Vanguard Interm.-Term Corp.	1-800-662-7447
Vanguard Total Bond Market Index	(same as above)

Muni National Long: Asset size $2.0 billion +, expense ratio max 0.50%

Vanguard Insured Long-Term T/E   1-800-622-7447

Vanguard Long-Term Tax Exempt   (same as above)

Muni National Intermediate: Asset Size $2.0 billion +, expense ratio max. 0.50%

Vanguard Intermediate-Term Tax-Exempt   1-800-662-7447

College Contacts

Involve your child in the decision about where to go to college by getting him or her a copy of a great reference guide: *The College Handbook*, published by the College Entrance Examination Board. The handbook profiles 3,215 colleges.

Unique College Investing Plan, sponsored by the State of New Hampshire and managed by Strategic Advisors, Inc., a part of Fidelity Investments, 1-800-544-1722.

Internet Brokers

Ameritrade	www.ameritrade.com	1-800-454-9272
Datek Online	www.datek.com	1-888-463-2835
E*TRADE	www.etrade.com	1-800-387-2331
Fidelity	www.fidelity.com	1-800-544-5555
Harris Direct	www.harrisdirect.com	1-800-825-5723
TD Waterhouse	www.waterhouse.com	1-800-934-4410
WebStreet	www.webstreet.com	1-800-932-8723
Muriel Siebert & Co.	www.siebertnet.com	1-800-872-0444
National Discount Brokers	www.ndb.com	1-800-888-3999
Brown	www.brownco.com	1-800-822-2021
Fidelity	www.fidelity.com	1-800-544-7272
Schwab	www.schwab.com	1-800-435-4000
Scottrade	www.scottrade.com	1-800-619-SAVE
Quick & Reilly	www.quick-reilly.com	1-800-837-7220

Mortgages

Want to use the Internet for online mortgage quotes? Here are three websites:

◆ E-loan at www.eloan.com

◆ Quicken Home and Mortgage at www.quicken.com/mortgage/

◆ HomeShark at www.homeshark.com

Glossary

adjustable-rate mortgage (ARM)   A mortgage with an interest rate priced off the yield for the 10-year Treasury note. Since the yield on the note changes every six months, so will the interest rate on the ARM. There are also longer-term ARMs with yields that change after three, five, or seven years.

adjusted gross income   AGI is gross income from your W-2 form, plus interest income, rents, royalties, etc., minus medical account deductions, alimony payments, and other adjustments.

alternative investment   An equity-based investment, such as a hedge fund or venture capital fund. Alternative investments used to be available only to very wealthy investors.

amortize   To write off a debt or fee over time.

annual report   Report, prepared by a corporation, that includes full dis-closure of its financial statements.

annuity   An investment that yields fixed payments during the investment holder's lifetime or for a stated number of years.

asked price   The price that an owner of stock is asking for it in the market.

assets   Any item of value—from baseball cards to stocks—that you own.

back-end load   Fee charged when you redeem (sell) your shares in a mutual fund. Also referred to as "back-end," "back-door" load, or "deferred sales charges."

balance sheet   A financial statement that shows what you own (your assets) and what you owe (your liabilities) at a given point in time.

bid price   The price a buyer is willing to pay for a stock.

bill   An IOU that the U.S. government issues when it wants to borrow money for one year or less. The government agrees to pay back the lender at a specified maturity date, with interest.

bond   An IOU that a corporation or government agency issues when it wants to borrow money for more than 10 years. The issuer agrees to pay back the lender at a specified maturity date, with interest.

broker   A generic name for middlemen who facilitate trades between buyers and sellers.

browser   Software that enables your computer to surf the web and read all those groovy HTML documents. Popular browsers include Netscape and Microsoft's Internet Explorer.

business plan   Document prepared by entrepreneur to show exactly how a new business will be operated; includes projections for sales and profits.

call option   Contract giving the contract holder the right to purchase a stock at a set price, called the strike price, for a specified period of time, usually a few months.

capital   A fancy word for money that is used for business purposes. Corporations issue stock to raise capital, for example.

capital gain   Any money you make from an investment—from selling a stock for a profit, for example. If you've held the investment longer than one year, the capital gain is not subject to income tax; instead, it's subject to capital gains tax, which is typically lower.

cash equivalent   Investment that can be turned into cash within 24 hours. Treasury bills, CDs, savings accounts, and money market funds are examples of highly liquid cash equivalents.

certificates of deposit   Money market instruments typically sold by banks in three-month, six-month, or one-year maturities. CDs are very safe investments because they are fully insured by the Federal government, up to $100,000.

charge card   An account that allows you to carry debt for a specified time, after which you incur fees and penalties.

collateral   Something you own that can be pledged against a loan.

combined income   Adjusted gross income plus nontaxable interest (interest on municipal bonds, for example) plus half of your Social Security benefits.

commission   A percentage fee paid to a broker for executing a trade.

commodity   Any product sold in the financial markets that can actually be weighed, such as gold, silver, pork bellies, sugar, or grain.

compound interest   The money you earn on interest (or dividends or capital gains) that you earned in a previous period. Compound interest enables your money to grow exponentially.

corporation   A business structure composed of stockholders who all share in its owner-ship. Because no one person "owns" a corporation, the people who work for it are protected if the corporation is sued.

credit card   An account that enables you to carry a debt indefinitely, as long as you pay interest.

credit report   Report created by private credit reporting agency (CRA) that is based on what creditors have said about you.

debit card   Card that enables you to make purchases with a direct deduction from your checking account.

deductible   The amount of expense you agree to cover before your insurance kicks in.

defined benefit plan   An employer-financed retirement plan that pays you an annual sum upon retirement.

depreciation   The loss in value of an item over time, due to wear and tear.

discount   The amount a bond is trading below par (100).

discount broker   Broker who simply executes trades, for a lower commission and without the additional services provided by a full-service broker.

diversification   A method of decreasing risk by increasing the variety of assets in a portfolio. If you own lots of different stocks, for example, your whole portfolio won't tank if one company goes bankrupt.

dividend   A payment to the owner of a share of corporation's stock; represents the owner's portion of the corporation's profits.

Dow Jones Average (DJIA)   An average of thirty well-known companies, such as AT&T or McDonald's, chosen by Dow Jones & Company to represent trends in the stock market.

education IRA   Introduced in 1998, and now called "Coverdell ESA," this is an IRA to which you can make tax-deferred contributions of up to $500 per year, per beneficiary, until your kids are 18. Withdrawals for qualified educational purposes are tax-free.

e-mail   Electronic mail, sent via modem over the Internet.

encryption   The scrambling of information as it is transmitted over the Internet to ensure your privacy and confidentiality.

equity   Ownership of property, such as stock or a house.

executor   Person who makes sure that the provisions of a will are carried out.

expiration date   Date by which an option contract must be exercised or lose its value.

fiduciary   A person or entity responsible for investing money on behalf of another person or entity and expected to earn a reasonable rate of return on the investments made.

fixed-income   Investment that provides income that remains constant and doesn't fluctuate (like stock prices do, for example). Bonds are fixed-income investments because when you buy a bond you are promised regular, steady interest payments.

fixed annuity   An annuity that promises to provide a fixed (predetermined) sum in an annual or other regular (e.g., monthly) interval.

401(k)   Retirement savings plan that allows employees who are eligible to choose how much of their pay is to be deducted for investment purposes and how the dollars are to be invested.

403(b)   A version of the 401(k) used by public employers, such as schools, hospitals, and other not-for-profit organizations.

front-end load   Sales charge deducted from the principal invested in a mutual fund.

future or **futures contract**   An agreement between a buyer and seller to make a specific trade at a specified future date and price.

general obligation bond   A bond backed by the tax-raising ability of the issuing state or municipality.

hedge fund   An unregistered investment fund whose managers can pretty much do whatever they want—invest in currencies or commodities, go short or long, use options and futures, etc.

HTML (Hypertext Markup Language)   A computer language that enables programmers to include graphics and sound in documents.

income statement   A financial statement that compares income and expenses.

index fund   A mutual fund designed to mimic the performance of a given set of securities.

inflation   A general rise in prices.

initial public offering (IPO)   A corporation's first stock sale.

institutional investor   As opposed to an individual investor, an institutional investor is an institution, such as a corporation, hospital, city government, or other large entity that has a portfolio.

interest   Payment you receive for lending someone your money. Interest is also the fee you pay when you borrow money.

Internet (the 'Net)   A computer network developed in 1969 as a way for government scientists and military departments to communicate with each other via computer and access information stored on computers around the world. Today more than 30 million people use the Internet.

Internet Service Provider (ISP)   A company, such as America Online or CompuServe, that provides you with access to the Internet for a fee.

IRA   An Individual Retirement Account, which is basically a shell that protects money you put in it from taxation until you start to take money out.

Keogh   Pension plan that allows business owners to shelter more income than SEPs or SIMPLEs do and to create vesting schedules for employees.

layaway   Plan that allows you to make a down payment and monthly payments toward the purchase of an item.

leverage   A way to finance the purchase of something with debt.

leveraged buyout fund   Fund that borrows money to buy a company, revamp it, and take it public. Investors profit from what the LBO fund makes when it resells the company's stock.

liability   A debt you owe. The opposite of an asset, which is something you own.

lien   A legal right to take someone's property and hold it until the owner pays a debt.

liquidity   The ease with which an investment can be converted to cash.

living trust   Legal document that names someone to manage your assets if you die or are incapacitated.

load   Sales fees and commissions charged to investors in a mutual fund.

long bond   The 30-year Treasury bond.

Long-Term Equity Anticipation Security (LEAPS)   Long-term option contracts that are very popular with individual investors.

lump sum   The entire value of an investment taken in cash at once.

margin   Deposit put down by both parties in a futures contract.

marginal tax rate   The tax rate you pay on the last few dollars you earn.

Medicare   A national health program that pays certain medical and hospital expenses for elderly and disabled people.

modem   Device used to connect a computer to a phone line.

money market   Instruments highly liquid investments with rates that vary from day to day, week to week, or month to month.

municipal bond   A bond issued by a "municipality," like your city, town, or county. The interest paid by municipal bonds is, with a few exceptions, not taxed by the federal government.

mutual fund   A company that collects money from investors and invests on their behalf, usually in diversified securities.

net asset value (NAV)   The dollar value of all the marketable securities (stocks, for example) owned by a mutual fund, less expenses and divided by the number of the fund's shares outstanding.

net earnings from self-employment   The amount of income on which you pay self-employment tax, minus the tax itself.

note   An IOU that a corporation or government agency issues when it wants to borrow money for between one and five years. The issuer agrees to pay back the lender at a specified maturity date, with interest.

option   A contract that states what is to be delivered for what price and what time period. The option is a right, but not an obligation, to exercise the rights stated in the options contract. At the end of the designated time period, the option loses all its value.

options buyer or **"holder"**   Pays an options writer a premium for the right to exercise the option contract created by the options writer.

options writer or **"seller"** or **"issuer"**   Creates an options contract, and must stand ready to honor the terms of the contract.

par   The original price of a bond, note, or bill. It is also the amount that the security will pay back at maturity and is referred to as "100."

penny stock   Stock sold for under a dollar.

pension   A regular payment made to you (or your family, if you pass away) by your employer that reflects how much you earned and how many years you worked at your job.

portfolio   The mix of assets in which you've invested. A portfolio contains investment instruments that you've selected to achieve your financial goals.

premium   The amount that a bond is trading above par (over 100).

prenuptial agreement   A legally binding document signed by two people before they get married. Most prenuptial agreements simply spell out who owns what and who will get what in a divorce.

pre-tax   Describes dollars that are deducted from your pay before taxes are applied. Pre-tax contributions to a 401(k) or 403(b), for example, are deducted from your pay before it is taxed.

principal   The original dollar amount of a fixed-income investment; the amount received upon maturity.

probate   State court that decides how an estate will be distributed when the deceased person's will is nonexistent or unclear.

prospectus   A legal document prepared by a mutual fund and sent out to potential investors that describes the fund and its operations.

put option   A contract that gives you the option to sell a security at a specified price until the contract's expiration date.

return on investment (ROI)   The amount you expect to earn from an investment over a given period of time. ROI is also called rate of return (ROR) and is expressed as a percentage of your original investment.

revenue bond   A bond issued by an agency of a city, county, or state for a specific purpose. Revenues from that agency pay the interest on bonds that are outstanding.

revolving line of credit   Credit that puts an upper limit on what you can borrow. You can borrow up to that amount, and you pay interest only on what you actually draw down.

rollover IRA   Used to shelter money that's in a 401(k) if you change jobs and can't put the money in your new job's retirement plan.

Roth IRA   A new type of IRA that is more flexible than the traditional IRA but is only available to families earning under $100,000 a year. As long as your Roth IRA has been open for at least five years, you can withdraw up to $10,000 to buy a first home.

round lot   One hundred shares of stock.

Savings Incentive Match Plan for Employees (SIMPLE) IRA   A new option for self-employed people and small businesses with few employees, growing in popularity because it's very easy to use.

search engine   Also called a portal; a business that collects and indexes web pages. You can access search engines online and use them for free to look for web pages on topics that you specify.

securities and Exchange Commission (SEC)   Regulatory agency started in 1933 by Congress to protect investors.

self-employment tax   A tax self-employed people have to pay into Social Security because they don't have an employer contributing on their behalf.

Simplified Employee Pension (SEP) IRA   Essentially an IRA for someone who is self-employed, and small businesses with few employees. A SEP is like a 401(k), but contributions are limited to 15 percent or $30,000, whichever is less. A good retirement plan for a sole proprietor who doesn't have employees.

Social Security   A system managed by the federal government, which provides money to people who are retired or are not able to work because of disability.

sole proprietor   Someone who owns a business alone, without partners.

spread   The difference between the asked and the bid price of a security or between interest rates.

Standard & Poor's Depository Receipts (SPDRs)   A subset of Unit Investment Trusts, or UITS. Both are mutual fund hybrids that trade for a fixed period of time.

stock market   The stock market doesn't exist as a physical place—stocks are traded at various stock exchanges, such as the New York Stock Exchange or The American Stock Exchange. All the exchanges together are considered the stock market.

stock option   The right, but not the obligation, to buy a stock at a fixed price after a fixed period of time (usually 12 months) for a fixed period of time (10 years).

stock split   A division of stock that increases the number of shares outstanding and decreases share price of the stock.

strike price   Also called the exercise price; the price at which the holder of an option contract can buy (call) or sell (put) the underlying security.

trade   To buy or sell securities on the financial markets.

Treasury bill securities   Securities issued by the U.S. Treasury that mature in one year or less. Treasury securities are fully guaranteed by the government and can be sold within 24 hours.

Treasury bonds   Long-term securities issued by the U.S. Treasury with maturities over 10 years. Historically, the Treasury has issued 20- or 30-year bonds.

Treasury notes   Securities issued by the U.S. Treasury that offer maturities from 2 years to 10 years.

Treasury strip   A piece of a Treasury security, such as a coupon or principal payment, that has been stripped from the original security.

12b-1   Shareholding servicing fee charged on mutual fund.

Unit Investment Trust (UITS)   Hybrid mutual funds that invest like mutual funds but, unlike them, have a fixed termination date.

URL (Uniform Resource Locator)   Address for a document on the Internet.

variable annuity   An annuity that provides an undetermined amount that depends upon the return of the annuity's underlying mutual fund; basically a mutual fund wrapped around an insurance contract.

venture capital fund   Fund that invests in new businesses by providing start-up capital. The investors in a venture capital fund are limited partners in the businesses in which the fund invests and are entitled to a share of its profits.

vested   Eligible to receive a pension. An employee is typically considered vested after five years at a company.

will   A legal document, signed by you and witnessed, that gives explicit directions as to who or what is to get whatever specific assets of yours you choose to list.

World Wide Web (the web)   A subset of the Internet organized by an organization called the World Wide Web Consortium. Documents on the web, called home pages, include graphics and sound.

yield   The return on an investment expressed as a percentage.

How to Avoid Turning the Stock Market into Your Own Personal Emotional Roller Coaster

We all have friends who freak out over the stock market constantly. Guess what? Freaking out doesn't make your investments grow one whit faster.

Admittedly, buying and selling stock can be a very emotional game. It's like betting at the racetrack or rooting for your home team(s). At the end of the trading day, the race, or the game, you know whether you were a winner or a loser. You experience either instant gratification or instant remorse.

What's wrong with that? Nothing, if you can keep a single day or event in perspective. But most of us can't. When we turn to the next trading day, race, or game, our decision-making process is influenced strongly by the previous day's wins or losses. Winners get elated (and reckless); losers get depressed (and overly cautious).

These dramatic ups and downs are what make sports and the racetrack such glorious entertainments. But this is not the way to approach the stock market, unless you are investing merely for entertainment. If you are investing to meet your financial goals, however, you need to avoid using the stock market as your own personal emotional roller coaster.

How to do this? First, recognize that emotion comes from the heart and logic from the brain. In games of chance, emotion usually overcomes logic. So you need to come up with ways to block your emotions from affecting your logical decisions. Start by becoming an investor, not a trader. Traders live and die on the gains and losses they experience in the stock market each day; you don't have to do that, and you shouldn't. You are (or should be!) a long-term investor. Forget about day trading—that's an emotional game. If you need some drama in your life, go to the racetrack—it's a lot cheaper!

Market Timing Doesn't Pay

The best way to short-circuit an emotional response to the ups and downs of the stock market is with cold, hard facts. Earlier in this book, we gave you several examples of how short-term market declines did not detract from superior 10-year returns (we discussed the 10 years through October 31, 1987, and the most recent 10-year period). If you're going to invest in the stock market, start thinking in 10-year time chunks. Don't even pay attention to what the market is doing day to day.

Still don't believe us? Okay, assume that on December 31, 1990, you invested $5,000 in an S&P 500 Index Fund. Ten years later, on December 31, 2000, that $5,000 would have grown to approximately $25,000, assuming you did nothing more than reinvest the cash dividends in additional fund shares. Now, 10 years equates to about 2,500 trading days. If you were out of the market for the 20 best trading days, your $25,000 would have only grown to $12,500—that's right, less than 1 percent of the trading days during that decade accounted for half of the stock market return! Do you think you (or anyone else) could have picked those 20 days in advance? Do you think you can pick the 20 best trading days for this decade? Don't kid yourself, kid!

Here's the best part: Sure, there are a lot of pros out there who have access to better immediate information than you do. They could maybe beat you on day-to-day trading. Over 10 years, however, you and the pros are pretty much on equal footing. So stay calm, cool and collected, no matter what the market does from day to day.

Here's the best piece of advice we can give you: Don't even bother to look at the price of your stocks and/or mutual funds every day. If you're a long-term investor, why do you care what happened yesterday? If you're at a cocktail party and somebody asks you how your stocks are doing, just say, "I don't know; I'll check at the end of the month." Won't get their attention!

Stick to the Plan, Stan!

In this book we taught you two strategies to control that 'ol devil emotion. The first is dollar cost averaging. You invest a fixed sum of money on a regular basis (every month, every paycheck, and so on). When prices are low, your fixed sum will buy more shares;

when they are high, you buy fewer shares. This technique is a time-proven variation of the Holy Grail of investing: Buy low, sell high. In this case, it's buy more stocks lower, buy fewer stocks higher. Second, rebalance your portfolio back to the initial target levels once a year (on your birthday, for example). Once again, you're cutting back on recent winners and adding to recent losers. It's like buy low, sell high. In both cases, you don't have to think about what you're doing, thereby keeping the emotion locked up. You just do it. Your 401(k) (or 403[b] or 457 plan) is the easiest example of these concepts. You automatically have a fixed sum deducted from your paycheck each payday (dollar cost averaging), and it is invested according to your standing instructions. And once per year, you rebalance and inform the plan administrator of your decisions.

Diversify!

Finally, don't put all your eggs in one basket. That's really exposing yourself to emotional highs and lows. Owning just one or a few stocks leaves you vulnerable to bad news that is company-specific, rather than stock market nonspecific. During the year 2002 so many employees lost so much money because they were heavily invested in their company's stock. They lost two ways: in their 401(k) plan and with their jobs. Never invest more than 5 percent of your stock dollars in one stock. Just don't do it.

So, be a savvy investor: Invest long term (10-year time frame), dollar cost average, rebalance on a predetermined schedule, and stay diversified. All that logic will override any emotional reactions to stock market news that could derail your steady ride toward achieving your investment goals. It's called savvy investing!

Index